ON THE
GANGES

ON THE GANGES

ENCOUNTERS WITH SAINTS AND SINNERS

ON INDIA'S MYTHIC RIVER

GEORGE BLACK

ST. MARTIN'S PRESS ⚛ NEW YORK

Portions of this book originally appeared in a different form in *The New Yorker*, newyorker.com, *OnEarth*, onearth.org, and the *Times of India*.

www.stmartins.com

Designed by Steven Seighman

The Library of Congress Cataloging-in-Publication Data is available upon request.

ISBN 978-1-250-05735-8 (hardcover)
ISBN 978-1-4668-6111-4 (ebook)

Our books may be purchased in bulk for promotional, educational, or business use. Please contact your local bookseller or the Macmillan Corporate and Premium Sales Department at 1-800-221-7945, extension 5442, or by email at MacmillanSpecialMarkets@macmillan.com.

First Edition: July 2018

10   9   8   7   6   5   4   3   2   1

CONTENTS

PART THREE: *DELTA*

ACKNOWLEDGMENTS

For bridging the language gap and opening locked doors, thanks to Mostafizur Rahman Jewel, Praveen Kaushal, Damayanti Lahiri, Ajay Pandey, Pallavi Sharma, and Pranav Sharma.

For lending me an extra pair of eyes, thanks to Agnès Dherbeys, a brilliant photographer and awesome traveling companion, and to Diane Cook and Len Jenshel.

For helping to usher earlier versions of some of these stories into print, thanks to Doug Barasch, John Bennet, Alan Burdick, Scott Dodd, Mac Funk, Janet Gold, David Kortava, David Remnick, and Dorothy Wickenden.

For creating Paragraph Writers Space, where all this eventually came together, thanks to Joy Parisi, for her vision and her friendship. And for keeping the ship sailing smoothly and the jar of Hershey's Kisses always filled, thanks to Lee Bob Black, Ryan Davenport, Maya Macdonald, Ilana Masad, and Amy Meng.

For teaching me new things about our shared craft (even if you didn't realize it at the time), and for listening to my lamentations when the going was rough, thanks to all my fellow *paragrafistas*. It's impossible to name everyone, but I'd be remiss not to give a special tip of the hat to Saul Anton, Zaina Arafat, Kavita Das, Lisa Dierbeck, Elyssa East, Will Heinrich, Sophie Jaff, Anne-Sophie Jouhanneau, George Kyrtsis, Tim Mangin, Ruth Margalit, Sam Nigro, Susanna Schellenberg, Kaushik Shridharani, Kathleen Smith, Sarah-Jane Stratford, Laura Strausfeld, and Cynthia Weiner. Aurvi Sharma has been a particular friend to this project, and her kindness, sharp intelligence, and sense of humor have saved me from countless errors, both large and small.

For sharing their time, advice, hospitality, and encouragement, and for putting up with my insatiable curiosity and often ill-informed questions, thanks to Anupam Agarwal, Fatima Halima Ahmed, Shirin Akhter, Babu Alam, Firoz Alam, Taj Alam, Abdullah Ansari, Alyssa Ayres, Jugal Giri Baba, Acharya Balkrishna, Adam Barlow, Rajiv Bawa, Martin Brading, David Bruce, Vidyawati Chaudhary, the myriad Chowdhurys of Varanasi, Akanksha Chaurey, Prateek Chawla, Dilip Chenoy, Sarat Dash, Kaushal Deb, Bibek Debroy, Paula Devi, Sumant Dubey, Michael Duffy, R. K. Dwivedi, Jennifer Fowler, Atanu Ganguli, Anshul Garg, Anchita Ghatak, Vignesh Gowrishankar, Tapati Guha-Thakurta, Hafizurrahman, Saleemul Haq, Kanupriya Harish, Syed Iqbal Hasnain, Shahidul Islam, Ramaswamy Iyer, Anjali Jaiswal, Rakesh Jaiswal, Maj. Rajinder Singh Jamnal, Jesmin and the women of Savar and Mirpur, Tara Joy, Babar Kabir, Kushi Kabir, Bonani Kakkar, Pradeep Kakkar, Capt. Mostafa Kamal, Abhishek Kar, Raju Keshri, Meeta Khilnani, Radhika Khosla, Zakir Kibria, Sivarma Krishnan, Col. Manoj Kumar, Nitish Kumar, Anil Kuriyal, Bharat Lal, Anuradha Lohia, Arun Lohia, Munmun Maharaj, Iftekhar Mahmud, Petra Manefeld, Elisabeth Fahrni Mansur, Yvonne McPherson, Brij Mehra, Mike Metrik, Vishwanbharnath Mishra, Ramgopal Mohley, Partha Mukhopadhyay, Mukhti, Bob Nickelsberg, Simon Norfolk, Martina Odermatt, Ragini Pandey, Deependar Panwar, Priya Patel, Ajay Puri, Prema Ram, Navneet Raman, Nithya Ramanathan, Jairam Ramesh, Anita Rana, Haroon ur Rashid, Mariam Rashid, Deepak Rathor, Shruti Ravindran, Shravya Reddy, Ibrahim Hafeez Rehman, Rahim Riyaz, Pallavi Sah, Arvind Sand, Ravindra Sand, Benedict Poresh Sardar, Suresh Semwal, Shabnam, A. K. Sharma, Mourvi Sharma, R. P. Sharma, Shashi Shekhar, A. C. Shukla, Ajeet Singh, Arun Singh, Mahavir Singh, Minijit Singh, Rakesh Singh, S. N. Singh, Violet Smith, Salma Sobhan (who left us much too soon), Leena Srivastava, Meera Subramanian, Mahmudul Suman, S. Sundar, Michael Thompson, Sir Crispin Tickell, Vijay Shankar Tiwari, Raitis Vaivods, Annapurna Vankeshwaran, B. G. Verghese, and Petra Wolf.

For the beautiful maps, thanks to Joe Lemonnier.

For Anne, David, and Julia, thanks for your collective creative energy, intellectual and moral curiosity, and regard for fine writing.

For sixteen years of friendship, advice, and support, thanks to my incomparable agent, Henry Dunow. Long-lasting relationships and personal loyalties are increasingly rare in this business, and writers can often feel like relief pitchers in baseball, bouncing from one team to another in search of the best contract for each new season. For that reason, it's a special pleasure to work twice in a row with the same house. Thanks then to Sara Ensey, Meryl Gross, Gwen Hawkes, Steven Seighman, Dori Weintraub, Michelle Cashman, Rob Grom, and the rest of the fine team at St. Martin's Press, but above all to Michael Flamini, who came up with the idea for this book in the first place. Michael, this one's for you.

A NOTE ON LANGUAGE

For anyone with a love of language, India is a special delight. Indian English is deeply idiosyncratic, filled with quirky turns of phrase and archaisms from the days of colonial rule. For a speaker of "standard" English—whatever that may mean—the effect can sometimes be unintentionally comic, and in reproducing conversations verbatim, it's easy for the writer to come across as condescending. I'm fully aware of those pitfalls, but my overriding goal was to capture and respect the authenticity of the voices of those I met on my travels along the Ganges.

Contrary to popular belief, only about ten percent of Indians speak English, and not always fluently. Many of the conversations in this book were with people who spoke only rudimentary English, or none at all. Some switched back and forth between English and their own language. Many spoke only Hindi, or in some cases Urdu. In these situations, the writer is at the mercy of the translator, and inevitably some translators are better than others. Again, I have done my best to convey the speaker's voice as accurately as possible.

Since Independence in 1947, the anglicized names of more than a hundred Indian towns and cities have been changed. The effects of this on popular usage have been uneven. Madras has all but given way to Chennai, yet very few people refer to its southern neighbor as Bengaluru; it's still Bangalore. While some argue for Mumbai, others stay loyal to Bombay. There's a similar tension between the new Kolkata and the old Calcutta—a matter that is debated by residents of the city, fueled by vodka mojitos and *bhang* pakoras, at my Holi party. The most extreme case of all is Varanasi—aka Benares, Banaras, and Kashi. In writing about these places, I've used different variants according to the context, the source, or the speaker.

Above all, of course, there is the name of the great river itself. Is it the Ganges or Ganga? If it's the river goddess, I've always used Ganga, or Ma Ganga. Otherwise, I've used both names, depending on the context and the speaker. When in doubt, my default has been to call it the Ganges, simply because it's more familiar that way to non-Indian readers.

Calamity-averting Ganesh!

Salam!!

Thou who art invoked on the commencement of a journey,

the writing of a book,

Salam!!

Oh! Ganesh, put not thine ears to sleep!

Encourage me, and then behold my bravery.

—FANNY PARKES, *Wanderings of a Pilgrim in Search of the Picturesque*, 1850

PART ONE

MOUNTAINS

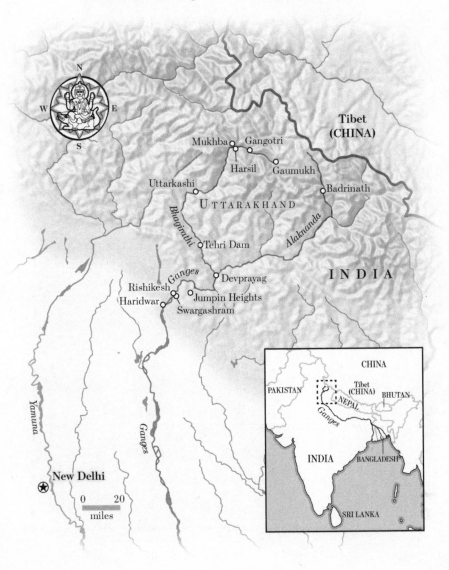

TRAVELERS' TALES

Month after month, snow blankets the great wall of rock that separates India from China and Tibet. It settles, compacts, changes its crystalline structure, freezes solid. The mountain peaks, the highest on earth, are covered with endless fields of ice. Sometimes people call them the Third Pole.

No one really knows how many glaciers there are in the Himalayas. Some say ten thousand; some say more. In India, the second largest is the Gangotri Glacier. In our warming world, it isn't as big as it used to be. Before I left New Delhi for the mountains, I went to see India's best-known glaciologist, Syed Iqbal Hasnain. A jovial, white-haired, grandfatherly man, he told me that the glacier used to cover more than two hundred and fifty square kilometers—about a hundred square miles. "But now it's breaking up in many places. You will see blocks of dead ice that are no longer connected to the main ice body." He chuckled, which seemed odd for someone who was so alarmed by his own findings. But I've often found that maintaining a sense of humor is a common trait among scientists engaged in possibly hopeless endeavors.

The tip of the Gangotri Glacier—what scientists call its toe, or its snout—has receded by about two miles since the first European explorers reached it two hundred years ago. It loses another sixty feet every year. When glaciers decay, they become sad, derelict things. The ice cracks and crumbles and turns a dirty pale blue before melting away altogether. At the snout of the Gangotri Glacier, a thin stream of gray, silt-laden water trickles from a cave surrounded by a bleak, colorless rubble field. So much of the ice is gone that you would have to use your poetic imagination, or look at a very old photograph that shows the long-vanished arch of the cave, to understand why, for centuries, Indians have called it Gaumukh: the Cow's Mouth.

Two hundred miles downstream, the stream reaches a town called Devprayag, which sits on a triangular promontory. By now it has picked up countless tributaries, passed through innumerable villages and pilgrimage towns and a couple of dams, and become a broad, whitecapped torrent. At Devprayag, it is joined by another river of roughly equal size, the Alaknanda, which flows deep and green from the east. From there to the Indian Ocean, another thirteen hundred miles, it is Ma Ganga—Mother Ganga, or, as the British chose to call it, the Ganges.

At Haridwar, the "Gateway of God" and one of the holiest places in Hinduism, the Ganges leaves the mountains and enters the endless dusty plains of North India. Its main tributary, the Yamuna, runs dead and black through Delhi, then skirts the walls of the Taj Mahal in Agra before eventually joining the Ganges in a place that is sacred to Hindus but carries the name it was given by an invading Muslim emperor: Allahabad, City of God. Farther on, bodies burn around the clock in another city, one that has four names: Kashi, Benares, Banaras, Varanasi. The hinterland towns and villages of the great Gangetic Plain seem sometimes to encapsulate everything that ails India: caste prejudice, corruption, rape and sex trafficking, Hindu-Muslim violence, poverty, and pollution. A pall of brown dust and soot hangs over the fields for most of the year, rising from the cookstoves that burn firewood, kerosene, and cow dung in tens of thousands of villages. Three kilometers thick, the brown cloud drifts northward to the Himalayas, turning the ice dark, increasing the speed at which it is melting. But the northern plains, especially the state of Uttar Pradesh with its two hundred million people, also control India's political destiny.

When the river finally approaches its delta—the Hundred Mouths of the Ganges—geographers and believers part company. The Ganges divides. Names change. Swollen by the power of the Brahmaputra, the Son of Brahma, the main stem sweeps eastward into what used to be East Bengal and is now Bangladesh. From the geographer's point of view, this is the true Ganges. It picks up the Jamuna, becomes the Padma, morphs finally into the Meghna, whose estuary is twenty miles wide. But the sacred Ganges of Hinduism—which is also to say the secular Ganges of the British East India Company and the Raj—peels off before the border and heads south, changing its name again as it cuts through the fertile rice fields and palm groves of West Bengal. By the time it reaches Calcutta, present-day Kolkata, it has become the Hooghly.

Seventy miles south of the megacity, and one thousand, five hundred and sixty-nine from the Gangotri Glacier, the Hooghly arrives at last at a flat, oval island, the final point of land. At its southernmost tip is Gangasagar, the last of the river's innumerable pilgrimage sites, where the river dumps a coffee-colored plume of silt a mile long into the Indian Ocean.

By the time it reaches the Bay of Bengal, Ma Ganga has fed half a billion people. The great river is the source of their rice, their wheat, the sole guarantor of their two-dollar-a-day survival. But it is also a seducer, a magnetic field that for centuries has drawn in millions more—empire builders and seekers after enlightenment, butchers and plunderers, scholars and teachers, painters and poets and moviemakers, curiosity seekers and consumers of poverty porn, package-tour pilgrims and yoga-mat carriers and bungee jumpers and drug-addled Deadheads, devotees of the sacred and the profane. They come to witness ineffable beauty and surpassing ugliness, the river as goddess and place of worship and the river as open sewer and factory drain.

Most leave as bewildered as when they arrived. Invariably they report, record, scribble down their thoughts. They contemplate the incomprehensible. How can there be thirty-three million gods? And why do others of the same religion say thirty-three? Why is it auspicious this year to marry between 3:48:16 P.M. on February 14 and 5:29:37 A.M. on the following day? How can an open sewer be holy? They struggle to make sense of the endless conundrum of India.

This place! How can we describe it to you?

They write reports to their imperial masters, newspaper stories, magazine articles and travel journals, scholarly histories, ecstatic poems, catalogs of fish, inventories of temples, lists of the hundred and eight names of Ganga, the thousand and eight names of Lord Shiva, analyses of dissolved oxygen and fecal coliform bacteria. They send prayers to heaven. They write emails home, groping for words. They take countless photographs. They make feature films and reverent documentaries. They post jerky amateur videos on YouTube.

In their suitcases and backpacks, the travelers carry the tales of those who traveled before them. I still remember the first time I read about the Ganges. For an eleven-year-old, I had an odd assortment of passions: soccer, stamp-collecting, and scouring junk shops for antique books and prints. One day, for a few pennies, I bought a slim, leather-bound volume with its title gold-tooled on the spine: *Strange Lands and Their People*. Published in 1827, its purpose was to edify, horrify, excite curiosity, but above all to rally the reader behind the civilizing mission of Christianity. The text was broken up every few pages with a woodblock print showing some piece of local exotica: a sled pulled by reindeer in Lapland, ranks of Muslims pressing their foreheads to the ground in prayer, the skeleton of a woolly mammoth encased in Siberian ice. In the chapter on India, the image was of a widow throwing herself on her husband's funeral pyre on the banks of the Ganges in Benares. Formally dressed Englishmen stood off at a distance, clapping their hands to their mouths in horror.

I thought of that woodcut often as I traveled along the Ganges, imagining that this might have been one of the books that early English travelers packed in their portmanteaus and steamer trunks for the three-week journey from Calcutta to Allahabad, whiling away the long hours under a sunshade on the sweltering deck of a budgerow or swaying from side to side in a palanquin. Today's travelers do their reading on the long flight to Delhi, by the dim night-light in the 2AC coach of the Shiv Ganga Express as it clatters across the endless plains of Uttar Pradesh, or sitting cross-legged on the ghats of Varanasi, the steep steps and platforms where the pilgrims come at dawn for their holy dip. The books they carry could stock a small library. There are accounts by those who have traveled all the way from the Cow's Mouth to the ocean on foot, sunburned, stricken with dysentery, sleeping every night in a different but identical village, getting by on a dozen words of Hindi, starting with *chapati* and *dal* and *chai*. Others have made the journey by boat and where necessary by bus, nostalgic for the days of the Raj, tossing out droll asides about impassive or incompetent oarsmen and native bearers. Others have sailed the whole way. Some have struck off on side trips through the labyrinthine channels of the delta in Bangladesh. Others have attempted the journey to the Himalayas in reverse, fighting against the current in jet boats, until they had to admit defeat when faced with the last of the rapids.

As I traveled the Ganges from source to mouth—not in a single journey but in many discontinuous ones—I carried my own share of these books, with each of the authors leaving something new imprinted on the long chain of narrative, adding their own notes of curiosity, distaste, cynicism, ecstasy, and reverence.

Rudyard Kipling, writing for *The Pioneer*, the newspaper that briefly employed him in Allahabad, hated the sight of dead bodies floating in the river.

Mark Twain wrote the line that has been quoted more than any other: "Benares is older than history, older than tradition, older even than legend, and looks twice as old as all of them put together."

Seventy years later, Allen Ginsberg would sit for hours in a kind of morbid trance among the naked sadhus on the cremation ghats. One night, stoned as usual on ganja, he watched, fascinated, as "the middle corpse had burst through the belly which fell out, intestines sprang up (that is) like a jack in the box charcoal glumpf."

George Harrison spent equally long hours in the beehive-shaped meditation chambers of the Maharishi Mahesh Yogi's ashram in Rishikesh, composing songs for the Beatles' *White Album*. "That Maharishi's a nice man, but he's not for me," said Ringo Starr, who was homesick for Liverpool and tired of eating eggs and beans.

When Poland opened its borders in the 1950s after the death of Stalin, the journalist Ryszard Kapuściński's first trip was to India. Like everyone, he watched the bodies burning on the ghats of Varanasi. From there he took the train to Calcutta, where he struggled through the crowds sleeping on the floor of Sealdah Station in the floodwaters of the monsoon.

Kapuściński, who carried with him *The Histories of Herodotus*, the first travel reporter, understood the nature of journeys better than anyone. "A journey, after all, neither begins in the instant we set out, nor ends when we have reached our doorstep once again," he wrote. "It starts much earlier and is really never over, because the film of memory continues running on inside of us long after we have come to a physical standstill."

Part of my own film of memory was made up of stories that were drawn from other authors whose names would never be known, those who wrote the great legends of Hinduism: the Mahābhārata, the Rāmāyaṇa, and the Puranas. They were a constant reminder that the Ganges is no ordinary river and that a physical journey is not the only way of going to its source. I found its beginnings in the unlikeliest of places, as far as you can get from the glaciers and the ocean and the cremation fires, in a land that had no rivers at all.

PRESENT AT THE CREATION

Turn left at the monkeys," said Sumant, an affable young man with the face of a cherub, who had come to the burning Thar Desert of Rajasthan to explore the possibilities of solar energy.

Sure enough, a mile or two on, we came upon the monkeys, a pack of a hundred or more scavengers at a dirt truck stop, pouncing on plastic bags and mango skins and evading kicks and swipes from the drivers of the big painted Tata trucks. We turned left and headed deeper into the desert toward Jodhpur, the Blue City, where I was going to meet a woman named Kanupriya Harish.

In the world of water, Kanupriya was something of a celebrity. She was a brisk young woman with sensible glasses and a laptop full of PowerPoint presentations. She was the head of the Jal Bhagirathi Foundation, which had its offices in the converted nineteenth-century summer palace of Maharaja Takhat Singh, a sand-brown building on a low, sand-brown hill on the outskirts of Jodhpur. Twice she had hosted Prince Charles. The first time, he came with Camilla Parker-Bowles. The second time, he arrived in time for Holi, the spring festival of colors. Kanupriya invited him to join a celebratory dance with a group of local men. They wore turbans, earrings, and memorable Rajasthani mustaches. The prince wore a gray double-breasted suit. He twirled around for a couple of minutes, holding a brightly striped parasol. When they complimented him on his moves, he said, "It's hereditary."

Kanupriya fired up her slideshow. A woman scrabbled a hole in the sand in search of seepage. Girls trudged through the desert with battered aluminum water pots on their heads. Men dug fathomless tube wells, going deeper each year. "There is nothing harder than finding water in the desert," Kanupriya said, "and that is how we got our name."

You could have written my Hindi vocabulary on the back of a postage stamp and still had room for a shopping list, but one of the few words I did know was *jal*—water. So what about the *Bhagirathi* part? Desert?

She shook her head. "Something that is very hard to do, a task that requires a lot of effort and brings praise and honor to the one who carries it out: this is called *Bhagirath Prayatna*."

"So *Jal Bhagirathi* is the task of finding water?"

"In a way. But Bhagiratha was a king. Let me tell you the story."

Every Hindu knows the legend, which is recounted in the scriptures with innumerable variants and sub-variants, elaborated and embroidered down the centuries by oral transmission. This is the version that Kanupriya Harish told me.

There was once a king of Ayodhya, the birthplace of Lord Ram, named Sagara. He was a generous and judicious ruler, but his great misfortune was to be childless. However, the gods eventually granted his wish for an heir—which is something of an understatement, since one of his two wives gave birth to sixty thousand sons. Their seeds were nurtured in a gourd, and when they were born, a nurse tended to each of them in a jar of ghee, or clarified butter.

Toward the end of his reign, Sagara decided to perform the traditional horse sacrifice, the *aswamedha*. This involved sending out a white stallion to roam the land for a year, at the end of which it would be sacrificed to propitiate the gods. The territories through which it wandered would be brought under the king's sovereign rule. Those in its path would be offered a choice: succumb or fight. But somewhere along the way, the horse went missing, abducted by the gods because they were fearful that King Sagara's power might come to extend as far as the heavens.

Where was the horse? Puzzled and angry, Sagara dispatched his sons to search for the missing animal. They scoured the high mountains and tore apart the forests. By some accounts they dug deep into the underworld, until eventually they came to the ocean, or perhaps it was their digging and delving that created the oceans in the first place. On the farthest shore, they found the horse grazing peacefully by the ashram of a great sage, a rishi, named Kapila. They cursed him as the thief. Kapila flew into a rage at being disturbed during his meditation, at the insult to his good name. He opened his eyes and shot bolts of fire at the intruders, or perhaps the fierceness of his gaze was enough to produce spontaneous combustion. Whatever the case, the sons of King Sagara, all sixty thousand of them, were incinerated on the spot.

Kapila said that only one thing could redeem their ashes and allow them to enter heaven. The goddess Ganga would have to be called down from her celestial realm, where she had issued from the big toe of the left foot of Vishnu, preserver of the universe, and wash them clean of their sins.

King Sagara tried for thirty thousand years to persuade the goddess to come to earth, but she refused. In the course of time, his great-great-grandson, Bhagiratha, took up the problem. He journeyed to the snowbound peaks of the Himalayas near Mount Kailash, the home of Lord Shiva, where he stood on a rock on one leg for a thousand years in a place that is now called Gangotri. Brahma, the creator, was so impressed that he agreed to summon Ganga to earth. But her descent, the *Gangavatarana*, was no simple matter; even if the impetuous young goddess agreed, she might crack apart the universe with the power of her flood.

The dilemma was resolved by Shiva, the blue-skinned, trident-wielding destroyer of worlds, the god who was both benign and fearsome, ascetic and voluptuary, with the moon on his head. Curling around the moon, the temperamental goddess came down from the Milky Way in a frothing fury, her waters teeming with fish, but Shiva broke her fall by entangling her in his thick, matted dreadlocks. When he had tamed the flood, he channeled it into seven rivers. The most important of these issued from Gaumukh, the snout of the Gangotri Glacier, where it took the name of King Bhagiratha. From there to Devprayag, where it joins the Alaknanda, the river is still called the Bhagirathi.

Ganga's journey from there to the ocean was not without incident. As she crossed the plains, preceded by King Bhagiratha in his chariot, the torrent so upset a young ascetic that he swallowed her to the last drop. The gods were forced to intercede again, prevailing on him to release her, by way of his ear. Eventually the river reached its great delta, where it braided itself into a labyrinth of channels and distributaries as dense and tangled as Shiva's hair. In the end, it came to Gangasagar, where today there is a simple, modern temple dedicated to Kapila, the sage who turned the sons of Sagara to a smoking heap of ash. The name can be translated in two ways: as the marriage of river and ocean or the union of goddess and king.

THE WATER PYRAMID

The road west from Jodhpur became narrower and emptier, threading its way through an infinite landscape of sand dunes, wild peacocks that erupted suddenly from the shade of *khejri* thorn trees, and plodding camel carts pulling water tanks with swastikas daubed on the sides for good luck.

A few miles short of the border with Pakistan, we ran into a line of a dozen tanks performing maneuvers across a crunching salt flat. A soldier gave us a baleful look, hoisted his weapon, and signaled us to circle around the convoy at a safe distance.

"Will there be war?" I asked our taciturn driver. India and Pakistan were in one of those cycles where the sabers were being rattled.

"Most definitely," he said. His expression suggested that if he had been on the other side of hostilities, he would have added *insh'allah*.

"But both of your countries have nuclear weapons," I said.

The response to this was an enthusiastic nod. "Yes, and we will drop one on Islamabad."

"But then they will drop one on Delhi."

"But if they do that, we will destroy all of their cities," he said. A beatific look spread across his broad features. "And then there will be peace forever."

We came to a collection of round mud huts with conical thatch roofs, encircled in a thorn break. We might have been in Africa, but for the barefooted women in rainbow saris who were stamping cow dung into a flat surface for their yards. When they were done, it had the look of poured and polished concrete.

Beyond this compound, out in the open desert, sat the miraculous machine that the Dutch engineers had brought to the remote village of Roopji Raja Beri. It was a sleek mushroom cap of silvery plastic, thirty feet high. It looked as if the pilot of a UFO had set his machine down for refueling among the sand dunes, and it was Prema Ram's pride and joy.

Prema Ram was the *sarpanch*, a figure of some considerable authority, acting as the intermediary between the village and the government. He was a tall, beefy man, draped in loose white cotton, his big head encased in a turban of red, green, purple, and gold. He wore small, petal-patterned earrings and an extravagant mustache. He was a proud twenty-year veteran of the Indian Army, and his barrel chest seemed to expand visibly as he recounted the particulars of his service, nose to nose with the enemy in the freezing altitudes of Kashmir. It seemed best to keep him away from the driver; I had no stomach for further talk of war.

Prema Ram cleaned out some stainless-steel thimble cups with the meat of his thumb, and we drank the obligatory chai, tooth-rottingly sweet, and nibbled on the obligatory dry biscuits that are one of the minor legacies of the Raj. Prema Ram turned morose. Hearts and sometimes bones were broken over water here, he said. Four inches of rainfall amounted to a good year. What little remained in the ground was so salty it could burn your tongue. "The natural order is breaking," he said.

Then he led us across to the silvery structure, where he cheered up. He peeled back two flaps of heavy plastic film, like a conjurer demonstrating a magic trick. A blast of heat and humidity hit me in the face. He waved his hand at a shimmering sheet of water inside, which was the size and depth of a small backyard swimming pool. He thumped his fist on the side, and sparkling droplets trickled down the interior walls. It was an exercise in physics and chemistry, elementary but ingenious. You pumped the brackish water from the ground, used the blazing heat of the desert sun to evaporate it, drew off the salt to sell later, and collected the distilled drinking water as it ran down into a storage tank.

"We call it the water pyramid," Kanupriya told me. But it had another name, too: *Shiv Jaldhara*—Shiva's constant flow of water, the guarantee of all life. Having brought the Ganges down to earth from the Milky Way, the great god is worshipped in every rock and ripple of the river, all the way from its source in the glaciers of the Himalayas to its Hundred Mouths in the Bay of Bengal, and out here in the farthest reaches of Rajasthan.

The reason for this second name was that the water pyramid had been inaugurated a few years earlier on the Mahashivaratri, the Great Night of Shiva—the night, some say, of his *nataraja*, his whirling cosmic dance in a ring of fire. A statue of the *nataraja* stands outside the headquarters of CERN, the European Organization for Nuclear Research in Geneva. For physicists, it is a symbol of the dance of subatomic matter, although others see it as the dance of divine creation and destruction. Which may arguably be two ways of saying the same thing.

It was time for my journey to take a more conventional form, so I left the desert behind and headed for the mountains. The timing was good, for I arrived just in time for the Mahashivaratri. But that part of the story comes a little later.

THE COW'S MOUTH

When Warren Hastings, the first governor-general of India, arrived in Calcutta in 1772, the place was in turmoil. A parliamentary committee had recently accused the British East India Company of "the most atrocious abuses that ever stained the name of civil government." All that mattered to the officers of the Hon'ble Company was the rapacious pursuit of private wealth. India was an unlocked store waiting for the shelves to be looted. "We have outdone the Spaniards in Peru," said the politician and writer Horace Walpole. "They were at least butchers on a religious principle, however diabolical their zeal."

Hastings came in to clean the slate. If you were to rule a country, did you not have an obligation to understand it? He took pains to learn passable Hindi and Urdu. It might have been the Age of Empire, but it was also the Age of Enlightenment, although sometimes it was hard to know where to draw the line between the two. The Orientalists, as men like Hastings came to be known, wanted to know the size, weight, and value in pounds sterling of all things. They sought out intelligence on the riches that could be extracted from the lands they had conquered and the strength, location, and disposition of potential competitors. But at the same time, they were serious scholars of religion, promoters of Sanskrit literature, historians, geologists, philologists, archaeologists, antiquarians. In 1784, Sir William Jones, the very epitome of the Orientalist, founded the Asiatic Society of Bengal. "The intended objects of the Asiatic Society," he wrote, "were Man and Nature—whatever is performed by the one, or produced by the other—within the geographic limits of Asia, with Hindustan as a centre."

Of all the scholarly disciplines Hastings had at his disposal, the most important was cartography. If you wanted to understand the country you were ruling, the first thing you had to do was map it, and much of India remained terra incognita, especially its great northern barrier wall of rock and snow. The greatest mystery of all concerned the source of the Ganges. The Orientalists were familiar with the rudiments of its creation myth, but renderings of the upper course of the Ganges in eighteenth-century maps might just as well have been labeled "Here Be Dragons." What little the mapmakers knew was drawn from travelers' tales and anecdotes, not from science or firsthand observation—and that had remained true since the days of Ptolemy, fifteen hundred years earlier.

Drawing on the accounts of early Greek and Roman writers, Ptolemy made a map that showed the Ganges flowing in a southeasterly direction from the Himalayas to the ocean. He distinguished the regions to the west and the east of the river. *India intra Gangem, India extra Gangem.* There was general agreement that neither the Danube nor the Nile could bear comparison. Pliny the Elder had heard that the Ganges "bursts at once with thundering roar from its fountain." Downstream there was a giant lake. After that, the river was never less than eight miles wide, he reported, and never less than twenty fathoms deep. The third-century poet Dionysius Periegete seems to have been the first to comment on the spiritual significance of the river as well as its physical character. "Hard by the fair-flowing Ganges is a wondrous spot of holy ground greatly honored," he wrote.

The seventh-century pilgrim Xuanzang was one of many Chinese who made their way at the time to the holiest Buddhist sites in India, bringing back manuscripts and artifacts. The most notable of these sites was Sarnath, six or seven miles outside Varanasi, where the Buddha had preached his first sermon and the two great religions, Buddhism and Hinduism, diverged to follow radically different paths, one serene and contemplative and the other clamorous and charged with myths and epic stories. Xuanzang reached the Ganges after spending two years in Kashmir. "The water of the river is blue, like the ocean, and its waves are wide-rolling as the sea," he wrote. He also wrote about the funeral rites that were conducted on its banks, describing it as "the river of religious merit, which can wash away countless sins. Those who are weary of life, if they end their days in it, are borne to heaven and receive happiness."

Muslim travelers arrived with the Mughal invaders who swept down from the plains of Central Asia, beginning in the eleventh century, put North India to the sword, and razed thousands of its temples. Al-Biruni synthesized accounts of the "River of Paradise" from Hindu scripture. Ibn Baṭṭūṭah described how water from the Ganges, *gangajal*, was transported overland for forty days for the delectation of the sultan of Delhi. Later, the Muslim emperor Akbar, who gave Allahabad its name, employed specially designated servants to carry it in fine copper jars all the way from the holy city of Haridwar to his court at Agra, where his grandson, Shah Jahan, would later build the Taj Mahal.

Akbar ruled in the seventeenth century, and the accounts of his high regard for the "water of immortality" come from the first European writer-travelers in India, who arrived at around the same time. The Englishman Nicholas Withington was probably the first to add scientific curiosity to what was by now a good number of generally repetitive accounts of the river's religious attributes. What struck him most was that the water of the Ganges "will never stinke, though kepte never so longe, neyther will any wormes or vermine breede therein." The Frenchman Jean-Baptiste Tavernier was skeptical of this theory, "taking into consideration the number of bodies which are constantly being thrown into the Ganges." Dr. E. Hanbury Hankin, chief medical officer for Agra, was still puzzling over the phenomenon in 1896, when the Institut Pasteur in Paris published the results of his investigation. Hankin described how he had collected cholera-infected bodies thrown into the river at Varanasi and found that the microbes died within a few hours of contact with water.

The Orientalists' first great mapping effort was conducted by the surveyor general of Bengal, Major James Rennell. *A Bengal Atlas and Map of Hindoostan*, which he published in 1781, gave a strikingly accurate picture of the Ganges south of Haridwar. But in the mountains to the north, he was as lost as anyone. All he had to go on was scripture, myth, and hearsay. Where was the rock on which King Bhagiratha had stood for a thousand years? Where was Shiva standing when the goddess came hurtling down from heaven through his dreadlocks? This part of his map was drawn with frowns of puzzlement.

Conventional wisdom, such as it was, held that Ganga must have come to earth in or around Shiva's Himalayan abode, Mount Kailash, a great pyramidal slab of black rock, twenty-two thousand feet high, in western Tibet. Tibetan Buddhists also held the mountain sacred, and they reinforced this legend in their conversations with the first European missionaries to reach the secretive kingdom. Perhaps the river did not spring from the mountain itself, the lamas said, but from nearby Mansarovar, the Lake of Consciousness, or from a smaller body of water next to it, Rakshastal.

Rennell went along with the Mansarovar theory but added one intriguing detail:

> *This great body of water now forces a passage through the ridge of mount Himmaleh, and sapping its very foundation, rushes through a cavern, and precipitates itself into a vast bason which it has worn in the rock, at the hither foot of the mountains. The Ganges thus appears to incurious spectators, to derive its original springs from this chain of mountains: and the mind of superstition has given the mouth of the cavern, the form of the head of a cow, an animal held by the Hindoos, in a degree of veneration, almost equal to that, in which the Egyptians of old, held their god Apis.*

For a generation of British explorers, that detail—the cavern and the cow's head—was like the first clue in a treasure hunt that became an obsession.

In 1808, Robert Colebrooke, a military surveyor and talented watercolorist, planned the first official expedition to find the source of the Ganges. He fell ill and died before the mission could depart, but Captain William Webb and the unfortunately named Captain William Raper took up the mantle. They passed through Haridwar, cut across country, and reached the ruined town of Uttarkashi, which had been flattened by a great earthquake five years earlier. They made notes on local cultural practices and agricultural methods. They calculated the height of mountains by triangulation. They labored on for another twenty miles or more upriver. Their equipment was burdensome. Should they leave their tents behind? No, the spring weather was too fickle. The march was slower, more arduous, and more perilous each day, before finally they decided to abandon the expedition, across the river from a village called Salang and still five or six days short of Gangotri.

They persuaded one of their local guides to go on alone, however. They gave him a compass and instructed him in its use, and with his help, they eventually produced a map that traced another thirty miles or so of the river before dribbling away into uncertainties: the word *Gangotri* floats among some vague contour lines showing the "Himalaya or Snowy Range of Mountains" and then, somewhere to the north, is *Mahádéva ca linga*—a reference to Mount Kailash.

In the reports they published in Calcutta in *Asiatick Researches*, Webb and Raper discounted Rennell's notion of the curiously shaped cavern. Webb wrote, "Every account agreed that the Source of the River is . . . not, as it is related, through a Secret passage or Cavern bearing any similitude to a cow's mouth." Raper concurred: "With respect to the Cow's Mouth, we had the most convincing testimony to confirm us in the idea that its existence is entirely fabulous, and that it is found only in the Hindu book of faith."

The first European finally reached Gangotri in 1815: the intrepid Scottish painter and travel writer James Baillie Fraser, fifteenth laird of Reelig. Along the way, he created a series of paintings and aquatints that gave interested parties in Calcutta and London their first sight of the inspirational landscapes of the upper Bhagirathi, subtly enhanced in the best Romantic manner: the peaks always steeper and sharper than they are in reality, the chasms deeper and darker, the torrents fiercer and more tumultuous, and the colorful locals looking like extras in a production of *Ali Baba and the Forty Thieves*. Fraser, too, had heard the stories of the Cow's Mouth. "Enquiries were made into the origin of this fable," he wrote, but a priest at the Gangotri temple "gravely assured us that no such thing happened." No doubt, like Raper's informants, he had his reasons for trying to throw sacrilegious foreigners off the scent.

By 1817, two things had changed. After a two-year war, the recalcitrant Gurkhas had been put in their place, and the British took over direct rule of the mountainous region. With this came an end to the local maharaja's divinely ordained monopoly of the right to enlist porters without pay. Tourists and explorers took full advantage of the change, and if a porter protested, one of the standard punishments was to have a commode stuck on his head.

On May 31, 1817, Captains John Hodgson and James Herbert finally proved that the Cow's Mouth was no fable. After reaching Gangotri, they pressed on for five days to the western tip of the Gangotri Glacier, where they found the Bhagirathi gushing out of its low-arched cave, surrounded by forbidding snow peaks. Hodgson took out his measuring chain. The stream was twenty-seven feet wide and eighteen inches deep. This was the true source of the Ganges, he decided. "There is every reason to suppose, its first appearance is at the *debouche*, which I will call MAHA'DE'O's hair." This is the strangest detail of all. Mahadeo, or Mahadev, is Shiva. But why his hair? Because of the icicles hanging down from the cow's mouth. According to a contemporary account, this notion came from an illiterate Brahmin whom Hodgson met in Gangotri: the icicles were the dreadlocks of Shiva.

THE TEMPLE ON THE ROCK

On the way to Gangotri, I fell in with a motley group of assorted nationalities, two Americans, two Indians, and a German. The Indian woman was named Pallavi, and her son, Pranav, drove us up there. One of the Americans, Paula, was a serious student of Ayurvedic medicine who had rented a tiny cottage on the riverbank in Uttarkashi. Petra, the German, and her American husband, Mike, were traveling around India on foot, but the road to Gangotri was steep and winding and crowded with buses, and even though the buses had a disturbing tendency to barrel around blind corners, they'd hopped aboard one of them to spare their tired legs.

Other than the caves and rough shelters that house a handful of sadhus, Gangotri is the first human habitation on the Ganges. At the northernmost extension of the town, a swami had painted his house electric blue and set out a La-Z-Boy recliner on the deck so he could enjoy an unobstructed view of the river. Behind his home, the head of the valley was closed off by formidable snow peaks.

The river is still named the Bhagirathi here, honoring the king who impressed the gods by standing on one leg for a thousand years. It is a modest stream that runs blue gray with silt from the glacier. Pilgrims were clustered on the rocky bank. Some were swallowing mouthfuls of the icy water as an elixir. They call it *amrit*, nectar. Women in bright saris waded out knee-deep, filling small plastic flasks to take home. Indians living abroad can buy a bottle on Amazon or eBay for $9.95.

The town itself was similarly modest. An open area for the buses to park, a narrow main street lined with guesthouses and stalls selling religious items and trinkets, leading to a flagstone square with a squat white temple where the effigy of the goddess Ganga is housed until the first snows, when she is carried farther down the valley for safekeeping in the village of Mukhba. Pilgrims were lined up in single file behind a chain barrier, waiting their turn to squeeze between the iron concertina gates that guarded the entrance to the temple. Children dressed up as gods patrolled the crowd with begging bowls.

The goddess was still inside, because we were in the brief window between the snowmelt and the onset of the monsoon when it's safe to travel up here without the risk of floods and landslides that can block the road for weeks. Even so, the nights were bitingly cold, and I slept fully clothed under a pair of rough, scratchy blankets in a guesthouse called the Ganga Nivas, the Ganges Residence. It had a dozen rooms. *Spartan* would be a kind word. The only light was a feeble bulb on the balcony, powered by a diesel generator that ticked all night. The room keys hung from hooks on a wooden board right out on the street. We were above eleven thousand feet, and a sign on the facing wall advertised Free Oxygen Service.

In the morning, we found a restaurant that served regional specialties for pilgrims from South India. It had bathroom-tile walls and a kitchen open to the dining area, where the waiters shoveled *masala dosa* and *idli* onto stainless-steel plates. A tourist poster showed men playing golf at the old British hill station of Ranikhet. The *dosa* were fragrant and spicy; the *idli* were as insipid as always. We drank watery Nescafé against the cold, and the women wore heavy shawls over their heads.

Petra did a lot of the talking. She had a square, jolly face with glittering eyes and a pronounced gap in her front teeth, which put me in mind of Chaucer's garrulous and sensual Wife of Bath. "Gat-tothed was she, soothly for to seye. . . . Housbondes at chirche dore she hadde fyve."

The Wife of Bath was also a traveler. "Thries hadde she been at Jerusalem," Chaucer wrote, and Petra said she had also been there. In fact, she and her husband had just completed the second edition of their book, which was called *Encounters on the Road to Jerusalem*. They also had a website called walkingwithawareness.com. They had been bitten by the walking bug after meeting on the pilgrim road to Santiago de Compostela, and after marrying, they walked across the United States from their home in Paso Robles, California. When they got to the other side of the Atlantic, they kept going all the way to the Holy Land. The whole journey took them a month short of two years, and they arrived in Bethlehem on Christmas Day. Now they walked everywhere.

After breakfast, we went up the square and stopped at the home of one of the temple priests. Several soldiers were standing around inside. They wore patches on their uniforms identifying them as grenadiers, and they were looking for a place to sleep. The priest, who was wearing a scarlet scarf over a yellow cotton shirt, asked me to sit next to him on a sort of low platform. He had a kind and gentle face.

His name was Suresh Semwal. He told me that like all the Semwals, he came from Mukhba, twenty-five kilometers downstream, where the effigy of the goddess spent the winter months. The priesthood was hereditary and had been passed down through at least fifteen generations of Semwals and perhaps twenty. I asked if he had a son, and his expression turned despondent.

He said the young man had moved away and was studying engineering. "He can choose his own career," he said. "The income here is not good."

He leaned over and patted my arm. "But our faith is very strong. Ma Ganga flows in us like your blood is flowing through your body. It is our lifeline."

I asked him how many priests served in the temple.

"Two hundred gents are doing worship here," he said. They worked on a rota system, and their main source of income was donations from pilgrims. Five hundred people ate in the temple kitchen each day, and the money went into the temple trust. The pilgrims came from all over India, from Madras, from Bombay, from faraway Bengal. The most pious or energetic ones did the full *char dham yatra*, which took them to four sacred sites on the headwaters of the river. These days many of them came on package tours. The wealthiest ones even came by helicopter. But then the state of Uttarakhand had been struck by disaster. In 2013, six thousand people had died in freak monsoon floods that came in June, a month earlier than usual; the roads were impassable for weeks. Two years later, the *yatra* had still not recovered. Before the catastrophe, as many as a million and a half people had come each year; now there were barely a tenth of that number.

We went outside, and I told the priest that I wanted to see the rock on which King Bhagiratha had performed his one-legged austerities. I imagined a flat boulder in midstream. But perhaps it was no longer there? Those events had happened in ancient times. He smiled and walked me over to an enclosure where a small area of bedrock had been left deliberately exposed among the flagstones. He waved an arm around the square. "All of this is the rock on which King Bhagiratha stood," he said. "The whole town of Gangotri is founded upon it."

"Yes," Pallavi said under her breath, "and every building here is illegal, but what can you do about it?"

Semwal introduced us to a group of three fellow priests who were chatting on a green-painted bench that would not have been out of place in an English park. On the wall behind them, the words *Record Room* were written in faded red paint. One of the other priests, an imposing middle-aged man with a large nose and a clipped gray mustache, took me inside. There was hardly any room to move about, because the floor was almost entirely covered with large wooden crates. We sat on one of them, and he opened the one next to it. It was filled with dog-eared ledgers, the pages densely covered with spidery writing, figures, and dates. They were records of those who had made the pilgrimage, organized by family and place of origin; you could trace when your ancestors had visited.

The priest sighed. "There used to be records here that went back more than two hundred years," he said. "But they were stored in a wooden hut that burned down fifty years ago." He closed the lid of the crate and pushed it back into its corner.

Records that burned; pilgrims who drowned; a temple too poor to sustain its hereditary traditions. It was a day of brilliant spring sunshine, but I found Gangotri to be a melancholy place.

CAVE DWELLERS

Suresh Semwal said that about twenty sadhus lived year-round in caves in the mountains around Gangotri. We went to see one of them.

"A sadhu's only connection is with the underlying reality, the truth eternal," said a woman who lived in a nearby ashram. "He renounces all worldly things and severs all ties to society. This is why he wears saffron, because it's the color of fire, the fire that burns away all bonds."

In the narrow streets of Gangotri, there are blind sadhus and sighted sadhus, sadhus with one arm, sadhus with one leg, sadhus with no legs at all who propel themselves around on little wheelie carts, and sadhus with the physiques of Olympic athletes. There are sadhus who will happily tell you the story of their past lives, a disgruntled high school teacher from Kolkata, a widowed company executive from Mumbai. There are sadhus who will answer your greeting with a stare as icy as the glaciers, and sadhus who will respond with bursts of stoned hilarity.

We crossed a small bridge and hiked along the east bank of the river for a couple of miles. It had cut its passage through the bedrock in a thunderous series of channels, chutes, caverns, and waterfalls. The rough trail took us through an airy forest of deodar cedars and chir pines, and along the way, Pallavi told me that this was no ordinary cave we were visiting. It made a cameo in a story from one of the two great Sanskrit epics, the Mahābhārata.

A king named Yudhishthira, his wife, his four brothers, and his dog decided to renounce the world and walk all the way to heaven, passing through Gangotri. This cave was one of their resting places. After they moved on, they began to fall off the cliffs to their death, one after another, failing to reach heaven because of one sin or another—gluttony, narcissism, overweening pride. Only the unblemished Yudhishthira and his dog were spared. When they reached the highest peak, Indra told the king that he had passed the test and was free to enter heaven, but it was no place for dogs. Yudhishthira refused to leave the animal behind; it was his faithful and devoted companion. Indra relented, saying that the dog must be the incarnation of dharma, the divine principle of righteousness. So both of them climbed into Indra's chariot for the ascent to heaven. The moral of the story appeared to be that dharma will follow you to the end.

Dark smoke was wafting from the mouth of the cave, which had a heavy, barred iron door. Inside it was pitch-black apart from the red glow of the sadhu's fire, and the air was thick with woodsmoke and reefer. We felt our way to a flat outcrop of rock. The sadhu cackled and chanted *Om, Jai Ram Shri Ram* in the darkness.

"Why did you become a sadhu?" Pallavi asked him after a decent interval of silence.

He chanted some more of his devotion to Lord Ram, then finally said he had been born in the town of Muzaffarnagar, down in the plains, halfway between Delhi and the sacred city of Haridwar, where he went to college and studied Sanskrit. He had come to Gangotri ten years ago. "You ask why I became a sadhu?" he said, cackling again. "Well, everyone has to do something in life. Most people get married and have babies. I decided to do something different."

Pallavi asked him who his guru was. This is a matter of deep significance, and she and her English husband, Michael, had told me the story of how they had found theirs. Pallavi was a journalist. Michael was working for a small environmental organization in Vrindavan, which stands on the Yamuna near its confluence with the Ganges and is the place where Lord Krishna played his flute for the milkmaids. They met online, just before Michael turned fifty. He was searching for something that was still elusive. In Haridwar, he found a sadhu named Jagdish Giri, who agreed to take them on. Michael was his only Western initiate; Pallavi became his first woman initiate.

"Your guru sees you, he judges you, he whispers a mantra that he thinks will help you," Pallavi said. "Michael and I were initiated at the same time, so we probably have the same mantra. But you never divulge it to anyone, not even to your spouse."

Jagdish had lived for thirty years in a cave in the mountains above Gangotri. He was a warrior sadhu, a member of the fearsome Juna Akhara. "They're trained to be very hard-core, trained in martial arts, then given weapons," Michael said. "They're the protectors of other sadhus. They have fortified areas up in the mountains, and they'll drive away outsiders with slingshots."

But Jagdish was anything but a forbidding character. "He's about seventy now," Michael said. "He's a virgin, never touched cigarettes or booze. Lives in a hut under two trees that are intertwined, a peepul and a neem.

Terribly eco-conscious. He's a simple person. You know, suffer the little children, no skullduggery, no agenda. We don't even see him that often, but we don't really need to. When your guru is spiritually attuned to you, it's like remote sensing."

The sadhu in the cave seemed to be evading Pallavi's question. Eventually he mumbled that his guru was dead. A cloud of ganja smoke drifted across the cave. He started praising Lord Ram again. My questions seemed to irritate him. I asked if he found visitors an inconvenience. He grunted. "I just sit in my corner and do my own thing. I sleep peaceful at night. I don't like to chitchat with people." He grew agitated when I told him about my conversation with the priests in Gangotri. "This is not a place you should come to play or enjoy yourself. You should come here for your penance. This is the realm of the gods. The celestial beings roam around here in the shape of the air and the sunlight."

Suddenly, the cave was illuminated. The light was only from two low-wattage bulbs, but the abruptness of it was dazzling. He giggled; this was his party trick. He was sitting behind the fire on a cement platform. His eyes were staring wide, his teeth were startlingly white, and he wore a manic grin. His beard was tumultuous. He breathed out a lungful of ganja.

"Look at this!" he said. There were two long shelves filled with stainless-steel tableware. The lightbulbs hung from a wire that snaked across the wall, pilfering electricity from a tiny hydropower plant on the river. "Lots of people used to stay in this cave for a short time," he said. "I've been here seven years and one month. I've improved the whole thing. Look at these walls! They used to leak, but I brought in cement and stone to seal the cracks. I like it here. I prefer to not be around other people."

The lights went out again, and the silence returned. The embers burned low.

"What a phony," Pallavi muttered. "Ninety percent of them are into drugs.

They say it makes it easier for them to connect with their inner self. Such bullshit. He probably can't afford his habit, just hangs around with the *babas* smoking theirs."

We took our leave, but he seemed to have forgotten all about us. As we walked away from the cave, the chant of *Jai Ram Shri Ram* started up again, a low, steady drone over the muffled roar of the river.

THE RAJA OF HARSIL

For Pranav, as for many Indian drivers, the most important instrument in any vehicle was the horn, and he had a deeply adversarial relationship with trucks and buses. These part company with Indian roads with some regularity, despite the best efforts of government sign painters, who leave their warnings inscribed at intervals on the roads into the Himalayas.

BETTER TO BE MR. LATE THAN THE LATE MR.

AFTER WHISKY, DRIVING RISKY

ROAD IS HILLY, DON'T DRIVE SILLY

On the way down the mountain from Gangotri, we overtook an ancient bus belching out black diesel smoke. We passed donkey trains carrying sacks of sand and gravel from the river and a woman who was stumbling along the side of the road, carrying a dead goat on her shoulders. We stopped to ask what had happened. The animal had fallen off a cliff, but no matter, she was taking it home for dinner. The bus drove past us in a black cloud. A little later, we passed it again. This game of leapfrog went on for some time. "*Chutiya!*" Pallavi snapped as the bus accelerated on a bend to overtake us again. She groped for an accurate translation. *Total moron* came close. Or maybe *douche-bag* was better. (Pallavi was a decorous translator, another Indian friend told me later with some embarrassment; literally, it's *cunt*.)

"If you really want to insult someone, *bhenchod* is worse," Pranav remarked from the driver's seat. "*Sisterfucker.*"

"Well, you can also say *maderchod*," Pallavi said after a moment's reflection. "That's *motherfucker.*"

They debated which was worse. Pranav voted for *maderchod*. His reasoning was that mothers were deserving of greater respect than sisters.

We passed the bus again on a long downhill. Pallavi rolled down the window and yelled, "*Maderchod!*"

Later that day, we learned that the bus had become one more traffic statistic. One of the signs said, "Safety on the Road Is Safe Tea at Home," but this advice seemed to have been lost on the driver, who had pulled over for a bathroom stop but neglected to apply the parking brake. The bus slid into a ravine, although by Himalayan standards, the consequences were minor: six passengers were seriously injured; none died.

We crossed a deep gorge on a rattling bridge over a tributary of the Bhagirathi, the Jadh Ganga, and Pallavi pointed out some ancient, rotted pilings on the hillside far below us. These were the remnants of a wire-cable suspension bridge built by an English adventurer named Frederick Wilson, who settled here in the early 1840s. When he arrived in the Himalayas, he became known as Hulson Sahib. He was also referred to as the Raja of Harsil, a nearby village where he took up residence. There is some evidence that he was the model for Kipling's story *The Man Who Would Be King*, which would make him the Sean Connery character in the movie version.

Harsil means "Rock of the Gods," a name supposedly bestowed on it by Lord Vishnu. It was nestled in a valley of astonishing beauty, where the Bhagirathi follows a sinuous path framed by steep forested slopes and vertiginous walls of rock and snow. One of the more risqué wet-sari scenes in Indian cinema was filmed here on the river for a movie called *Ram Teri Ganga Maili*.

On the way down, we passed the twisted wreckage of an orange truck that was improbably pinioned on a tree stump halfway up the hillside, like a victim of Vlad the Impaler. A group of workers were standing around and scratching their heads about how to get it down. The passengers had been less fortunate than those on the bus. Four had died, Russian devotees of Hare Krishna, a cult that had flourished in the Soviet republics during the 1960s and 1970s when there was close cooperation between India and the USSR.

Pallavi knew the story of the Raja of Harsil in some detail, having researched it for an English author who later published a gloriously lurid pseudo-biography of Wilson, filled with invented scenes and imagined dialogue.

Wilson is described by one source as "a short, wiry, hard man" who stood about five feet seven inches tall. He was already a minor legend by the time he reached Harsil. He had worked his passage to Calcutta, joined the Queen's Eleventh Light Dragoons, then walked all the way to the garrison town of Meerut, near Delhi, almost nine hundred miles in thirty days, and then reaching the Himalayas in another four. He was a ferocious hunter and angler and a taxidermist with a taste for ecocide. He caught a sixty-three-pound specimen of India's great freshwater game fish, the mahseer. In one single season, he and his men shot 150 musk deer, musk selling at the time for thirty shillings an ounce on the London market. He liked to pick off exotic birds like the red-plumed pheasant, *Satyr tragopan*, and the iridescent, rainbow-colored monal, *Lophophorus impejanus*, and take them home to his workbench, where scissors, tweezers, and arsenical salts turned them into mementos for English naturalists and collectors.

Wilson was also a horticultural pioneer with an eye for the economic possibilities of the valley. The villagers grew barley, buckwheat, and amaranth; he taught them to cultivate an exotic delicacy, the apple, and Harsil is still famous for its orchards.

He paid close attention to the seasons of the river, which turned his mind to larger ambitions. When the monsoon began in July, he wrote, the Bhagirathi became "a large river rolling on an immense volume of muddy water, and rushing over the rapids with such impetuosity as to be for miles like a great cataract." By December, it had shrunk to "a moderate-sized, clear, and by no means rapid mountain stream sleeping in glassy pools, and gently rippling over the shallows and rapids." At the right time of year, Wilson decided, it would be perfect for floating logs, and the surrounding mountains were full of timber. The trees could be cut in winter and sent downriver in springtime.

And there was always his boisterous love life to consider, because the Raja of Harsil is described as "a randy goat with a wandering eye," which allowed free rein to his biographer's imagination.

Wilson had married a local girl from Mukhba, on the opposite side of the river, the winter home of the goddess Ganga. When she turned out to be infertile, he married her aunt, who was fifteen and the daughter of a low-caste drummer who migrated seasonally back and forth between Mukhba and the Gangotri temple. He bought her from her husband, an abusive police constable, for sixty rupees and paid an additional tax that the local raja, hereditary ruler of the princely state of Tehri Garhwal, levied for adultery. But two teenage brides were not enough.

The raja was a retiring septuagenarian Sanskrit scholar and poet named Sudarshan Shah. He was fervently pro-British. However, Lord Dalhousie, the governor-general of India at the time, had invented something called the doctrine of lapse, a threatening piece of legislation to the royal house because the raja's wife, the Maharani Khaneti, was unable to bear children. She was also petite and large-breasted, according to Wilson's biographer, and he lusted after her for five years until, one day in 1854, she arrived on his veranda disguised in a hooded riding cape, a tight-fitting jacket, a long pleated skirt, and leather riding boots. She asked him for twenty thousand rupees to open an academy for young ladies on a hillside overlooking the Ganges. Within minutes, the biographer says, the check was in her hands, her clothes were on the floor, and "she was on him like a panther. By the time they reached the settee, she had unbuttoned his trousers and wrapped her fingers around his throbbing cock."

The aging raja was oblivious to this hanky-panky, and in 1858, he granted Wilson a concession for the unlimited exploitation of timber on the banks of the Bhagirathi. There were chir pines everywhere, but the choicest logs came from the deodar cedars. The deodars—the "wood of God"—were majestic trees, some hundreds of years old and soaring as tall as two hundred and fifty feet, their average girth close to twenty. They were considered sacred. Their fragrant sawdust was used as incense. Their densely colored, pollen-laden catkins were used to anoint the forehead. In Hindu tradition, a deodar is sometimes planted as protection for a temple; to fell one is a grievous sin, and Wilson felled them by the tens of thousands. His men built wooden sluices and dynamited rocks that blocked the passage of the logs downriver. Before long, he had a thousand workers on his payroll, bringing the logic of a modern industrial economy to a valley that had known only subsistence farming, petty local trading, and temple donations. He became so powerful that he struck his own coinage, challenging the divine right of the raja to this monopoly. The face of the brass coins was stamped, "F. Wilson—Harsil—One Rupee." They had a hole in the middle so that women could string them together as a necklace.

Farther downstream, the officers of the Raj were busy. The Upper Ganges Canal was nearing completion, running three hundred and fifty miles from the gates of the mountains at Haridwar to Kanpur, in the heart of the Gangetic Plain. It had been designed for famine relief and for transportation, but it was also perfect for floating logs. What really made Wilson's fortune, however, was the Indian railway, another idea from the fertile mind of Lord Dalhousie. Railways needed sleepers, seventeen hundred of them for every mile of track; sleepers were made of wood; and the wood came from Wilson. Deodar had the great virtue of being oily, easy to work, and termite-proof, and unlike pine, it didn't require a coat of creosote to protect it from rot. By 1865, the railway stretched all the way from Calcutta to Delhi. By 1870, it covered sixty-four hundred miles, calling for more than ten million sleepers, and Wilson—Wilson & Sons by now—was supplying 80 percent of them.

By the time he was done, the Raja of Harsil, who had set out from Calcutta thirty years earlier with nothing more than five rupees and a gun, was said to be the richest man in North India.

Eventually his dalliance with the Maharani Khaneti came to an end, as such things will. But one day, on impulse, he decided to pay her one last visit. He burst into her chambers unannounced to find her entwined with another woman. Khaneti, the biographer writes, "bolted upright in bed, quickly drawing a cover over her lover's bare rump while demanding an explanation for his rude intrusion. 'I could have you flogged for this,' she fumed."

But Wilson found the whole thing a great lark, not to mention arousing, so they had sex again instead. Whether the Maharani's girlfriend joined them is not recorded.

WINTER QUARTERS

The idol of the goddess Ganga comes down the mountain on the first day of Diwali, the festival of lights, when the first snows begin to seal Gangotri off from the outside world. Borne on a palanquin and accompanied by handbells, drums, and red-uniformed bagpipers of the Garhwal Rifles, she crosses the Bhagirathi on the iron-girder bridge at Harsil and then winds her way uphill again to her winter home, a small white temple in the village of Mukhba.

I reached Mukhba by an alarming apology for a road, nothing more than a thin scar blasted out of the mountainside between a vertical rock face and a steep scree slope that dropped away to the valley floor hundreds of feet below. The road ended at a small concrete structure that housed a pair of latrines. The village was a scattered collection of wooden houses with steeply pitched roofs and ornately carved eaves, the kind of houses you might find anywhere in the high Himalayas, from Tibet to Kashmir. A few had satellite dishes. The houses were linked to one another by a series of rough flagstone steps, and at the top of one flight, looking down on the temple, was the home of the village head, Anita Rana.

It was chilly in the house, and she wore a scarf and a crocheted cardigan over her mustard-colored *shalwar kameez*. Her hair was pulled back in a tight bun, and she had a tiny nose stud. We sat in her spartan living room and sipped strong black tea.

She said that when she was a child, her father, who was a schoolteacher in Harsil, had slipped and fallen into the river and was swept away in the fierce currents. His body was never recovered. The family was left destitute. Anita was ten, the eldest of five children; the youngest was six months.

She and her mother labored in the fields for an uncle. At fifteen, Anita went to Gangotri and opened a small puja store for pilgrims. She kept on working until she was well past the age when a woman was considered to be marriageable. She turned down one suitor after another; supporting her brothers' education was the only thing that mattered to her.

All three brothers eventually moved away, one to Delhi, one to Gujarat, and one to another Himalayan village. Anita never did marry. Now she was the elected head of the panchayat, the village council, a job that consumed all her waking hours. "People keep coming to me with one thing or another; I get no time to myself. Fencing, street lighting, problems at home. 'My wall is falling down.' But the thing they complain about most of all is that road you came in on."

We walked down the steep steps to the temple. In the crystalline mountain air, you could see forever, across the sheer drop to Harsil to the terraced slopes and waterfalls on the opposite side of the valley and westward to snow peaks that rose to more than twenty thousand feet.

"The goddess Ganga is everything for us," Anita said, smiling. "This village is like her mother's home, so when she is here, we treat her like a daughter. There's a tradition here in the mountains that when the daughter leaves her mother's house, we give her gifts and food for the journey, and then the food is distributed in her husband's village. So in springtime, when they take Gangaji back to the temple in Gangotri, we send her off in exactly that way. Then, when she comes back on Diwali, everyone stays with her and cooks special dishes to celebrate her return."

She said the bagpipers of the Garhwal Rifles were a fairly recent innovation, a respectful gesture by the army, which has a base in Harsil. Before that, the goddess had been accompanied on her journey by musicians playing traditional brass horns and local drummers. Like the Brahmin priests of the Semwal family, the drummers, who belonged to the scheduled castes, or *dalits*, rotated seasonally between Gangotri and Mukhba.

But the bagpipers also spoke to the valley's long martial traditions. "Most people who settled here were soldiers who were being hounded by the British after the War of Independence in 1857," she said. Many of them were from the state of Maharashtra on the west coast; Rana in fact was a Maharashtran name. Garhwalis were always considered to be ferocious warriors, comparable to the Gurkhas in the eyes of their British officers. More than a thousand men of the Garhwal Rifles died in the two world wars. In the second, they had fought in the Burma and Malaya campaigns; in the first, they served in Flanders, France, and Turkey and won two Victoria Crosses, Britain's highest honor.

We came to a large house with a heavily grained door of deodar cedar, built to withstand the snows. It had a large iron ring for a handle and looked like something from a medieval shipwreck. "Frederick Wilson built this house for his in-laws, the family of Gulabi, his second wife," she said. "There's another one higher up on the mountain. But they've started dismantling them. They'll probably be gone within a few years." The family were still temple drummers, as they had been in Wilson's time. Supposedly, they still had a small collection of Wilsoniana inside, including one of his nine-foot crosscut saws. But the door was secured by a heavy padlock; no one was home.

Nearby was a second small temple. Ganga, it turned out, was not the only deity people worshipped in Mukhba. There was also a local god named Sameshwar, who was believed to be an incarnation of Lord Shiva, taking on human form during his festival, the Selku Mela, which was held every September. There was the usual singing and dancing, but the most dedicated worshippers showed their gratitude to the god for his gifts by walking to the temple on knife or ax blades set into the ground. "No, they don't get cut," Anita said. "There is some divine intervention that protects them."

Local legend says that when the Raja of Harsil came to the Selku Mela in 1865, Sameshwar appeared in the form of a servant, denounced him for his plunder of the forests, and pronounced a curse on him. *Your lineage will sink into oblivion. None of your sons will continue your race.*

The following year, Wilson's youngest son, Henry, fell off his horse and was swept away and drowned. His middle son, Charlie, went off into the mountains above Gangotri and disappeared. His eldest, Nathanial, was an alcoholic, a drug addict, a rapist, and perhaps a murderer. He was thrown in jail by the British and was never heard of again.

NOMADS

We stopped at a chai stall by a roadside shrine, where a red-headed, large-breasted, heavily tattooed young Western tourist, wearing a green halter top that left nothing to the imagination, was being ogled by a semicircle of Indian men with cell phone cameras. A sadhu was soaping his hands at a water pump, and some women were snapping and folding freshly washed saris. A little farther along the road, a large group of men, women, and children were trudging uphill with heavily laden packhorses. They were Van Gujjars, on their spring migration from the lowlands and the Shivalik Hills to the *bugyals*, the high Alpine meadows just below the snow line.

I'd first heard about the Van Gujjars, a seminomadic and mainly Muslim tribe, on an earlier trip to Devprayag. The man who told me about them was named Praveen, but his friends called him Manto. He was a beefy man with a dense mass of black curls, a Tom Selleck mustache, and a surfeit of nervous energy. His leg jiggled constantly, and he never stopped talking. He would fall silent for ten seconds and then he'd say, "Also . . . ," and off we'd go again. He had an active Facebook page where he liked to post photographs of shop signs that said, "FRESH VISITABLE JUICE," and, "SANTOSH TAILOR—SPECIALIST IN ALTERATION OF LADIES AND GENTS"; a notice on a hospital wall that said, "MEDICAL RAPES ARE NOT ALLOWED BEFORE 01:30 P.M."; radical Islamist protesters in Pakistan holding up misspelled posters that said things like "WE MUST BUM INFIDELS."

When someone took him to task for being politically incorrect, he had posted a reply:

> *I am Agnostic Atheist (Religeo-Philosophical position) Individualist (Social Outlook) Anarchist (Political Ideology) Un-Repentantly Right Libertarian (Political Philosophy) on Polity and Economics AND Extremely Conservative (Social Philosophy) Leftist on Social and Cultural Issues (Social Justice).*

"I'm a very restless person," he said to me. "Maybe this is why I like to travel around with nomads."

The lives of the Van Gujjars revolved around their water buffalo. What they lived on was the milk, selling and bartering it to chai stalls and small restaurants along the mountain roads. Because of the large number of pilgrims, milk was always in demand.

"You can tell where the Van Gujjars are at any given time by asking at the tea stalls," Manto said. "When they leave for the plains in winter, all you can find is black tea or tea with powdered milk."

India is not a country of skim or 1 percent, or soy or almond milk. The price of milk is determined by fat content, and the milk that the Van Gujjars sell is rich and creamy from grazing their buffalo for months in the high pastures.

"Sometimes they'll walk for a month to reach the snow line," he said. "I've walked with them from Simla to Dehradun, three hundred kilometers. I've stayed with them up at the snow line, up to forty-five days at a time, completely cut off from modern civilization. When they're down on the plains, they have to work hard, lopping the leaves for feed for their animals. In the hills, they just leave the animals to graze. It's a much easier life."

Not that their existence was entirely idyllic. "They lose one person every couple of years to wild elephants. Although they can hear the elephants, smell them, sense them. They know which trees to climb. If you climb up into a tree that's too small, the elephant will shake it until you fall like a ripe mango. An elephant will kill you not by trampling you but by wrapping you in its trunk and tossing you in the air."

On the way back downriver from Devprayag, Manto had turned morose. "Also, the government says the Gujjars can have land titles if they can produce papers to prove that they have occupied the land continuously for seventy-five years. But they're nomads, and they're illiterate! Then they go down to the towns, and we turn them into factory workers, or loaders and unloaders. We put them in a uniform and we call it development."

He stopped and stared out of the car window. "Frugality is our tradition," he said after a while. "There is an obsession in the Himalayas to give people electricity even when they don't ask for it. We used to have a school under a tree, but now it has to be in a cement building even if that's hot and uncomfortable. The Gandhian model of the village, that is the solution. You must not think that I want to turn the clock back five hundred years. It's just a matter of orientation. Happiness is not about piling up all the pleasures, the creamiest of the cream."

We passed a group of women in saris who were patching a torn-up section of road. The sight bothered me, but Manto shrugged. "An excavator can put hundreds of people out of work. We save them labor just so they can die."

I tried to find something that would lift his spirits, so I switched the conversation to the Raja of Harsil and his apples.

He grunted. "Why do I want to eat an Australian apple? I have tasty, juicy apples right here. An Australian apple may look beautiful, very red, but it tastes like paper. Not even paper. *Wastepaper*."

It was a hot afternoon, and it was a tiring drive along a narrow, twisting corniche high above the Ganges. There were more of those highway department signs:

EAGER TO LAST, THEN WHY FAST

MOUNTAINS ARE ONLY A PLEASURE, IF YOU DRIVE WITH LEISURE

Manto had fallen silent. There hadn't been an "also . . ." for a while.

We passed through a tract of forest, part of the Rajaji National Park. There was a commotion by the roadside. A wild elephant was crashing around in the trees, and a man was whacking it with a stick. We drove on. After a bit, Manto turned to me and said earnestly, "I'm glad you didn't ask to stop back there."

I asked why.

"Oh," he said, "because most people would probably have wanted to stop and take a picture and then post it on Facebook."

BIG FISH STORY

What was a well-bred Englishman in the colonies without his rod and gun? One missed the weekend shooting parties at one's country home, the ghillies and beaters on the grouse moors of Scotland, the stag at bay, the rivers alive with brown trout and silvery salmon. But India offered its own alternatives. The first tourists to follow in the footsteps of Captains Hodgson and Herbert after they reached the source of the Ganges rejoiced in the abundance of wild game. "Our party consisted of three European gentlemen, each taking ten servants, while our coolees, or porters, amounted to eighty at the least," wrote Lieutenant George Francis White of the Ninety-First Regiment in an account of his travels published in 1838. "Our sportsmen filled their game bags, after a very exhilarating pursuit of the furred and feathered race, most beautiful to the eye."

Calling it sport was a stretch; it was more like wholesale slaughter. Multitudes of partridges and pheasants fell to the gun. So did countless musk deer, goat-antelopes, and leopards, and above all tigers, which brought a government bounty, since killing them was considered a public service as well as the finest of sport. Captain James Forsyth, assistant conservator of forests for Central India and author of *The Sporting Rifle and Its Projectiles*, bagged twenty in a month. Roualeyn George Gordon-Cumming, an old Etonian with outlandish muttonchop whiskers, took his rifle to two continents. "A mad sort of Scotchman," said the explorer David Livingstone, after learning about his compatriot's rampages in East Africa. In India, Gordon-Cumming shot ten tigers in five days.

Lieutenant White was less impressed by the fish of the Himalayas, which were "usually the leather-mouthed kind." No doubt by this he meant that they were members of the carp family, which vacuumed up their food from the riverbed with their thick, rubbery lips and were regarded in England as fit only for "coarse fishing" for the lower classes. But others begged to disagree, for the biggest fish that swam in the Ganges and its tributaries was the "Mighty Mahseer." The largest member of the carp family, the mahseer could reach seventy-five pounds and tear a man's arm out of its socket. Best of all from a gentleman's point of view, it would rise to take a well-placed dry fly.

"What is wanted is not conquered worlds, but more worlds to conquer," said Henry Sullivan Thomas of the Madras Civil Service in 1873. "From this point of view it is that I say a Mahseer shows more sport than a salmon."

A mahseer made a tarpon look like a herring, wrote Rudyard Kipling in *The Jungle Book*. "He who catches him can call himself a fisherman."

Nonetheless, a fellow still missed his trout. While it would never grow to these monstrous proportions, the beautiful creature triggered a particular kind of nostalgia for the old country. And while salmon would never take to the upper Ganges, there was every reason to think that trout would thrive in the clear, cold mountain streams. The only question was how to get them there.

People told me that Dodital was the place to find trout. It was a small mountain tarn at the end of a well-trodden trekking route, barely a mile in circumference and the source of a tributary of the Ganges called the Assi Ganga. It was reputed to be the birthplace, or at least the favored retreat, of Ganesha, the elephant-headed son of Shiva and Parvati. Van Gujjars often camped in the meadows around it. *Tal* meant lake, and *dodi*, supposedly, was the local word for trout. Dodital was said to be home to the rare Himalayan golden trout. It was rumored that Frederick Wilson had stocked trout in the lake in the 1840s.

None of this made any sense. There's no such species as the Himalayan golden trout; the closest natural-born trout are in the tributaries of the Aral

Sea in Central Asia. And getting fragile eggs to a lake ten thousand feet up in the Himalayas in the 1840s would have taxed even the formidable talents of the Raja of Harsil. British sportsmen made their first attempt to export trout to the colonies in 1852. They chose Tasmania and finally succeeded on the third try, twelve years later. Organized in "acclimatisation societies," they moved on to New Zealand, Ceylon, Kenya, and South Africa—the portion that was then known as Zululand, to be exact, where the hills had a hint of the highlands and the green of the veld could be a stand-in for the water meadows of Hampshire. Whatever Henry Sullivan Thomas might say, there were always new worlds for trout to conquer. Finally, around 1900, the first eggs were brought from Scotland to a hatchery in Kashmir. If there were trout in Dodital and the Assi Ganga, Kashmir was where they must have come from.

It was a bit more than forty miles from Harsil to the mouth of the Assi Ganga, almost two hours down the twisting mountain road. The Harsil valley had been pristine, but that word no longer applied to this stretch of the Ganges. The landscape now was disfigured by disasters both natural and unnatural, and it was sometimes hard to tell the difference, since their common denominator was broken rocks and scarred earth. In a gorge at Loharinag Pala, there was an abandoned hydropower plant, left half-built since 2008, when India's Supreme Court barred any further construction within a hundred yards of this "eco-sensitive" section of the river. Below the ugly Maneri Dam, which dated from the 1960s, a furious cascade came hurtling into the Ganges in midair from a headrace tunnel cut through the solid rock. The surrounding mountainsides were disfigured by landslides. The upper Ganges ran through an active seismic zone, and the epicenter of the last big earthquake, in 1991, was just across the river from Maneri.

The 2013 floods that the priests had told me about in Gangotri had killed six thousand people in this region. A year earlier, another flash flood had been more localized but still devastating. That had been three years ago, but the steep valley of the Assi Ganga was still nothing but a boulder field split by a thread of gray water. Big orange JCB and Hyundai earthmovers were shunting the rubble around, and a steamroller was laying apparently random stretches of asphalt. Hard hats were reinforcing the foundations of a ruined bridge.

Four or five miles upstream, a steeply stepped path led uphill to a wilderness camp run by a sociable man named Anil Kuriyal. He had a bald dome, two large and exuberant dogs that gave me a slobbering welcome, and an expression that suggested perpetual optimism in the face of adversity.

He said he had grown up in Uttarkashi, a few miles farther down the Ganges, and moved away to go to college. "I went to Delhi. I worked as a naturalist. I ran a wildlife camp in Madhya Pradesh. But in 2004, I came back. I had to. I missed the beauty of the Himalaya." He found a place with a natural spring and built a few rooms for visitors, with space for tents on the grassy hillside. You could use his camp as a base for the trek to Dodital, twelve miles up the mountain, or to stretch out in a hammock and listen to the birdsong, or, until the disaster, to fish for trout in the Assi Ganga.

"There used to be two fish hatcheries on the river," he said. "The first one was built by the maharaja of Tehri in 1921, with brood stock from Kashmir. But they were destroyed in the earthquake in 1991. They were rebuilt, but then the floods destroyed them again. The cloudburst was right over Dodital. The fishing was wiped out. The river is now totally destroyed. You've seen it, nothing but boulders and scree. All the tree cover is gone."

Kuriyal got permission from the government to restock the lake with brown trout. "Sixteen boys carried them up to Dodital in oxygenated tanks. They walked all night. The lake is still swarming with fish. Just leave it to nature. They'll come down the river again eventually, although it may not be in my lifetime."

He'd never been much of a fisherman himself, just an amateur, and it didn't seem to matter much whether he caught anything. "I just love to cast the fly, see how it lands just where you want it. The ultimate is when the trout actually takes it, but if I just see the fish follow the fly, that's enough for me."

Although the river had been full of trout, few anglers had made it to this obscure and remote place. "I can count on my fingers. Probably, in all those years, seventy or eighty. Most of them were foreigners from Europe or America."

He showed me a photo album from the days before the flood. The river was an enticing series of emerald-green plunge pools and slick boulder runs, unrecognizable from its present ruinous state. The anglers were grinning as they held up huge, golden-brown fish for the camera, the kind of trout-porn images you see on the cover of fly-fishing magazines, usually taken in places like Montana or Patagonia.

Kuriyal knew that the sport would never catch on locally. For people here, fishing was a matter of nets or poison or dynamite. But there were tales of trout that migrated down to the Ganges and grew to a monstrous size. I told him I'd once seen a photograph of the biggest brown trout ever landed. It had come from an artificial canal in New Zealand, where the fish gorged on feed pellets that drifted downstream from a salmon farm. It weighed a little over forty-two pounds. The fisherman who caught it was standing under a sign that said, "Meat Supplied by the Happy Butcher Retail Shop. No Stress. No Mess. Mobile Abattoir." He'd told the local radio station, accurately, that "it looked like a submarine. Very ugly. Small head, big belly. Just amazing."

"The local butcher in Uttarkashi says he had one that was twice that size," Kuriyal said. "He caught it in a net in the big pool where the tunnel comes off the Maneri Dam. Most people are too afraid to fish there. They think the trout will bite off your fingers."

Twice as big? That was inconceivable.

He nodded. "Forty *kilograms*, not forty pounds. He swears that was how much it weighed, because he cut it up in his shop and sold it by the kilo. And he sold forty kilos. He kept count."

THE AGE OF KALI

In the village of Sangrali, sixty miles or so south of Gangotri, there is an outpost of the Indo-Tibetan Border Police and a tiny white temple with a single prayer flag, perched on a rocky promontory. It was an awkward place to reach, involving a hand-over-hand climb up a series of crude steps and notches cut into the hillside. You had to place your fingers with some care. Pallavi and Michael lived in the nearest house, and one of their dogs had a disconcerting habit of bringing home the gift of a snake clamped in his jaws. One recent sighting had been of *Trimeresurus albolabris septentrionalis*, the white-lipped pit viper, which they had found exploring their flower garden. A leopard they called "the princess of the night" prowled the hillside sometimes, but legend had it that only the big cats on the other side of the river had a taste for human flesh.

Paula and I went out onto a jutting platform of rock, where the ground dropped away sheer to the valley of the Ganges. The steep slopes in the foreground were sculpted into a green staircase of agricultural terraces. In the clear mountain air of early summer, the northern horizon was defined by a serrated line of snow peaks. Beyond them was Tibet. The only defect in the view was a thin column of gray smoke rising from a nearby ravine. When the breeze blew in from the east, it carried with it the unmistakable stink of burning plastic.

On the way up here, I'd passed a knot of grim-looking women clustered at the roadside. They were there to complain to anyone who would listen about the improvised garbage dump in the ravine. Three miles downstream was Uttarkashi, a grimy cement and cinder block town of eighteen thousand souls. Uttarkashi is the abode of Shiva. But holiness and cleanliness are not necessarily the same thing. Like most Indian municipalities, Uttarkashi has no organized means of disposing of its solid waste—or its nonsolid waste, for that matter. So at night, the trucks nudged the pigs out of the way and scooped up the filth from the streets and marketplaces. Then, groaning in low gear, they labored up the narrow, serpentine road that leads to Sangrali and tipped everything onto the huge, smoldering pile that scarred one side of the ravine. Rain and gravity would take over from there, and having slithered its way down into the clear stream that flows through the cleft in the mountain, the whole noisome mess would end up in the Ganges.

I heard later that the protest had succeeded. It was annoying to the authorities, all those angry women milling around. So the town identified another dump site, much closer to the river. The consequences were just the same.

One evening, I went down to Uttarkashi to see Ajay Puri, an intense, athletic man who wears many hats, both sacred and profane. He is a trekker, a skier, a photographer, and a hereditary priest of the town's Vishwanath temple, which is dedicated to Lord Shiva. Its construction was paid for in 1857 by the Maharani Khaneti, Frederick Wilson's bisexual lover. Puri is also the president of the Uttarkashi Hotel Association and owner of the Shivlinga Tourist Complex, which is named for the phallic representation of the god's cosmic energy and is one of the smarter accommodations for pilgrims on their way to Gangotri.

Late as it was, he was still in his office, clacking away at his desktop computer and answering multiple cell phones.

This place was just as important as Varanasi, which is generally regarded as the holiest city in India, he said at last after hanging up on a call. That city's original Sanskrit name was Kashi, and *Uttarkashi* means "Kashi of the North." Shiva himself resides here, among his close friends and other celestial beings. The Himalayas themselves are gods. And significantly, this is one of only two places where the river makes a northward turn, the other being Varanasi. "All this is authentic," he said. "This is not from my side. It is mentioned in the Skanda Purana, the biggest of the eight Puranas."

The *shivling* in the Vishwanath temple, which gives Puri's hotel its name, is no ordinary one. "It's a natural object," he said. "It has not been created or placed there by anyone." Also, it leans to the south. The reason for this is that Yama, the great lord of death, once came here to carry off an eight-year-old boy. The boy resisted, clinging on to the *shivling* and tilting it off its vertical axis.

The important thing about Shiva's relocation from Kashi to Uttarkashi was not only the *where* but also the *when*. He had told the sages that he would make his move at a time when India came under powerful foreign influence. That clearly referred to the time in which we were living now, the Kali Yuga, the age of the demon Kali (not to be confused with the goddess Kali), of the Mughal invasions and the East India Company and the Raj and the market economy and the forces of globalization.

"Our galaxies are in motion, and the solar system is in motion within the galaxy, and these movements are what decide the age," Puri said. The Age of Kali is the last of the four cycles in the evolution of humanity, the culmination of its long, slow slide from virtue into vice.

During the first age, the Satya Yuga, mankind existed in a state of pure goodness. "Everything was pure. Even this chai would have been golden!" he exclaimed, holding up his cup. The Treta Yuga brought silver and the beginnings of sin. The Dvapara Yuga was an era of brass, deceit, and disease. "And today in the Kali Yuga, only 10 percent of people are good, and 90 percent are bad," he went on, switching back and forth between animated Hindi and English. "This is the age of iron, terra-cotta, mud, and plastic. And plastic is the main thing now!"

I asked Puri when the age of Kali had begun. He answered by pulling out a fat three-ring binder filled with dense columns of figures and detailed notations. "I have extracted all this from the texts of the Vedas and the Puranas," he said. He scanned several pages and punched some numbers into a calculator. "Kali Yuga began 5,115 years ago," he said.

That was long before the foreigners began to arrive, of course, but they accelerated the process. Puri named some of them: first the Greeks and the Chinese, then Ibn Baṭṭūṭah and the English indigo trader William Finch, who arrived in 1608 and stayed for three years. The Frenchman François Bernier, during the reign of Shah Jahan, builder of the Taj Mahal. Father António de Andrade reached the upper Ganges valley in 1624, at the head of a group of Portuguese Jesuits who planned to cross the high passes into Tibet, open a mission there, and baptize the local ruler, who declined, saying that they made it sound as if this religion of theirs might get in the way of his belief in indiscriminate fornication.

After the misadventures of the Jesuits, there was a hiatus of almost two centuries until the second wave of Englishmen arrived, the big one. The soldiers and the landscape artists, the mapmakers and botanists and zoologists, the sportsmen and the taxidermists who stuffed the animals they shot, and Frederick Wilson, the Raja of Harsil, who cut down the ancient and sacred deodars and turned them into railway sleepers.

And now the descent into vice had given us the smoldering garbage dump in the ravine below Sangrali, which Puri saw as emblematic of the age of Kali. "People never used to think that the river could be for anything but getting your water and worshipping," he said. "But as we started all this so-called developing, we left our old traditions behind. Fifty years ago, we never saw this kind of thing, because people still had faith. In those times, people were not money-fuckers as they are today."

And when would the Kali Yuga end, I asked him, this era of filth, vice, and degradation? He went to his ledger again, fingers flying from line to line. "It will last a total of four lakh and thirty-two thousand years," he said at last. Indians count in crores, multiples of ten million, and lakhs, which are one hundred thousand. So the age of Kali would last another four hundred and thirty-two thousand years. He grinned. "As you see, we still have a long way to go."

ALL YOU NEED IS LOVE

Despite Ajay Puri's gallows humor, the age of Kali was also the age of peace, love, and understanding, and rootless young Westerners in search of illumination had been seeing the Ganges in that light for more than half a century. Few of them made it as far upstream as Uttarkashi, let alone Gangotri. Instead, they clustered in the ashrams and cheap hostels in the holy city of Rishikesh, yoga capital of the world, and, just across the river by a narrow hanging bridge that the British had built, the township of Swargashram.

Swargashram means "the rest house of heaven." It is also the title of a soft-core porn movie with the subtitle *Story of a Dirty Mind Guru*, which is about a lascivious swami who seduces his naïve female devotees.

It was drizzling when I got to Swargashram, and there were slops of orange shit all over the muddy slope from the sadhus who squatted under rough shelters between the riverbank and the mossy walls of the abandoned ashram of the Maharishi Mahesh Yogi. From the hillside above, there was the racket of teenage boys and young men on a pilgrimage to Haridwar, the Gateway to God, a dozen more miles downriver. Most of them were wearing identical orange T-shirts with screen-printed images of Shiva. Many were sottish with bhang, the slimy concoction of marijuana, yogurt, ghee, and spices, that was being ladled out from makeshift stalls. Others were measuring out their journey in body lengths, crawling along on their stomachs like inchworms. Music was blasting out of loudspeakers that went to eleven. A man told me that the song was in praise of Shiva and his fondness for ganja. The lyrics said, "I don't want sweet lassi; I just want cannabis."

There were rumors that the government was planning to restore the Maharishi's ashram and open it to tourists, but when I got there, the gates were still padlocked, and a sign said No Entry in English and Hindi. The walls were topped with broken glass and rusty barbed wire. But I found a place where the upper part of the wall had crumbled away and hoisted myself across and onto a slippery, overgrown path lined with pink-painted concrete benches and windowless, beehive-shaped chambers where the Beatles had gone to meditate and wean themselves off drugs and ended up writing most of the *White Album*.

The idea of going to see the Maharishi—the Great Sage—came from Pattie Boyd. She had met George Harrison in 1964 on the set of *A Hard Day's Night* and married him two years later. (Eventually his friend Eric Clapton would steal her away.) In 1965, the Beatles made *Help!*, whose plot revolved around a comical Indian cult. George found a sitar among the props, noodled around on it, added it to a song called "Norwegian Wood." Ravi Shankar heard the recording, said it sounded like an Indian villager trying to play the violin, and offered to give George lessons so that he could "feel the sweet pain of trying to reach out for the Supreme," like John Coltrane, who had already fallen under the sitar master's spell.

George and Pattie went to India, spending six weeks in Bombay, Kashmir, and Varanasi. Pattie joined the Maharishi's Spiritual Regeneration Movement. George's own spirituality became deep and lasting. In August 1967, just after the release of *Sgt. Pepper*, the Maharishi came to London to give a talk in the ballroom at the Hilton Hotel. The Beatles went at Pattie's urging, all but Ringo, whose wife, Maureen, had just given birth to their second child.

The Maharishi had grown up in Allahabad, where the Ganges meets the Yamuna. He studied physics, worked in a factory, found a guru, retreated for a while to the Himalayas, and developed a set of techniques he called Transcendental Meditation, or TM. One of his first pupils was a German cement manufacturer. "He taught the method to all his employees and thereby quadrupled the production of cement," the Maharishi said. Before long, he was giving classes under the redwoods in California and opening a Swiss bank account. When the Beatles met him at the Hilton, he was about to turn fifty. A tiny man with a white beard, he was described as resembling "a beatific nanny goat." He had a high, squeaky voice, and his laughter was like the twittering of birds. A close friend of John Lennon's said that the Maharishi "giggled and chattered like a mouse on speed." The Beatles were smitten.

Two days later, all four of them, together with Mick Jagger and Marianne Faithfull, boarded a train for Bangor, Wales, where the Maharishi was to give a weeklong workshop. For the first time in years, they traveled without their manager, Brian Epstein, which felt, John said, "like walking around without your trousers on." At a press conference, the Beatles pledged their allegiance to "the Big M," as George called him, and vowed to give up drugs. The Maharishi gave each of them his own mantra, "a password to get through into the other world." George assumed it would be in Sanskrit, but it turned out to be in English. He never revealed what it was, of course, although he did say enigmatically that it could be found in the lyrics of "I Am the Walrus." Expert-texpert? Semolina pilchard? Crabalocker fishwife? Pornographic priestess? Goo-goo-ga-joob?

But the Beatles were forced to cut short their Bangor trip when Epstein overdosed on a lethal mixture of barbiturates and alcohol. The Maharishi comforted them, but George said that it was okay, life would go on, because there was no such thing as death anyway. The Maharishi was now "the Beatles' Guru," appearing on the covers of *Time*, *Newsweek*, *Esquire*, *Look*, and *Life*. Six months later, the Fab Four were on a plane to New Delhi, en route to Swargashram. Philip Goldberg, the preeminent historian of Indian spirituality in the West, called it "the most momentous spiritual retreat since Jesus spent those forty days in the wilderness."

The ashram covered fourteen acres and was paid for with a gift of $100,000 from the American tobacco heiress and socialite Doris Duke. The Beatles lived in Block Six, which was more comfortably appointed than the other living quarters, with Western-style toilets, bathtubs, four-poster beds, and electric fires for the chilly nights of late winter. It was impossible, wandering around the ruins, to figure out where Block Six had been. Walls had been blown out as if by a bomb blast. Roofing had been scavenged. Trees grew up through the floors. Occasionally, through gaps in the dense forest, you could catch a glimpse of the temples and ashrams of Rishikesh on the far bank of the river. Accounts of the Beatles' stay described a jungle full of elephants and leopards and tigers and monkeys and peacocks, but I saw none of them. The damp woods seemed dead apart from the flitting of black crows and green parakeets. I kept an eye open for cobras in the undergrowth.

Nearby, there was an old-fashioned pillar box, its red paint peeling and its rusted door hanging open. Cynthia Lennon had hoped that the trip to India would quiet John's demons and repair their stumbling marriage. But within two weeks, he had moved into a separate room, claiming that it helped his meditation. Often he snuck down to the mailbox to send letters to Yoko Ono.

Other celebrities and demi-celebrities came and went. There was Donovan, Britain's pallid answer to Bob Dylan, sweet-faced and sweet-voiced. There was Mia Farrow, recently estranged from Frank Sinatra. "I'm flying from flower to flower, looking for a place where people will let me be," she said, but her experience of the place was mixed. One day she wrote a telegram to Sinatra that read FED UP WITH MEDITATION. AM LEAVING ASHRAM. WILL PHONE FROM DELHI, but she was persuaded not to send it for fear that it would leak to the press. There was Lewis Lapham, the patrician editor of *Harper's Magazine*. There was Mike Love, the lead singer of the Beach Boys, who wore a floor-length coat and a fur hat and communicated, Lapham said, in variants of "yeah" and "wow."

Farther along the path, I came upon a larger building, still mostly intact, that I guessed might have been the Maharishi's own quarters. It had two stories and was set back from the path. Near the flagstone walkway leading to the house was a small shrine with two black Shiva lingams. The Beatles had come here for private lessons once the day's organized program of lectures and meditation was over.

I stooped under the low doorway of one of the beehive chambers and went inside. The Maharishi had urged his students to sustain their meditation for four or five hours at a stretch. John eventually pushed it to fourteen. I imagined them sitting silently in the damp, claustrophobic space with songs taking shape in their heads: most of the *White Album*, a couple for *Abbey Road*, a few reserved for later solo albums. Early in their stay, John wrote "I'm So Tired," a response to his strung-out, drugged-out state. George wrote "Piggies." Paul wrote "Why Don't We Do It in the Road?" after watching two monkeys do just that. Even Ringo weighed in with his first composition, a cheerful little rockabilly number called "Don't Pass Me By."

Some of the songs, like "Dear Prudence," drew directly on their experiences in the ashram. Prudence Farrow was Mia's younger sister, still reeling from a drug-induced meltdown that involved institutionalization and electroshock therapy. For much of the time, she remained in her room, near-comatose, drooling, unable to feed herself. At night, she screamed like one of the wild peacocks in the forest. "Dear Prudence," John wrote, "won't you come out to play?"

I heard footsteps outside. It was a young American who had also climbed over the wall. He told me he was a student at the University of Texas in Austin. He was tall, clean-cut, and good-looking, wearing khakis and a Ralph Lauren Polo shirt. No one could have looked less like a hippie. He might have been on his way to a summer internship at a law firm. He was too young to remember the Beatles, of course, but he knew all the songs.

We walked over to the lecture and meditation hall, the largest building in the complex. It could seat two hundred, and the Maharishi's students gathered here three times a day to listen to him dispense his wisdom from a gold cloth-covered sofa on a raised platform, surrounded by potted plants. This was where he had organized the party to celebrate George's birthday, his twenty-fifth. So many garlands were draped around the birthday boy's neck that he looked as if was wearing a life jacket, Lapham wrote. The Maharishi said he felt the vibrations of angels and that the arrival of the Beatles heralded the rebirth of mankind on the banks of the Ganges. His birthday gift to George was a globe turned upside-down. This was the state of the world; it needed to be corrected. George said he would do his best.

The walls of the lecture hall were covered with graffiti from earlier visitors.

BEATLES 4 EVER

LOVE TRUTH

ONE LOVE

I AM HE AS YOU ARE HE AS YOU ARE ME AND

WE ARE ALL TOGETHER

SHE LOVES YOU, YEAH, YEAH, YEAH

LUCY IN THE SKY WITH DIAMONDS. LSD

I SEND THIS WITH PEAS AND LOVE

IMAGINE. IS IT REALLY SO DIFFICLT

CNOW YOUR SELF BY HAPPY

And wrapped around a heart in a swirl of psychedelic colors, ALL YOU NEED IS LOVE.

But of course it wasn't all peace and love. Paul was affable and open to the experience, but his girlfriend, Jane Asher, remained detached, even a little cynical. Ringo, who had brought a suitcase full of Heinz baked beans and eggs as a hedge against spicy food, left after ten days. He missed the Mersey and he missed his cats and he wondered why, if you were going to sit for hours in the lotus position, you couldn't do so equally well at home. He and Maureen were sick of checking the bathtub for scorpions. She hated the flies and spiders. The Maharishi told her that they would cease to bother her if she became a traveler in the world of pure consciousness, but she found this an unpersuasive line of argument. She was a hairdresser, not a mystic.

And there were scandals, real or invented. They were rock stars, and the press couldn't get near them, so inevitably there were rumors. Newspapers in Delhi carried headlines that read WILD ORGIES AT THE ASHRAM and BEATLE'S WIFE RAPED AT ASHRAM.

Some of the accusations were directed at the Maharishi himself. Mia Farrow said he had made inappropriate advances, although others reassured her that his stroking her hair was just part of the process of spiritual enlightenment. The more serious allegations came from a young man named Magic Alex, a self-described electronics and light-show wizard who had insinuated himself into the Beatles' inner circle. He told tales of an impressionable young blond nurse from California, who had been told several times by the Maharishi to lie back and let his spiritual power flow into her through pathways more intimate than holding her hand and caressing her hair.

George refused to believe a word of it, but John, who had adopted Magic Alex as a kind of court sorcerer, took the stories at face value and packed his bags in a rage, leaving a large photo of the Maharishi ripped in half on the floor of his room. The episode produced "Sexy Sadie," the most notorious of all the songs they wrote at the ashram. "What have you done? You've made a fool of everyone." John originally called it "Maharishi," but George persuaded him to change it, still defending "the Big M" and nervous about libel.

The Maharishi asked John why he was leaving. John replied, "If you're so cosmic, you'll know why."

Later, though, when Johnny Carson asked him about the incident on *The Tonight Show*, his tone had softened. "We made a mistake," he said. "He's human like the rest of us."

THE HAPPY ESCAPEE

Brij Mehra was about to turn eighty. Spondylitis had left him bent at the waist at a ninety-degree angle, and he lived in an ashram just up the hill from the Maharishi's with a teenage boy named Naveen and a dog who spent two hours humping my leg. "He's all right, he loves affection, he's quite happy, except when his season is on," Mehra said.

There were nineteenth-century paintings and engravings on the wall, some of European scenes and others of Calcutta and Ghazipur, a town fifty miles downstream from Varanasi that had been the center of the opium trade in the days of the East India Company. Brij Mehra dabbled in painting himself, and he wrote short stories that were set in Rishikesh and Swargashram, though he had no particular interest in publishing them. "Somebody said self-publish, but I hate that idea. It doesn't do much for my ego."

We sat drinking green tea, which he assured me was organic, and gave me one of his stories to read. It was called "Happy Escapee." This was the gist of it.

There was a man named Jim, who lived in suburban Virginia. He had everything he wanted in life: a loving wife, a wonderful family, great friends, and a good job with an engineering company. One day he was sent to India to explore a possible contract to build turbines for the new dams on the upper Ganges. He came to Rishikesh and walked across the footbridge to Swargashram, having heard about the visit of the famous Beatles.

That night he received an email from his boss. He'd been fired.

Wandering the streets of Rishikesh in shock, Jim ran into an apparently deranged man with ragged clothes, long hair, and a straggly beard. The man pointed a finger at Jim and said, "Beware the Ides of March." A shopkeeper told Jim that the man was from a wealthy family in Mumbai. His name was Rajesh, and he had the ability to see into the future because he had the third eye.

Jim went back to his hotel, opened his laptop, and found a second email. This one was from his wife. She had decided to leave him and run off with their next-door neighbor.

The next day, Jim tracked the madman down in an ashram, where he also met a swami dressed in spotless white who had a passing knowledge of Shakespeare. "What should I do now?" Jim asked. The swami smiled. "Get up, brush the dust off you, and rejoin the world. Do the creatures of the world sit and contemplate their failures? Ants and bees never stop trying, so why should you? Remember, when feeling frustrated and fretful by small cares, to look at the sky and the stars. It is then one realizes how insignificant we are and how minuscule our troubles really are."

Humbler and wiser, Jim headed home on the next available plane. He was astonished to find his wife and children waiting for him at Dulles Airport. She had made a dreadful mistake; all was forgiven. The boss had called with the offer of a new job. Jim's story had a happy ending.

Most of the stories we tell are in some way autobiographical. The only material differences in this case were that Brij Mehra was Indian, not American, and that he hadn't gone back to his wife and family. He had stayed on in Swargashram, the ashram of heaven.

GOOD VIBRATIONS

As befitted the son of a traditional anglophile family from Peshawar, in what is now Pakistan, Brij Mehra was sent away to be educated at St. Joseph's College, in the old British hill station of Nainital. The school was founded by the Congregation of Christian Brothers, and its motto was *Certa Bonum Certamen*—Fight the Good Fight. From there he went on to Delhi University, a degree in commerce, and a career with Air India. Successive transfers took him to Bombay, Calcutta, Australia, and the United States.

"When I got to New York, I stayed in a hotel near Grand Central Station. I had to find Park Avenue. I asked a nice gentleman, 'Do you know where is Park Avenue?' and he said yes and walked away. And there is New York for you."

I tried to mount a defense of the city, saying how kind people were to lost-looking visitors on the subway, but he was having none of it.

"As soon as I went to Los Angeles, my neighbor said, 'I'm Bob, welcome to California,' and that transformed the whole thing for me. I had a very colorful visit in California. I was there for five years. I met Mary Pickford. Does that name ring a bell?"

He befriended an elegant socialite-philanthropist named Nancy Cooke de Herrera, who had spent time at the Maharishi's ashram with the Beatles. "She was the only American I ever knew who had urine therapy. You drink your own urine in the morning, and it changes your complete life. When I saw this lady, it looked like about ten years of her life were taken away. I met her later when she was eighty-five years, ninety. She looked about seventy, sixty even. One's own urine! Not cow urine!"

We sipped our organic green tea.

"Naveen!" he called. The boy was in the kitchen. "Naveen! Naveen!" He set his cup down with a sigh. "I'm trying to teach him English."

Naveen appeared.

"Tell the gentleman where is your village."

Naveen looked at the floor and murmured, "Gauchar."

"It's on the Alaknanda, district of Chamoli," the old man said. "*Gau* means 'cow.' *Char* means 'grazing.'"

He got up and fetched a picture of the place to show me. It was more town than village, in a green valley surrounded by conical mountains. The Alaknanda was one of the two main branches of the upper Ganges.

"Imagine, he left this to come here. He was learning English and Sanskrit, but they didn't give him enough time. So I gave him a room here."

I asked him to tell me more about Air India.

"Well, I was in charge of cargo, and I did a great transformation of the company. You know that India is one of the original countries accepted by the United Nations to grow legal opium for medical use. It used to go by sea, in hermetically sealed containers with lots of security. So I went to the opium factory in Ghazipur, which was the second most important place in British India."

The British East India Company opened the factory in 1820. It occupied a forty-five-acre site on the banks of the Ganges, where it packed the drug for easy shipment downriver to Calcutta, hundreds of jars at a time. For twenty years, Ghazipur was the driver of the opium wars with China and the means of engineering the helpless addiction of millions of Chinese. When Kipling visited in 1888, it was still "an opium mint as it were, whence issue the precious cakes that are to replenish the coffers of the Indian government."

"I met the commissioner of Ghazipur and had a nice chat with him, and I said, 'We'll send it by air,'" Mehra went on. "And Air India immediately got a huge, massive business. I went to Boots the Chemist in Nottingham,

McFarlane's in Glasgow, and they were very grateful to get it this way. This was in the early sixties. The factory was still very archaic. There was a famous monkey there who used to come and drink the water that drained from the opium. The commissioner said, 'We took the monkey and sent him away, a hundred kilometers away. But he came back, because he'd become a drug addict.'"

After he retired from Air India, Mehra went to work for Bajaj, which manufactures motorcycles, scooters, and three-wheelers. "They sent me to a country called Belize, and I had the agency for all of Central America. Have you heard of Belize?"

I said I had. Not only that, but I'd been astonished to see Bajaj autorickshaws scooting around the mountain towns of northern Nicaragua.

"That's because of me!" he exclaimed.

He'd come to Rishikesh in the year 2000, plagued already by the spondylitis. Someone told him there was a doctor here who might not be able to cure the condition but could at least ease the pain of it.

"But also I said, the hell with the chasing of money. This isn't the answer. And an Australian lady who came here said as soon as you step here to Rishikesh, you get peace, because for hundreds of years there have been mantras going on here, and it's the vibration of all the mantras."

He pointed at the floor of his house. "The very land you are sitting on here, this land next to the river, the vibrations are coming out at this moment. All this land is owned by the Swargashram Trust, which was started in the fond memory of a swami who was known as Kali Kambliwale, which means 'the saint with a black blanket.' I was one of the earliest persons who came to Swargashram to live permanently. Then a European writer moved in next door with his wife about five or six years later. She was from Peshawar, like my family. He had a sister who was a remarkable woman. She married a Muslim from North Africa. She ate a ham sandwich on the day he died."

The dog was after my leg again. It was a large dog, not the kind you could kick away.

"All this land was bought up by the trust, about five hundred acres, and they control all building. Except they couldn't do anything about this dog, who always wants erection.

"Now lots of foreigners come here, of course. There's something about this place. Stay here for a while and you will get it. Some of them come for two or three weeks. We learn to ignore them. Then there are the Indian nouveaux riches. They come here because it's a holiday. But mainly it's Australians, Americans, French, Canadians, Netherlands. It's very cosmopolitan. Chinese have started coming also. Russians. Many Israelis."

This seemed to be an awkward subject, and he petted the annoying dog for a minute until it finally quieted down and curled up at his feet.

"Israelis unfortunately have picked up a very bad reputation all over India. The reason is that the ones who come here are barely out of that forced fighting, that military duty with the Israeli Defense Forces. It leaves a tremendous impact. They look upon the world as their enemy. So they behave in a very uncultured manner. They're very heavy on drugs. Not just marijuana. Heroin, everything. But the regular foreigners are sincere, they are here for yoga and teaching and the vibrations."

I wanted to know how you could actually know that a place had these vibrations, since I was something of a rationalist and not the kind to feel them myself.

"Okay, this is a true story. Did you see that coffee shop by the ATM? The big banyan tree there? Go and have a look at it. There was a young man, he was about twenty-one. He's in China now. One day, as he took a curve there, he got possessed. We all thought it was a big joke. He went down, and suddenly for twenty-four hours, this person possessed him. This person said, 'Look, I don't want to trouble anybody. I just want to meet my girlfriend.' The story was that a young couple from Moradabad had committed suicide here, by this tree. And the body of the boy was still here. It's in one of the stories I wrote. I'll send it along."

———

No matter how many foreigners came, they would never change India, he said. "India is a tremendous mystery."

I couldn't disagree with this.

"It's very irritating and extreme, but it's wonderful once you get used to it. You'll find Indians very hypocritical but at the same time very sincere. It's very difficult to fathom what an Indian is. But eventually the crux of an Indian is right inside. You must realize that five thousand, seven thousand years of civilization have gone into the genes."

Outside, another wave of orange-shirted Shiva devotees was surging past the house in a cacophony of chants and whistles and drums and music and motorbike horns and the hammering of the rain.

"I find it hard to imagine how you can find peace here," I said. And some of the foreigners who claimed to be in tune with the vibrations here could also be consumed by anger. Think of Allen Ginsberg. "Peace and flower power incarnate," one critic said of him. Yet, "America—Go fuck yourself with your atom bomb."

He smiled. "The question of what is peaceful is a relative question. You can be in the middle of Manhattan, honking away and everything, and you can be peaceful. Peaceful is here, inside." He touched a hand to his chest. That is what this place gives you. How to ignore all this. You must have the capacity to ignore. Look, evolution is taking place. Nothing is static. Animals will die, plants will die, new plants will come up. This earth is only a short time for us here. I am not the master of this world. I can only be the master of myself. I have to coexist with the good and the bad and the evil and the right and the temptations. All is part and parcel."

FROM OCEAN TO SKY

I f you were one of the first two men (and the first Westerner) to conquer Everest, what were you supposed to do as an encore? Sir Edmund Hillary, a New Zealander, spent a long time pondering the question. In 1958, five years after scaling the world's highest mountain, he reached the South Pole. In 1968, he and a group of companions took two jet boats 250 miles up the Sun Kosi River in Nepal. Five years after that, he settled on his next adventure: a similar ascent of the Ganges, "upstream against the current as far as we could go." It would be a mixture of cultural education and adrenaline rush, and when they hit the mountains "there would be all the action we could desire or handle." More than they could handle, as it turned out.

The trip took four years of elaborate planning and complex negotiations, and the timing was tricky. Leave toward the end of the monsoon, his Indian friends advised, when there would be enough water in the river for all fifteen hundred miles to be navigable. Hillary agreed.

He assembled a party of nineteen in three jet boats, including a documentary film crew. As cultural and religious adviser he took along Jim Wilson, who had lived for two years in Varanasi and written a doctoral thesis on Hindu religion and philosophy. A man with a titanic mess of a beard, he might easily have been taken for a sadhu. They left Gangasagar on August 24, 1977, with the Hooghly running high and the rains beginning to taper off.

Hillary read up on the creation myth of the river goddess. At Gangasagar, the expedition was blessed with a puja at the small temple that honors Kapila, the sage who had incinerated the sixty thousand sons of King Sagara. The priest thumbed a vermilion tilak on the forehead of each of the adventurers.

Hillary thought he looked like Merlin the Magician. The boats had a little difficulty in the booming surf.

In the tangled channels of the Sundarbans, they saw two Bengal tigers, a male and a female, prowling the shoreline at the edge of the mangrove forest.

Hillary disagreed with Kipling's description of Calcutta as "packed and pestilential." He found the city an endless fascination, although the journalists were tiresome. *Tell us about the tigers, Sir Edmund. Tell us about Everest.* He was offended when one of them reported that Sherpa Tenzing Norgay, who had reached the summit with him, had complained that "[my] friend has forgotten me" and "was fiddling with boats instead of running after the mountains."

In Patna, capital of the depressing state of Bihar, Hillary stopped for "a quiet beer" at the Bankipore Club, but found himself besieged by autograph hunters. Otherwise, the boats zipped through the bleak monotony of Bihar, where there was little to detain the visitor. At full throttle, they could hit more than forty miles per hour.

They spent three days in Varanasi and were awestruck, as everybody is. Hillary quoted the Bengali sage Ramakrishna: "As well try to draw a map of the universe as attempt to describe Varanasi in words." He abandoned Western dress; one of the other mountaineers in the group started referring to him as "Hillary in drag." Another member of the party was bitten by a monkey. A little girl on Dasaswamedh Ghat asked if they were the men who had been to the moon.

At Mirzapur, forty miles farther on, "a cluster of houses on top of an eroded bank 60 feet high" and a famous center of carpet-making, they met a yogi who dressed in yellow silk shorts patterned with stars and moons and who possessed extraordinary abilities that demonstrated the power of hatha-yoga. He could stop his heartbeat at will. He could stick a six-foot iron bar against the bone of his eye socket, ram the other end into the ground, and bend it double. Most impressive of all, he could stop a jet boat revved to full power by pulling on a rope looped around his chest. He was sixty-eight years old, or so he said.

In Allahabad, Hillary was invited to dinner with dignitaries from Indian Oil and the Rotary Club, and the expedition got its first packet of mail. Mike Gill, its deputy leader, had a letter from one of his children. "Dear Daddy," it said. "When Mummy tells me to go and do a pee, the pee always comes. Why is she always right?"

In Kanpur, they heard tales of the mutiny of 1857, which Indians call the First War of Independence.

Approaching Haridwar, they encountered their first fast water. They pressed on in driving rain, drenched and frozen to the bone.

Reaching Rishikesh, they admired the beauty of the river as it emerged from its gorge and took note of the large number of ashrams. In his journal, one of the mountaineers mentioned the Maharishi Mahesh Yogi and his ability to separate rich foreigners from their money. "Crafty old bugger," he wrote. More ominously, they received the news that two experienced canoeists, members of a Czech expedition, had drowned in the fierce headwaters of the river, which was where Hillary and his companions were headed next.

The big decision came when they reached Devprayag, where I had first set foot in the Ganges on one of my earliest trips to India. A *prayag* is the sacred confluence of two rivers. The holiest of them all is at Allahabad, where the Yamuna joins the Ganges, and Prayag, in fact, was the original name of the city.

The Bhagirathi and the Alaknanda combine at Devprayag to form the main stem of the Ganges, merging at a steep triangular flight of steps. A pilgrim could stand at the bottom with the left foot in emerald water and the right in blue. A priest beckoned me over, with a gesture that meant, take off your shoes and roll up your trouser legs. We stood together knee-deep in the water. I repeated the Sanskrit phrases he recited, undoubtedly making gibberish of them. He smeared the tilak on my forehead, then motioned me to stoop down and scoop up a handful of water and bring it to my lips. Then he leaned over and whispered, in serviceable English, "For this part you can pretend."

Hillary's boats bucked and thrashed in the turbulence of the *prayag*, but the decision had already been made for him. The deciding factor was not topography but national security. The Bhagirathi would have been his obvious preference. It was smaller water than the Alaknanda. It would take him to Gangotri, and from there he could make the trek to Gaumukh. But it was only fifteen years since India and China had fought a shooting war, and Gangotri, being so close to the border with Tibet, was still off limits to foreigners, so it had to be the Alaknanda. Hillary considered the sheer black walls that formed its gorge. "I never saw a less hospitable place," he wrote in his account of the expedition, which he called *From the Ocean to the Sky*.

The monsoon rains meant that the river was high enough to follow into the mountains, but they also meant that the class II rapids on the Alaknanda were now class Vs. The jet boats plowed into boiling chutes, slammed against hidden rocks, were spun around in whirlpools. They made it another seventy miles from Devprayag, but that was still forty short of their destination. Scouting from the riverbank, Hillary heard a roar of white water as loud as a jet plane, turned a corner, and found himself face-to-face with a ten-foot waterfall beneath a wooden footbridge. It was September 29; they had been on the river for thirty-six days. Hillary was philosophical. "In a way," he wrote, "Ganga had said, 'You can go no further!'"

In Swargashram, I'd mentioned Hillary's expedition to Brij Mehra. The old man had said there were rumors that one of the great explorer's jet boats had ended up somewhere in the vicinity of Rishikesh. Later, I heard it had been acquired by a wealthy businessman who lived near an ashram on the road to a place called Jumpin Heights and liked to give his friends joyrides. I never found the ashram, or the businessman, or the boat, but I did decide to go to Jumpin Heights. What I found there was that Sir Edmund was not the only New Zealander who had been drawn to the upper Ganges to satisfy a craving for adventure.

GOING TO EXTREMES

From a rocky promontory at the north end of Rishikesh, I watched a flotilla of inflatable rafts rounding a left-hand bend in the river half a mile away. Some were sky blue and some were tangerine. They made it easily past a cluster of rocks and through a couple of mild class II rapids. Faint whoops echoed across the valley.

There were signs everywhere in Rishikesh and Swargashram for companies with names like Himalayan Brave, Adventure Valley, and High Waves Expeditions. My hotel offered a nine-kilometer white-water rafting trip for four hundred rupees, not much more than six dollars, or you could go three times that distance for twice the price. There were billboards advertising hang gliding and others that said, "Battle Zone—Paint Ball Activity," with cartoonish figures that looked like a cross between ninjas and Navy SEALs. And there were posters here and there for Jumpin Heights, "India's First Extreme Adventure Zone—83 Mtrs Bungy Jump—1 km. Asia's Longest Flying Fox— Got Guts. . . ."

From Rishikesh it took almost an hour to drive the fifteen miles up a twisting mountain road to Jumpin Heights, which was on a steep, scrubby hillside above the Heval River, a modest tributary of the Ganges. The fixed jumping platform jutted out from a bright yellow gantry, eighty-three meters, as advertised—two hundred and seventy-two feet—above the rocky riverbed. In the waiting room, a little way up the hill, you could watch people jump on a live video feed.

"Before you will get butterflies," said a young man named Rohan, who was wearing a Manchester United shirt with sponsor logos for Nike and Chevrolet. The video showed a woman stepping toward the edge. The jumpmasters checked the buckles on her harness.

"This is moment of truth," said Rohan. "Just for five, ten seconds you must keep your peace of mind."

The woman went over the edge.

A young couple sat at a table, sipping coffee from paper cups. They had already faced the moment of truth, although whether it was worth three thousand rupees seemed to be a matter of debate. "It was nice," said the man, whose name was Gaurav. "It was okay," said his girlfriend, Isha. "I was scared for the first split second, but then it was not as exciting as I expected. But the important thing is that we can go back home and tell people we did it."

They were from the western state of Gujarat, where they worked at the giant Jamnagar oil refinery. "We also are from Gujarat," said Rohan, "from Ahmedabad. We Gujaratis go everywhere. Everywhere you go in India you will meet Gujaratis." Which turned out to be true, all the way to the ocean.

Rohan and his four friends had booked a two-day, three-night stay in Rishikesh. Brij Mehra's nouveaux riches at play. "All of us are going to business school, so we wanted to have an adventure trip before we start that other adventure. One of my friends in Ahmedabad told me about Jumpin Heights. It is quite famous. We have done also flying fox, rafting, cliff jumping when we were rafting only. There is a place where it is twenty, thirty feet also, just to take out the goose bumps. There was rain, so the river had come up. There were some rapids, class IV. They have given names to them: Three Blind Mice, Double Trouble. And even one was Roller Coaster."

"Lots of IT people fly in from Bangalore and Calcutta," said one of the jumpmasters, a blond Swiss woman named Martina, who had perfected her skills in New Zealand and Nepal. "Indians are earning good money these days, but what can they spend it on? A car, a cell phone, a computer. But if you want a passport, it takes two years, and it's expensive to go overseas. So they spend it on adventure sports. Weekends here are absolutely mad. We jump about a hundred people a day; that's where we max out."

Jumpin Heights was the creation of three retired military officers, and I called one of them, Colonel Manoj Kumar, on his cell phone as we waited for Rohan's turn to be called. After leaving the army, he had worked for a while in the auto industry, but his fascination was extreme sports. "I have a friend, Captain Rahul Nigam," he said. "We did basic training together. One day he asked me to quit my job so we could fulfill our dream. We spent almost two years looking for a site until we earmarked Rishikesh, because lots of trekking and rafting were already here. That was a different kind of adventure-seeking, and it added an attraction for people who come to Rishikesh for religious reasons. But we were not sure it would be safe in India. The only bungee jumps were in stadiums in Delhi and Bangalore, using cranes. But there was a safety incident."

The incident in question was the death in 2009 of a twenty-five-year-old marine engineer at an unlicensed club at a paintball range in Bangalore called the Centre for Adventure and Rejuvenation of Environment. His safety belt snapped, and he fell 150 feet. The owner of the company absconded, and the operation was closed down.

"So we contacted the New Zealanders," Colonel Kumar said. "That's the world capital of bungee jumping. The government mountaineering institute did an inspection of our equipment and procedures. They said they were up to the mark, and we started in 2010."

When Rohan's turn came, we walked downhill together to the gantry, along a steep, rocky path that wound through the trees. The woods were alive with the loud, melodic trill of the long-tailed rufous treepie, *Dendrocitta vagabunda*. "It's a beautiful paradise here," Martina said. "The bird life is incredible. There are leopards everywhere, mountain lizards."

Both the jumpmasters on the platform were Indians. Arun was from Rishikesh; Suresh was from the nearby village of Mohan Chatti. More than forty people worked at Jumpin Heights, and most of them were local. The captain and the colonel did most of the recruitment, and the New Zealanders did the training.

"There are forty families feeding off these jobs," Martina said. "At first they thought it was absolutely crazy, but we've never had any safety issues. So these young people are staying; they're not moving to Delhi and Mumbai. They can keep working in the fields, looking after the animals. If it's harvest time, they just ring up and say, 'I have to be two hours late because I'm in the fields.' It's family first."

Rohan was getting ready to jump, and his friends were teasing him. Ten percent of visitors lose their nerve at the last minute, Arun said. The air was thick with testosterone.

"I don't know what I would have done if this didn't exist," Suresh said. "I was thinking of networking, maybe hardware engineering. But this was kind of different, unique. I've done sixty, seventy jumps. I learned to do the jump backward from the roof, standing on one leg, holding a fifteen-kilo rock. At the bottom, you let it go, so you get a massive rebound. That was thrilling."

Rohan leaped off the platform with a rebel yell and a "whoo-hoooooo!" when he hit the rebound.

Next up was a young man who could have made an excellent living as a fashion model. He was six feet tall, dressed in a tight black T-shirt and dark blue pants, and his shoulder-length black hair was combed straight back from a high forehead. He was obviously not Indian. Latvian, he said. His name was Raitis. He'd met his two companions on the road. They were Ukrainian.

"A friend was coming with me, but he injured his knee," he said. "He knows India, knows the Ganga, worships some gods here, has a guru. The doctor said, 'You're crazy, with that knee you have to forget about going to India. Lie down and rest for two weeks.' But first day he just went to the Ganga, he felt the pain, he takes the bath, swims for five minutes, throws his crutch away. That is what you have to do, go to the river, take Ganga water. The river has the power, like all nature, but our belief inside of us is making that magic.

"In Latvia, it's very popular, Krishna and Shiva, there are little ashrams and restaurants and pujas. Of course yoga. It helps to keep my body in good shape. After thirty, I felt a little bit in my body, getting stiff."

In Rishikesh, he'd finally found the India he was looking for. He'd been to Mumbai, traveled around the south, spent time in Goa, where he went kite-surfing. "But what all people do, they go there to Goa, they go to drink, they go to fuck, but I'm not finding myself if I go to bars and hang out. I like true places like the ashram where we stay in Rishikesh."

He moved across to the edge of the platform, and Suresh and Arun fitted his harness. He paused for a few seconds, calm and serene, as I'd guessed he would be. Then he went over, executing a perfect swallow dive. He plunged two hundred feet, headfirst, then was hurled back a hundred feet on the rebound. He never made a sound.

GATEWAY TO GOD

Traveling with my nomadic friend Manto, I arrived in Haridwar in time for the start of the three-day Mahashivaratri, the Great Night of Shiva. A dozen miles downstream from Rishikesh, this is where the Himalayas taper off into the low Shivalik Hills and the Ganges begins its lazy meander across the boundless plains of North India.

Haridwar, one of the holiest cities in India, whose name means "Gateway to God," was like a theme park of statues and effigies. A multicolored Ganga, with her four arms, sat cross-legged midstream on a lotus flower on the back of an alligator, her vehicle, the whole affair mounted on a concrete plinth that looked as if it might have begun life in some heavy industrial facility. Nearby, on the riverbank, Shiva stood more than fifty feet tall, though that didn't qualify as the biggest statue of the great god in India. A Shiva in Karnataka, in the south, was more than twice as high. That one was shown in a sitting position; the Haridwar Shiva was standing. He was slim, vaguely androgynous, with a faint, almost Buddha-like smile, and his right hand was raised in a gesture of blessing. He had all his usual accoutrements: the raised trident in his left hand, the crescent moon on his head, the cobra Nag Vasuki coiled around his neck, the necklace of *rudraksha* beads, the hourglass-shaped drum, the *damaru*, which beats time to the rhythm of the human heartbeat and sounds out the mystic syllable of aum, or om. The first time I came to Haridwar, the statue was bronze-colored. The next time it was gray blue. Sometimes it's painted in all the colors of the rainbow.

All along the ghats, there were innumerable miniature shrines, arranged around the bases of trees, with garlanded statues of Shiva, Parvati, Ganesha, Krishna, the monkey god Hanuman, and other deities I couldn't immediately identify. Pilgrims were immersing idols in the river. Some of them had been dislodged by the current and damaged. A boy was looking out morosely at a life-sized Ganga who had lost her head and one foot. The back of his shirt was imprinted with the image of an eagle and text that seemed to have been composed by someone sticking a pin in the dictionary at random. LIFE GUARD—FORCES OF URBAN STREET—IN THIS PLACE YOU WILL FEEL 4TH ANNUAL DEATH RALLY.

All roads led to the main bathing ghat of Har Ki Pauri, where Lord Vishnu is said to have left his footprint. Even in February, with the water at its lowest, the monsoon long past and the snowmelt yet to begin, the current was strong enough to raise whitecaps, and the bathers kept close to the edge, clinging on to metal chains and posts topped with the sacred swastika. Even so, some teenage boys were moving around in midstream, launching *diyas*, small floating lamps of leaves and flowers. No matter where they waded, the water level remained constant, waist-deep. I imagined the current must have scoured the riverbed flat, but the next morning, I learned I was wrong.

As night fell, flames leaped from the camphor lamps that the priests were lighting for the evening worship of the river, the Ganga Aarti. Manto paid a boy a few rupees for a *diya* and let it slip away into the current. Then I did the same.

When the ceremony was over, the Mahashivaratri became less an act of devotion than a raucous, ecstatic dance party. The bazaar was filled with a discordant blast of trumpets and tubas from competing brass bands in uniforms of orange, silver, and gold: the Heera Band, the Raja Band, the Shiv Band. Water buffalo plodded through the crowds, pulling carts with statues of Shiva and Ganga. Pilgrims clustered outside the Chotiwala Restaurant for a free meal, ladled out from giant vats of rice and dal. Others dropped coins into the charity box at the Shri Ganga Maa temple. A woman ran at me with a small basket, whisked off the lid, and a cobra lunged out in my face, its hood flaring. She cackled. The endless gullibility of the foreigner.

The goddess Mansa Devi is the sister of Nag Vasuki, Shiva's cobra, and the next morning we took a cable car—Indians call it a ropeway—up to her temple, which is perched six hundred feet above the river on a bare pinnacle of rock, like a crusader castle. I handed over some small bills for a plate of flowers, the *prasad*, my gift to the deity. In return, I would be granted *darshan*, an auspicious sight of her effigy. An attendant channeled the crowd into a snaking line, organized on the same principle as an airport check-in line but with metal fences, head-high, that forced you to inch forward in single file. There were signs warning against pickpockets. Sticky bodies were crushed up against me. It was easy to imagine a stampede. We passed four exit doors, but three of them were padlocked. "Oh, those are for VIPs," Manto said.

Eventually we reached the goddess. I handed my *prasad* to the priest, who gave me a perfunctory blessing and passed the flowers back to another man, who would pass them back to the vendor at the entrance to be sold again.

Outside on the rocks, there were more monkeys than I'd ever seen in one place, even more than at the truck stop in Rajasthan, and a vertiginous view over the river and the city. Before it reached Har Ki Pauri, I could see that the Ganges split in two. A sluice gate on the east side of the river channeled part of the flow into its original bed, while another two diverted a larger volume to the west, where it ran swiftly along the ghats. I realized that the boys at the Ganga Aarti had not been wading in the river but on the level bed of an artificial canal, the start of an irrigation system that feeds tens of millions in the plains of the Doab, the arid triangle of land between the Ganges and the Yamuna.

Sir Proby Thomas Cautley was the man who built the canal. He was a disputatious polymath with a bald head, rimless glasses, and the mild face of a poet. He was also a humanitarian, bent on avoiding a repetition of the periodic famines that plagued the Doab. The most recent, in 1838, had taken eight hundred thousand lives, one in every seven of the population. Cautley broke ground four years later.

First, he scouted every inch of the terrain in the Shivalik Hills, "wandering into every accessible ravine, valley, or river, that I could find, with my gun and geological hammer as companions." His fossil discoveries included a saber-toothed tiger and an ancestor of the elephant with a trunk ten feet long. His critics said he was mad. Building dams in the fast mountain currents would be too difficult, not to mention too expensive; they should be built only in the flat, sandy plains, as the East India Company was doing in the south. "Idle calumny," Cautley replied. The prodigious floods on the Gangetic Plain would sweep them away. Agreed, the spring torrents of snowmelt in Haridwar were "a constant source of anxiety," but he designed his sluice gates in such a way that an alert operator could throw them open in time to prevent a catastrophe.

To the priests of Haridwar, all this was sacrilege. The mad Englishman was desecrating their goddess. But he listened to their complaints and offered concessions. He would refurbish Har Ki Pauri and the other bathing ghats to make them safer for pilgrims, and the inauguration ceremony would honor Ganesha, who removes obstacles and blesses new projects. This "may be received by the Hindoo as some atonement for the liberties taken with the Ganges," Cautley wrote. By the time his great project was done, it ran for more than 350 miles, all the way to Kanpur.

WHY SHIVA TURNED BLUE

B ack in the bazaar, a shopkeeper was berating two men in orange shirts and orange shorts and flip-flops. "These people aren't pilgrims, they are nothing but *goondas*!" he was yelling to anyone who would listen. *Thugs, bullies.* "They make a big problem of law and order. This young man comes up to me and says, 'Heat my milk!' I say, 'Heat your milk? No!' He asks why not. I say, 'Because I have other customers waiting!'"

Manto shook his head. "The locals become very bad-tempered when the *kanwarias* come here," he said.

Kanwarias?

There were groups of them lined up all along the edge of the canal, young men dressed all in orange with strange, gaudy contraptions that I'd noticed when we arrived in town the previous day. They were the size and shape of a stretcher or a cremation bier, on a frame of bamboo, curved on top. They were *kanwars*, and the men who carried them were the *kanwarias*.

"We have made this pilgrimage eight times before," said a man named Bittu, who had come here with his best friend, Sanjay, and four companions from a village near Moradabad, about a hundred miles east of Delhi. "We came by train, but we will walk back. We will carry the *kanwar* on our shoulders. It will take five days."

The most fervent devotees might do the journey in twenty-four hours, Manto said, running all the way, passing the *kanwar* from one man to the next in a relay with only brief rest stops.

"It is all for Lord Shiva," Sanjay said. "But we are not from any special temple. We are all from different castes. We are just neighbors. I am an office worker, Bittu is a driver. Sometimes we run into friends along the way also. People are coming from Delhi, from UP [Uttar Pradesh], from Haryana, from Rajasthan, from Uttarakhand. Some are even going all the way to Gaumukh, actually, more than five hundred kilometers."

They showed me some of the things they'd used to decorate their *kanwar*: a postcard-size portrait of Shiva, a small trident, a plastic cobra, a miniature *damaru* drum, a CD cover showing a Bollywood star with slicked-back hair, strips of gold and silver tinsel, some pink handkerchiefs, an aluminum teaspoon, and two wicker baskets with water pots inside, one at each end. The water pots and the teaspoon were the main point of the exercise, and naturally there was a legend behind it.

"It is a story in the scriptures of an obedient son named Shravan," Manto said. "A very ancient story from before the time of Lord Ram. It is very popular. You can see it on TV or buy a DVD. Shravan's parents were old and blind, and they wanted to go on a pilgrimage before they died. But they were too frail to walk, so he made a palanquin that he could carry on his shoulders and a basket on each end for them to sit in. So the baskets that these boys carry on their *kanwar* are a symbol of this story, and they will use them to take some *gangajal* back to their homes."

"Once we have the water, it can never touch the ground until we reach our village," Sanjay said. "It must be always hanging on our shoulders."

That accounted for the two baskets, but what about the aluminum teaspoon?

"For this you must know another legend also," Manto said.

The gods and the demons were at war, each of them wanting to possess the nectar of immortality. To find it, they had to churn one of the seven oceans, the Ocean of Milk. They used Shiva's cobra, Nag Vasuki, as a rope to do the churning. The gods held his tail, the demons held his head, and they swished the snake around in the milk. But the nectar of immortality was not the only thing that emerged from the struggle.

"A pot of poison also came out," Manto said. "It was a poison so powerful that it could destroy the universe. Someone had to consume it, but no one could agree on who should do it. Finally, Shiva said, 'Okay, I will volunteer.' He kept the poison in his throat, and that is why Shiva turned blue. For this reason, sometimes he is called *neelakantha*, the one with the blue throat."

"And the teaspoon?"

"Because the poison made so much heat and energy in Shiva that he had to be cooled down. So in Haridwar twice a day, the *kanwarias* will sprinkle water on the *shivling* to cool down the fire in him."

"When we reach our homes again, we must also pour the water on the *shivling*," Sanjay said. "And then we will make a big feast for the girls in our village."

"What happens to the rest of the *kanwar*?"

"We are keeping the frame for next year. And we are giving this decoration to the kids." He pointed to the tinsel.

"And what about the handkerchiefs?"

Sanjay and Bittu looked at each other and giggled. "These we are giving to the girls."

MRS. CHAUREY'S GLASSES

At the cremation ghat of Kankhal, on the southern outskirts of the city, in the direction of Yama, the terrible lord of death, an old woman's body was laid out on a compact pyre of logs and branches. Two other pyres were burning brightly, and another had been reduced to a pile of cooling ashes. A fourth was set and ready, evidently belonging to a poorer family since much of it was constructed from plywood planking and handfuls of straw.

The old woman's name was Ambika Chaurey, and she had died that morning, in the hour before dawn. She was eighty-two. After the body was cleaned, her male relatives had loaded it onto a garishly painted flatbed truck that looked more suited to a circus than to a funeral and made the four-hour drive to Haridwar from their hometown of Meerut, north of Delhi, arriving in midafternoon. They shopped at one of the stalls that lined the alleyway leading to the cremation ground, buying the wood they needed and some small blocks of camphor that would be unwrapped like sugar cubes and added to the fire as an accelerant.

Two priests were in attendance, and the family slipped them some money. One was a grizzled older man with several missing teeth. He was wearing a blue striped sweater despite the intense heat from the pyres. The other was no more than thirty. He introduced himself as Hari Om Shastri. He wore a black nylon zippered jacket over his dhoti. He had a bright vermilion tilak on his forehead, his hair was heavily pomaded, and he had a five o'clock shadow that was worthy of a young Richard Nixon.

At the foot of the steps, the river's edge was a dark ebb of marigolds, plastic bags, food wrappers, cigarette packets, chunks of Styrofoam, half-liquified dung from a couple of cows that were standing nearby, and a couple of uneaten chapatis. The river was braided into channels here, and cormorants were circling over a gravel bar, which might more accurately have been described as a garbage bar. A few yards away, a worker began shoveling cold ashes into the water.

I told the young priest that the plywood pyre bothered me. What if the body was left only half-burned? "The bones will purify the river and make the pollution less," he answered with the manner of a science teacher at an elementary school. "The individual human being is purified, and the river is purified. The bones will gradually disintegrate and get diluted. The body will be returned to air, water, earth, fire, and ether. Otherwise the river would be full of bones right now."

Mrs. Chaurey's body was adorned like that of a bride and garlanded with flowers. A frame of branches formed a kind a canopy above her, and it was hung with yellow, red, and blue plastic ornaments that resembled small balloons. Two of the men removed this now and tossed it into the river, where it drifted away in the lazy current. The eldest son knelt and kissed his mother's feet. Then he lit a couple of matches and tossed them on the pyre. There was a *whomp* of orange flame, and I noticed, as the burning branches fell in across the old lady's face, that they had not removed her glasses.

Greasy particles of black ash began to drift toward us, settling on our skin and clothing. "You'd better go down to the river and wash before you leave," the young priest said.

THE BEST MEDICINE

The Mahashivaratri had been in February. The next time I went to Haridwar, it was July, and the monsoon had just broken. The streets were awash, shin-deep in floodwater, and it was a fifteen-minute walk to the center from the vast parking area at the edge of town. My hotel had a large balcony overlooking the river, with a sign that said, "To Avoid Monkey Menace Please Do Not Dry Clothes on the Terrace." The rain came down like a fist and hammered on the roof all night. But by the next morning, the skies had cleared, and I went out to look for the celebrated Baba Ramdev.

I'd been corresponding with the *baba*'s office for weeks, hoping to be granted an audience with the most popular TV guru in India, the man who had brought yoga to the masses. His show has eighty million viewers—more when he's doing a special event, such as a multilingual simulcast when a hundred million people all over India sit at home in front of the tube, doing the same yoga exercises in unison. He'd also hosted rallies with other celebrity gurus to give his blessing to Narendra Modi, the Hindu nationalist candidate for prime minister. I'd seen film of Ramdev's mass open-air yoga sessions in Haridwar, which attracted thousands. Sometimes he was wrapped in robes that were the color of a ripe tangerine. Sometimes he was naked to the waist apart from the sacred thread draped over his shoulder, displaying a mat of black chest hair to match his prodigious beard. His teeth could have lit up a darkened room. Yoga had extraordinary powers, he told his followers. It could cure brain tumors, leukemia, swine flu, and homosexuality, a practice that was "unscientific, unnatural, uncivilized, immoral, irreligious, and abnormal." Breathing exercises could also be helpful in fighting this loathsome disease. So could locking up two people of the same sex in a room for a few days: salvation through aversion therapy.

It was late morning when I got to the headquarters of Baba Ramdev's yoga empire, Patanjali Yogpeeth, a five hundred–acre campus a few miles outside Haridwar, on the road to Delhi. Patanjali was a fourth-century sage; *Yogpeeth* means "seat of yoga." It was like a small city radiating out from a crescent-shaped administration building. There were neat rows of apartment blocks to house thousands of devotees, an artificial lake, ornamental trees, and neatly groomed lawns. There was the University of Patanjali, the Patanjali Bio Research Institute, a hospital, a hospice, a high-tech facility for the production of Ayurvedic medicines and health foods, and an agricultural research center housed in a building that looked like a stately English home in the Tudor style. You could go online (www.ramdevproducts.com) and buy the *baba*'s skin- and face-care products, shampoos, herbal remedies, food supplements, and cures for bleeding gums and premature ejaculation.

But Baba Ramdev himself wasn't at home. His gatekeepers said he was stuck in Gangotri with five hundred followers. After the previous day's downpour, the roads into the mountains were blocked by dozens of mudslides, maybe hundreds. When would he be back? Shrugs. No idea. Could be days, could be weeks.

I went down to the canteen, ate a bland lunch of organic dal and chapatis, made without onion or garlic that might have overheated my blood, then headed back upstairs to see who else I might find to talk to in the *baba*'s absence.

The gatekeepers disappeared behind closed doors, came back, held whispered conferences. But eventually, yes, Baba Ramdev's closest associate would receive me. His name was Vaidyaraj Acharya Balkrishna. *Acharya* means "teacher." He was the cofounder of Patanjali Yogpeeth; but more than that, he held a 97 percent share in its Ayurvedic medicine business, which has ten thousand stores across the country. He was, in fact, number forty-eight on the *Forbes* list of the wealthiest people in India, with an estimated net worth of $2.5 billion.

If you'd added a stuffed and mounted sailfish and a couple of signed photographs of the occupant shaking hands with Donald Trump and George W. Bush, you might have mistaken Balkrishna's office for that of a successful businessman in Florida. He was sitting in a high-backed chair behind a huge glass-topped desk with three phones. One or another of them rang constantly. He was a small, trim man, robed in pure white, with short, coal-black hair that looked painted on his head and teeth like tombstones. He was in his midforties, but he might have been a decade younger. A balance of serenity and nervous energy, kept youthful by the wonders of Ayurveda. He gave me a stack of glossy brochures with photos of yoga positions and medicinal herbs and a handout that listed his credentials and accomplishments, which ran to eight pages of very small type.

The handout described him as "a great visionary, highly ascetic, energetic, diligent, and a simple man with multi-dimensional skills who is selflessly engaged in the service of mankind." There was evidence of serious scholarship: thirty books he'd written or edited; forty coauthored articles, mainly on the health impacts of yoga and Ayurveda, in peer-reviewed journals like *Medical Science Monitor*, *Child and Adolescent Psychiatry and Mental Health*, and the *International Journal of Current Trends in Pharmaceutical Research*. The fact sheet also said he had "directly treated more than five million patients suffering from various chronic to complex diseases."

I had no quarrel with Ayurvedic medicine—a friend had told me that it definitely helped his asthma. But five million? And curing brain tumors with yoga? "Oh, yes, yes, yes," Balkrishna said. "Definitely." Other countries, too, had experienced the benefits of Patanjali yoga camps: Japan, South Africa, the United Arab Emirates. The Ayurveda business was now expanding into the United States. "We have online sales through Atlanta, and we just opened a store in Houston, Texas." Swamiji, Baba Ramdev, had made a personal appearance at the grand opening.

What about Swamiji's involvement in the swamps of secular politics? I asked. He'd always been revered by the militant right-wing Hindu nationalist organization, the Rashtriya Swayamsevak Sangh, or RSS. I'd read about one rally where he had called for an army of youth to be trained in *shaastra-shastra*—the study of weapons. The police had broken it up; the *baba* had made a B-movie escape dressed in women's clothes.

"When we started Patanjali Yogpeeth twenty years ago, it was not business for us," Balkrishna said. "It was not politics for us. It was for people to have more faith in their own culture and their system of health. But we realized after some point of time that there are also problems with the political system, like so much corruption. So we aspired toward changing that. But if the government works on these things, we can focus again on the work we were doing before."

He lit up when I said that the idea of bringing people to God through mass rallies was very different from having a one-on-one relationship with your guru, or going to the temple, or doing your own private puja at home before you left for work. It reminded me of American megachurches and televangelists, and he didn't take issue with the comparison.

"This is an important question!" he exclaimed. "This is my field. My brain will turn the other way around! Hinduism is about the unity of God. If you go back to the original texts, the Vedas and the Upanishads, it is only one God that Hindus believe in. It's like I may be husband, I may be father, I may be son, but I am still one individual. God is one, but people give different forms to God. God is also worshipped in the form of shakti, in the form of energy. But the most important thing, if you go back to history, is behavior. Worshipping is not just going to the temple. If you are not improving your behavior, it is just becoming a ritual. If religion becomes a ritual, it becomes a task. It is not the path to self-improvement. Meditation also will not lead to self-improvement, because it is not a group activity. In a group activity, you learn, you get information. Worshipping is about self-progress. How I can endure my sorrows, how I can increase my happiness, how I can remove my doubts?"

But the mass worship side of Patanjali Yogpeeth was less his role than Baba Ramdev's; his energies were devoted mainly to Ayurveda. Much of his time was taken up these days with compiling a monumental encyclopedia of all the known herbs in the world and their medicinal properties. "This has not been done till date," he said. "We have done the collection. One hundred scientists are working with us. Not only this local area, entire world. Forty thousand plants! If you see in the scriptures and historical books related to herbs, there are only eight hundred. So forty thousand is a big number!"

As I was leaving, he remembered one more thing. "The *gaushala*, the cowshed! You must go there also. It is three, four kilometers only. You will see the interesting things we are doing with cow urine. They will feed you organic mangoes also, which are coming down naturally from the trees!" He burst out in peals of laughter. For some reason, the idea of mangoes plummeting to earth seemed to tickle a funny bone that hadn't been evident before.

FIZZY WHIZZY

It was Baba Ramdev who had come up with the idea of selling *gaujal*, or cow water. It would affirm the spiritual identity of Hindus. It would have miraculous curative properties. It could be bottled and marketed as a healthy and patriotic alternative to Pepsi and Coke. I wondered if they made it at the gaushala.

A boy was assigned to show me around the shed. The cows were lined up on either side, and a man was collecting the precious liquid in a reeking bucket. It was a pungent brownish yellow. When his bucket was full, he carried it over to a large metal tank to be distilled and turned into concentrate. It was also purchased from nearby villages, where farmers left it for pickup by the roadside in big blue plastic barrels. They got twenty rupees a liter, about thirty cents, which was a nice income supplement if you were living on two or three dollars a day.

The boy took me upstairs to meet the manager, Mr. Jain. "From six cows at the beginning, we now have four hundred," he said. They were from four native Indian breeds, which were considered more desirable than Jerseys and Holsteins in a kind of bovine caste system. One breed was famous for being resistant to disease, another for its aggressive personality. Some people believed that urine from a pregnant cow had special properties, though others said it was better if the cow had never calved.

There were so many beneficial uses, Mr. Jain said: washing soap, turpentine, and floor cleaner; biofertilizers, biopesticides, biogas. Toothpaste, eye drops. You could add it to food: porridge, for example. You could add cow feces, too, for that matter. But medicine was the main thing. Homosexuality was not on the list of diseases it could cure—yoga was better for that. But it worked for everything else, from acne and constipation to cancer and AIDS.

It was a natural antioxidant. It was loaded with minerals and vitamins. One drug had even been granted a patent in the United States.

"People are coming also to the gaushala to buy the cow urine from us," he said. "They take it home to drink it first thing in the morning because it is very good for acidity problem." Some people liked to splash it on their faces.

What about cow urine cola? That part of the operation wasn't conducted here, he said, but at the Cow Protection Department of the RSS in Haridwar. Its director had announced the initiative several years earlier. All the necessary lab tests had been done. They'd figured out how to purify it, how to preserve it, and, most important, how to mask the taste. The cola had been test-marketed by a company in Kanpur in two flavors, orange and lemon, mixed with a variety of sacred herbs. But bringing the stuff to the masses had been a slow process. The idea had met with a certain skepticism. The president of one marketing firm had suggested it could be sold under the name of Fizzy Whizzy.

Mr. Jain asked if I'd like to have some refreshment. A cold drink, perhaps? I looked at him warily. "Cow urine cola?"

He was apologetic, but with the flicker of a smile. "Unfortunately not. We have only bottled water."

It came with a basketful of organic mangoes, which had thudded to the ground only minutes earlier. They were sublime, a quintessence of mangoness, and I ate three.

PART TWO

PLAINS

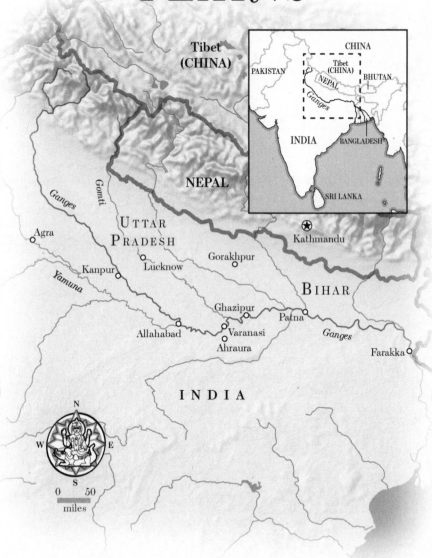

CAPSTAN BABA

South of Haridwar and east of Delhi, heat, dust, and unending flatness. Horizon lines pierced by minarets as well as temple spires and English clock towers. Black burkas in the streets and beards dyed orange with henna. Portraits of the Ayatollah Khomeini and other Shi'a Muslim icons outside the opulent Asifi Masjid mosque in the city of Lucknow, erected during the Persian dynasty that ruled the kingdom of Oudh, or Awadh, until 1856, when the East India Company decided that it had ruled long enough. British bureaucratic efficiency could no longer abide the indolence of the last of the nawabs of Oudh, the obese Wajid Ali Shah, who was "sunk in the uttermost abysses of enfeebling debauchery," dedicated not to statesmanship but to "the delights of dancing, and drumming, and drawing, and manufacturing small rhymes."

The Gomti River rises in the foothills of the Himalayas and winds for 560 miles southeast across the North Indian plain until it empties into the Ganges a short distance downstream from Varanasi. Close to the halfway point, it meanders through Lucknow, which nowadays is capital of the state of Uttar Pradesh, which has a population of two hundred million. The reason I'd made this small detour was to educate myself about the great rebellion against British rule in 1857, which came on the heels of the dissolution of the power of the nawabs.

I went to see the ruins of Musa Bagh, which lie on the outskirts of the city, on one of the many lazy bends of the Gomti. A rutted dirt track branched off from the highway at a noisome garbage dump. Ditchdiggers were at work by the roadside, and speakers on a handcart were blasting out tinny *filmi* music.

The track ended at a village called Bari, a straggle of houses and snack stalls with a small mosque that was painted green and white, with a gold crescent and star above the entrance. The usual yellow dog was sprawled out in the sun by a dripping water pump, to all appearances dead. The place was essentially a squatter colony, said a bony old man with a white goatee who was standing nearby. The villagers had no title to the land, which had been targeted by the city authorities and real-estate speculators for the next wave of urban sprawl. Government trucks arrived periodically and dug up the topsoil from their fields in a hapless effort to cap the mountain of garbage. "That dump makes us sick," the old man said. "The flies and mosquitoes are killing us whenever the wind blows from that direction."

He turned out to be the caretaker of the mosque, which was dedicated to Hazrat Syed Imam Ali Shah Baba, a miracle-working thirteenth-century divine. In a neighboring field was the tomb of another revered imam, adorned with a picture of the Kaaba. The caretaker slept here all night to guard the shrine. Not that he seemed overly concerned. "If anyone comes in the night, the dead will rise from their graves and take care of them."

Behind the mosque were the remains of a mud-brick wall that had largely dissolved in three hundred years of rain. "It used to go all the way around the palace of Musa Bagh," the caretaker said. "In those times, they had as much confidence in mud as we have in cement."

The word *bagh*, which is of Persian origin, refers to a formal garden. The *musa* part is a matter of debate. Some say it alludes to a rat that was killed here by one of the nawabs; others believe, improbably, that it derives from Moses. The most convincing explanation was that it's a corruption of the word *monsieur*, since the gardens are thought to have been laid out by Major General Claude Martin, the French-born soldier-architect who designed a number of impressive buildings in Lucknow, including the famous private school known as La Martinière. What the old caretaker called the "palace," a three-story summer retreat in the Indo-European style, was built in 1803, three years after Martin's death, for the fifth nawab of Oudh, Saadat Ali Khan.

The ruins were on a low rise, notched into the hillside. The formal gardens, divided by walkways and water channels into four symmetrical squares like those of the Taj Mahal, had originally extended as far as the river's edge, and the nawabs and their English guests would walk down there to watch the stag fights that were organized on the opposite bank for their entertainment. But the Gomti had changed its course since 1803, its old course was silted up, and the river was now almost a mile away, hidden away behind high levees. The gardens were long gone, repurposed as fields of mustard and wheat and animal fodder, while war, weather, and the pillaging of bricks hadn't left much of the building itself. There was still just enough for your imagination to play with: two domed kiosks or lookout towers, a few freestanding pillars and archways with remnants of ornate stucco work, and a sunken colonnaded courtyard. Someone had scratched graffiti on one of the walls.

NASEEM

MANTHASA

I LOVE YOU

Oudh was the heart of the 1857 revolt, and for readers of *The Illustrated London News* and *The Boy's Own Magazine*, no event during that year quickened the patriotic pulse more than the six-month siege of the British Residency in Lucknow, whose battered ruins now occupy an immaculately groomed public park and are floodlit at night.

The immediate trigger for the rebellion was the perverse decision by British officers to issue native troops, who made up more than 80 percent of the East India Company's Bengal Army, with paper cartridges greased with beef tallow, the vilest of insults to Hindus, or pork fat, anathema to Muslims. But as Benjamin Disraeli observed, "The decline and fall of empires are not affairs of greased cartridges. Such results are occasioned by adequate causes." New military rules had the Brahmins who dominated the army worrying about the loss of their caste privileges. No one had much affection for the Christian missionaries who scurried around seeking converts to their barbaric religion. The royal court and its loyalists fretted and plotted, as anciens régimes invariably will after they are ejected from power. Shi'a clerics issued fatwas and called for jihad.

The rebels were finally driven out of Lucknow in January 1858, and their main force fled to Musa Bagh, where they made their last stand. There were as many as nine thousand men under arms, led by begum Hazrat Mahal, the junior wife of the slothful ex-nawab. The begum was considered a beauty; portraits show a fine-featured woman in her late thirties with a small, pinched mouth and a long nose. She was also scheming and ambitious, with plans to restore the royal family to the throne of Oudh in the person of her beardless twelve-year-old son, Birjis Qadr. Accompanying the begum to Musa Bagh was one of her lovers, Mammu Khan, perhaps the boy's biological father.

It wasn't much of a battle. By some accounts, four or five hundred rebels were killed. Their commander was decapitated, his body burned, and his headless remains tossed into the river. The begum's lover went to the gallows. She and the boy king ended up in exile in Kathmandu.

In a field next to the ruins, I found a blue sign, pitted with rust, that said,

NATIONALY PROTECTED MONUMENT

CEMETRY MOOSABAUGH

In fact, there was nothing that resembled a cemetery, only a single weatherbeaten white tomb surrounded by a low stone wall and partly shaded by a scrawny tree. Yet for all its modesty, it was no ordinary grave. It was a mazar, a shrine, a term commonly reserved for a saint or a person deserving of special reverence.

There were two inscriptions on the slab, roughly incised by hand. One read,

TO THE MEMORY OF
CAPTAIN F. WALES [*SIC*]
WHO RAISED AND COMMANDED
THE FIRST SIKH IRREGULAR CAVALRY
KILLED IN ACTION AT LUCKNOW
ON THE 21ST MARCH 1858

The other had eroded with time, and the last few words were the only part that was still legible:

. . . LIVED AND DIED AS A CHRISTIAN SOLDIER

The First Sikh Irregular Cavalry had been part of the assault force under Sir James Outram. It had been hastily assembled by an infantry captain named Frederick Wale, and for that reason it was also known as "Wale's Horse." *Irregular* was the right word, said one military historian. The Sikhs sported "every variety of bit and bridle, saddle and tulwar [a kind of curved saber]; every variety of horse, entire, mare, and gelding; of all heights from fifteen hands to animals little bigger than ponies." But the British admired the Sikhs, like the Gurkhas, as one of the "martial races." They could ride, they had a taste for heroic violence, and they hated the Moghuls.

The fact that Wale's was the only grave or monument in a place that had witnessed the deaths of hundreds of Muslims who were regarded as freedom fighters was strange enough in itself. Stranger still was the detritus around the mazar. The signboard was decorated with strips of yellow, blue, and green cloth. The tree was decked out in more green cloth, fringed with tinsel. Someone had pinned a handwritten note to the trunk that said, in Hindi, "I have three sick children and two adults. Please heal them. Give the kids a good education, give my family prosperity and good fortune." On the ground, there were broken bottles of Old Monk whiskey and a number of clay incense burn-ers. Each stick was tipped with a burned-down cigarette butt, with the brand name still visible just above the filter: Capstan. There were several empty packs nearby, all of the same brand and stamped in bold black capital letters with the warning, SMOKING KILLS.

I stopped a graybeard farmer in a purple shirt who was carrying his hoe to the mustard fields. "Who was Captain Wales?" I asked him.

"Captain Baba was an English saint who lived five hundred years ago," he answered. "People bring him gifts. They also bring him bread and butter and hard-boiled eggs. When there is a festival, they bring a harmonium to play music. Once Captain Baba knows you are in trouble, he will bring you here."

"So he has special powers? How did he get them?"

He shrugged. "People just know about them by word of mouth."

I walked back to the mosque, where a small crowd had gathered after noon prayers. An old man came over and asked me what I was up to. He had two yellow teeth that were escaping from his mouth in opposite directions. He said he was the owner of the field where the mazar of the saint stood. "Captain Baba? Everyone comes to worship him, Hindu and Muslim alike, every caste and religion. If you are possessed by a devil and come close to the tomb, the devil will try to leave your body."

More men joined us.

"This was where he died in battle. Part of his cavalry fled, and he was one of the handful who were left."

"We don't know when this happened because there was no village here at that time. Some of the old *babas* guess maybe three hundred years ago. But even they don't know."

The *babas'* guess was closer to the mark than the old farmer's, but the date on the tombstone didn't seem to have caught their attention.

"People also come at night if they're sick, just like you'd go to a doctor."

They discussed the captain's various powers and attributes. He could heal the sick, soothe the troubled, improve your love life, help young women to become pregnant. Apparently, this was an area in which he had some expertise.

"Today is Sunday. You should have come on Thursday. It is more auspicious."

During the festival of Nauchandi, one of the biggest in Uttar Pradesh, as many as two thousand people come to pay homage.

"You can see the video on the internet," someone said.

There was an inconclusive debate. Was it more correct to call him Captain Baba or Capstan Baba?

"That was his favorite cigarette. He liked to smoke and he liked whiskey, so we bring him this also."

I saw another man frown at this, and I raised an eyebrow.

"Yes, it's true," he said. "I take him whiskey, and then I come home and I think he is blessing me. But then, when I go back to the mazar, the bottle is empty. So I ask myself, who is actually drinking that whiskey?"

BUTCHERS

Brigadier General James George Smith Neill, commanding officer of the Madras Fusiliers, a lugubrious Scotsman with a great shaggy mustache and muttonchop whiskers, died in battle six months before Capstan Baba. Neill is described as a religious zealot, a ferocious warrior, and a chivalrous protector of the honor of women. In the summer before his death, he had a chance to display all three of these qualities.

Having put down a brief revolt in Varanasi, Neill proceeded upriver to deal with the rebellion in Allahabad. On June 5, 1857, the British residents of the city had taken refuge in the massive, squat fort that the Mughal emperor Akbar had constructed on the Yamuna, just above its confluence with the Ganges and the mythical underground Saraswati, named for the goddess of knowledge, wisdom, music, and the creative arts. Neill reached the city on the seventh day of the siege and dealt with the problem with his customary thoroughness.

Twelve years later, in *The Travels of a Hindoo to Various Parts of Bengal and Upper India*, an Indian writer named Bholanauth Chunder was still scouring his Victorian phrase book for the right words to convey the extent of Neill's retribution.

The Martial Law was an outlandish demon, the like of which had not been dreamt of in Oriental demonology. Rampant and ubiquitous it stalked over the land devouring hundreds of victims at a meal. . . . To 'bag the nigger' had become a favourite phrase of the military sportsmen of that day. Pea-fowls, partridges, and Pandies rose together, but the latter gave the best sport. . . . Scouring through the town and suburbs, they caught all on whom they could lay their hands—porter or pedlar, shopkeeper or artisan, and hurrying them on through a mock-trial, made them dangle on the nearest tree. Near six thousand beings had been thus summarily disposed of and launched into eternity. Their corpses hanging by twos and threes from branch and sign-post all over the town, speedily contributed to frighten down the country into submission and tranquility. For three months did eight dead-carts daily go their rounds from sunrise to sunset, to take down the corpses which hung at the cross-roads and market places, poisoning the air of the city, and to throw their loathsome burdens into the Ganges.

It was capital sport, one British officer wrote. "One trip I enjoyed amazingly. We got on board a steamer with a gun, while the Sikhs and the fusiliers marched up to the city. We steamed up throwing shots right and left till we got up the bad places, when we went on the shore and peppered away with our guns, my old double-barrel bringing down several niggers."

"God grant I may have acted with justice," Neill said. "I have done all for my country, to re-establish its prestige and power."

The next place for prestige and power to be reestablished was Kanpur, or, as the British preferred it, Cawnpore, a hundred and twenty miles up the Ganges from Allahabad and sixty from Lucknow. Neill had to delay his own departure for Cawnpore by a few days to deal with an outbreak of cholera among his troops, but one of his subordinates, Major Sydenham Renaud, made a more than adequate substitute, marching his men up the Grand Trunk Road and being "rather inclined to hang all black creation." The height at which he hanged them allowed the local pigs to feast on their feet and ankles.

In Kanpur, the leader of the uprising was one Nana Sahib, or Nana Rao, a hereditary maharaja who had been considered loyal to the crown. He enjoyed nothing more than a game of billiards with his English visitors, followed by a dinner of pork or beef with fine china and bone-handled silverware on damask tablecloths, washed down with claret in crystal champagne glasses. After all this amiable socializing, the local military commander, Sir Hugh Wheeler, assumed he had a natural ally against the rebels. Instead, Nana Sahib turned his coat and laid siege to the British garrison. After three weeks, Wheeler surrendered in exchange for a promise of safe passage to Allahabad. Boats would be waiting at the Satī Caurā Ghat on the Ganges, so named because this was where widows had once committed sati, immolating themselves on the funeral pyres of their husbands, a practice that the East India Company had first deplored and then, in 1829, banned.

Down at the ghat, the fog of war was especially thick. No one ever established who fired the first shot. Perhaps it was a jittery soldier from the Bengal

Army. Perhaps a sepoy taking matters into his own hands. Perhaps a horse startled and the rider dropped his rifle. Whatever the cause, the result was mayhem. The monsoon had barely started, and the river was only two feet deep. The boats were "crowded to suffocation," so heavy that they bogged down in the mud. The boatmen jumped off and sprinted to safety, throwing away the oars and overturning stoves and oil lamps. The vessels began to burn. Rebels raked them with gunfire; others rode into the shallow water swinging their sabers.

When the slaughter was done, the surviving women and children were brought ashore and marched to a villa named Bibighar in the compound of the local magistrate. The decorous translation of *Bibighar* is "house of the ladies," the ladies in question, the bibis, being the Indian mistresses of British officials starved for female companionship of their own race.

The prisoners were kept there for two weeks, under the supervision of a woman named Hussaini Khanum, who is variously described as a courtesan or a common prostitute. What to do with them? Dysentery and cholera were already reducing their numbers. News came that the British relief force was bearing down on the city, and word had surely reached Nana Sahib of the horrors General Neill had inflicted on Allahabad. Wheeler had died in the massacre at the ghat, and there was no one to negotiate with in Kanpur. The women and children were no longer a bargaining chip but a burden. Who gave the order to kill them? Perhaps it was Nana Sahib himself, perhaps Hussaini the courtesan.

The sepoys were ordered to fire on the prisoners but found the screams more than they could bear, so Hussaini called upon her lover to assemble an execution squad. He rounded up two willing Hindus and a pair of Muslim butchers, who arrived dressed in their white work aprons and carrying meat cleavers. It took them half an hour to work their way through the seventy-three women and one hundred and twenty-four children imprisoned in the Bibighar. When they were done, they stripped the bodies and body parts naked and tossed them into a dry well. When the well was full, they were thrown into the Ganges.

Neill and his Madras Fusiliers arrived two days later. Nana Sahib, or Nana Rao, had vanished after faking his suicide in the river. Neill found the floor of the Bibighar strewn with torn clothing, bonnets, bloody clumps of hair, daguerreotypes, bloodstained pages from the women's diaries.

June 17, Aunt Lily died. June 18, Uncle Willy died. June 22, George died. July 9, Alice died. July 12, Mamma died.

The rank-and-file rebels were summarily hanged, but for the Brahmin leaders of the revolt, hanging was not enough. Neill contrived ingenious forms of caste pollution as a punishment that would follow them through the endless cycles of reincarnation. Beef was forced down their throats. British soldiers called it a Cawnpore dinner. Prisoners were strapped to a cannon and blown to shreds, not knowing whether the blood that was already smeared on the cannon's mouth was Hindu or Muslim. The floor and walls of the Bibighar were thick with the blood of Christians. Neill had it watered down by lower-caste Indians, adding to its polluting qualities, and then, with the assistance of a cat o' nine tails, forced the Brahmins to lick it from the floor.

"To touch blood is most abhorrent to high-caste natives, they think that by doing so they doom their souls to perdition," Neill wrote. "Let them think so."

Two months later, Neill led his Madras Fusiliers into battle to relieve the siege of the Lucknow residency. On September 25, he took a sniper's bullet to the brain.

MASSACRE GHAT

In the weeks and months that followed, the Victorian imagination, with its fever dreams of barbarism and sex, was a beast that demanded feeding. "Such atrocities as those committed by Nana Saheb [*sic*] are almost unparalleled in the history of the world," said *The Sheffield Daily Telegraph* on August 31. The dastardly Hussaini Khanum was most assuredly a prostitute. The women in the Bibighar had been "sold by public auction" and subjected to abuses that could not be named to refined English audiences.

Punch published a cartoon by John Tenniel that showed the British lion hurling itself on the Bengal tiger as it crouched over the swooning body of a young Englishwoman who belonged in a pre-Raphaelite painting. Edward Armitage, in a work called *Retribution*, preferred to have Britannia plunge her sword into the tiger's throat. Charles Ball came up with a specious image of the lissome Miss Wheeler, daughter of the late general, felling a murderous rebel with a pistol shot; another of her attackers is already lying dead on the floor, with a third apparently wounded. Ball also gave his imagination free rein on the topography of the slaughter. His *Massacre in the Boats off Cawnpore* depicted the riverbank by the ghat as a jungled mass of palm trees, creepers, and giant ferns. *The Treacherous Massacre of Women & Children at Cawnpore*, a tinted lithograph by a certain T. Packer, conflated the killings at the ghat and those at the Bibighar in a single horrific scene. The Kanpur riverfront was rendered as an Oriental phantasmagoria of low mountains, islands studded with palm trees, opulent pleasure gardens, ornate mosques with towering minarets, and the tapered spires of Shiva temples apparently imported from contemporary paintings of Varanasi.

I went to see the place for myself. The sky was overcast, and Kanpur was shrouded in its usual haze of vehicle exhaust. In the low water of the post-monsoon "lean period," the Ganges was a hundred yards away across a bleak expanse of silt littered with garbage. A marauding pack of rhesus macaques was rooting around in the muck, looking for edibles. Raw sewage leaked onto the beach from a stinking drainage channel and, cut off from the river, it had collected in a stagnant, bubbling pool.

I squelched across the flats to the water's edge, where women were clustered in circles preparing offerings of coconuts, fruit, and marigold garlands. The river had divided into two channels, separated by a low sandbar. Groups of children were splashing around knee-deep in the shallows. I imagined that the conditions might have been similar on the day of massacre, with the overloaded boats stuck in the mud.

I squelched back to the ghat. There were no mountains, no pleasure gardens, no mosques. There was a temple with a small statue of Shiva, but it bore no resemblance to the fantastical spires of the Victorian imagination. It was a nondescript modern building, propped up above the flood line on concrete pillars, with an ugly onion dome that was painted cream with an orange trim. There was a small market area at the top of the steps, and I stopped at a chai stall to chat with a bearded man who was tending a couple of cows.

Satī Caurā Ghat was a name long forgotten, he said. Officially, it was Nana Rao Ghat these days, in honor of the leader of the Kanpur rebellion. But that name hadn't stuck either. People just called it the Massacre Ghat. There used to be a big Christian cross here, he said, but it had been destroyed during Independence celebrations.

The British had indeed built a monument to the massacre, three years after it happened. It was a marble Gothic screen, and in front of it was a cross and the figure of an angel, "the mourning seraph." But it hadn't been destroyed. After Independence, it had been carefully dismantled and moved from the bricked-up well at the Bibighar to the gardens of All Souls' Cathedral, which is now known as the Kanpur Memorial Church. Inside the church, there was a marble tablet with the names of the dead.

MRS. BERRILL—MRS. BORTHWICK—MRS. BRETT—MISS
BURN—MISS BURN. . . .
MISS GREENWAY—Y. GREENWAY—MARTHA GREENWAY—
JANE GREENWAY—JOHN GREENWAY—MARY GREENWAY. . . .
MRS. REED—JAMES REED—JULIA REED—C. REED—
CHARLES REED—BABY REED. . . .

And so on, almost two hundred names until the list finally came to the last item: three ayahs, who remained anonymous. And a verse from Romans 12:19. "Vengeance is Mine, Saith the Lord."

MANCHESTER OF THE EAST

Once the rebellion was put down, out went the British East India Company and in came the Raj—direct rule from London. The army was now formally in the service of the young queen and future empress of India, who had celebrated the twentieth anniversary of her accession to the throne on June 20, 1857, a week to the day before the women and children of Cawnpore were hauled off to the Bibighar.

If it was to avoid a repetition of the late unpleasantness, the army would need many things. It would need guns and bullets and cannons and horses; it would also need holsters and belts and boots, saddles and tack for the cavalry. All this called for a lot of leather, and the army needed a convenient place to produce it. Cawnpore was the obvious candidate.

In 1860, after the railway arrived, with the help of countless thousands of sleepers floated down the Ganga Canal by Frederick Wilson, the Raja of Harsil, the city was chosen as the site of the Government Harness and Saddlery Factory. In came the North West Tanning Company, the Cawnpore Tanning Company, Cooper, Allen & Co. In came cotton from the fields of the United Provinces, present-day Uttar Pradesh and known either way as UP. Cotton goods could now be transported more easily to Calcutta, destined in part for the American market after the Civil War. In came the Elgin Mills, Muir Mills, Cawnpore Woolen Mills. The last third of the nineteenth century was Kanpur's golden age. The British called the city the Manchester of the East.

Over the years, Cooper Allen became Allen Cooper, and upscale shoppers of Kanpur can still buy Allen Cooper shoes on the city's traffic-choked disaster of a main drag, Mall Road. A few hundred yards to the east, beyond Empire Lane, is the gigantic Z Square Mall, owned by the ZAZ Tannery and one of the biggest in the new India. It was the same dazzlingly lit, air-conditioned, multilevel labyrinth of familiar brands and corporate logos you might see in New Jersey or Minnesota or the duty-free section of the New Delhi airport—Tommy Hilfiger and Calvin Klein and the Body Shop and French Connection, as well as India's own Cocoberry Frozen Yogurt—but it was easy to find the coffee shop where I was going to meet a biologist named A. C. Shukla. All I had to do was tap the digital touch screen in the lobby for directions.

A good number of Indian men of a certain age and professional standing—engineers, scientists, government officials—have this odd habit of going by two initials instead of a single name. I'd already met an R. K. and an A. K. and a B. D., an R. P., an S. N. and a B. G. Now here was an A. C. It always felt to me like a small and stuffy holdover from the days before Independence, the formality of address that boys endured in England's great public schools, where brothers were referred to as *major* and *minor*.

Shukla was a thin, gaunt-featured man in his seventies who had taught for more than forty years at Christ Church College in Kanpur. An elite graduate school founded in 1866, its motto is *Ego Sum Lux Mundi*—"I Am the Light of the World." During one of the government's periodic, futile efforts to clean up the Ganges, he had led a team studying the most heavily industrialized stretch of the river, between Kanpur and Kannauj, fifty miles upstream.

He was a native of Kanpur, proud of his city and at the same time disgusted by what it had become, an urban hell of three or four million people—no one really knew how many, no matter what the census might say—befouled by its famous tanneries. There was something of the scholar-pedant in the stories he told over our espressos, but he also had an old man's misty-eyed nostalgia. "In my school days, Mall Road was ten feet broad, hardly a car passing in five to ten minutes. There was an irrigation canal. It was a beautiful sight to behold in the evening, with a small lake and gardens. So well I remember those happy days of Kanpur. You could drink water from the Ganges without any problems."

The obvious question was what he thought, as a biologist, of the mystery that had baffled everyone from the earliest European travelers to the medical men of the Raj—that *gangajal* would never spoil.

"Some people say this, some people say that," Shukla answered. "Someone is talking about sulfur springs, someone is talking about radioactive substances, someone is talking about bacteriophages, someone else is talking about ozone. We have found five hundred and sixty different kinds of algae in the Ganges, and all of them will contribute to increasing the amount of oxygen in the river. There are forty-three different river fungi, and they will work on the decomposition of dead bodies and plants and other debris. My concept is very clear, that all these things have been together in the mix since time immemorial. But today, it is so polluted that it has lost this capacity. It is an endangered river."

These days, he said, no one should think of taking a holy dip in the river south of Haridwar, or of cupping their hands for an *aachaman*—the purifying mouthful—south of the pilgrimage town of Badrinath, high in the Himalayas. It made me think of my encounter with the priest in Devprayag and my relief that he had exempted me from the *aachaman*. Shukla shook his head, like someone who had spent most of his life seeing his fact-based version of reality overwhelmed by a larger one. "To add a scientific outlook," he said, "you are going beyond faith. And you cannot challenge faith."

SCAVENGERS

All water buffalo," said Hafizurrahman, gesturing at the yard of his tannery. If there was any cowhide in there, it would most likely be from roadkill.

There are scholars on the academic fringe who say that Hindus once used to slaughter cows and eat beef and that the nation was never conquered by foreign invaders when this was the custom. Others debate whether the sacredness of the cow is actually rooted in scripture, like the complex taboos on menstrual blood, or in practical economics, reflecting the cow's value for milk, ghee, and dung for cooking fuel. But the same things could be said in favor of the water buffalo, first cousin to the cow, which has the additional virtue of being a tireless beast of burden. Some say the water buffalo is a lazy animal that likes nothing better than to lie around in a pond with an egret perched on its head, but then again, I'd never seen an energetic cow. Others say that the problem with the water buffalo is that it's the mount of Yama, the great lord of death. One way or another, no one's conscience is much troubled by the killing of one.

The great plain of the Ganges is the heart of what people sometimes call India's Cow Belt, although that term is considered politically incorrect. Cow killing is against the law in Uttar Pradesh, as it is in all but five Indian states, but here the enforcement can be especially savage. In UP, even the rumor of killing a cow, or the accusation that you're carrying the carcass of a cow in your truck, can invite attack by marauding gangs of *gau raksha*, cow vigilantes. A few weeks before I arrived in Kanpur, a Muslim man had been dragged from his home in the village of Bisara and beaten to death on the unfounded suspicion that he was storing and eating beef in his home.

Most of Kanpur's tanneries—there are more than four hundred of them, large and small—are clustered in the Jajmau district, just a few hundred yards downstream from the Massacre Ghat. Jajmau is a Muslim community. Even though there is no formal taboo, Hindus generally disdain the industry, which is defined by blood, death, and toxic chemicals. So the tanneries give the Muslims of Kanpur an unusual amount of economic power in a state where they are widely disliked and often the victims of spasms of mass violence.

On the way to see Hafizurrahman, I stopped at a nullah, a drainage channel, that carried waste from the tanneries to the Ganges. Half a dozen fat pigs were wallowing chin-deep in the blue-black liquid; one of them had its head fully submerged as it nosed around on the bottom. I wondered what a wine critic would say of the smell: decomposing animal matter and battery acid on the nose, a long, intense finish with lingering notes of ammonia, feces, and burned hair.

We pulled up at the gate of H. Rahman Tanning Industries. Crudely hand-painted on it, as required by law, was a NOTICE OF HAZARDOS CHEMICAL AND WASTES. There were spaces for the details to be filled out in various categories: tons of acids (sulfuric, formic, etc.), tons of chromium sulfate, liters or kilograms of thinners and dyes, and so forth. All of them had been left blank.

Hafizurrahman was a soft-spoken elderly Muslim with a white beard. He wore a pale pink long-sleeve shirt, black pants, black loafers, and an improbably natty suede porkpie hat. He said he had inherited the business from his father in 1968. In 1987, he was elected president of the Small Tanners

Association—"small" meaning a business that processed fewer than sixty hides a day—and he had held the job ever since.

"We work with offcuts that are discarded by the larger businesses," he said as he walked me around his tannery. The misshapen chunks of yellow-brown rawhide strewn around the yard were destined to become chew toys for dogs. In the main processing area, there were four large rotating wooden drums where the hides were softened with a mixture of lime and sodium sulfide and stripped of the last of their flesh and hair. Pickling the hides in a slush of chromium salts gives them a distinctive gray-blue color. A skinny teenage boy, glistening with sweat, was squelching around in a brick-lined pit, sorting pieces of this "wet blue." Recommended safety measures for working with wet blue include wearing protective gloves, safety goggles, and a face mask. The boy was naked apart from his shorts. The soles of my boots were coated in a rank gray slime. Dickens and Engels came to mind.

What passed as an office for Hafizurrahman was a large windowless shed with walls of rough cement. Flop-eared goats and quarrelsome geese rooted around on the floor among bright blue barrels of chemicals.

"The government!" he said. "Nothing but trouble! The Ganges gets polluted, and we're always the ones to blame. But they are the main culprits!" When the government opened a plant to treat waste from the tanneries, they had to contribute part of the cost themselves. But then the construction budget tripled, and so did the amount levied on the tanners; so many contractors, middlemen, and officials had to take their cut. "There were only 175 tanneries at that time," he said. "But then another 227 came up—and they asked them to pay again. But they never upgraded the plant! The money just went into their pockets!"

And then there was the mela. Each year, on a date determined by astrologers, millions of Hindus gather in Allahabad, farther downstream, for the Magh Mela, a bathing festival at the sacred confluence of the Ganges, the Yamuna, and the invisible Saraswati. Once every twelve years, it becomes the greatest of all the festivals, the Kumbh Mela, the largest assembly of humans anywhere on the planet. The last Kumbh Mela in Allahabad had been in 2013.

It lasted more than seven weeks; on one single day, thirty million people converged on the river. The government felt it was unreasonable to expect them to bathe in diluted tannery waste.

Hafizurrahman never raised his voice, but bitterness doesn't have to be loud. "'Close the tanneries yourselves, or we'll raid you and shut you down,' they said. So we came to an agreement. They gave us the dates, and we stopped work. But it didn't make any difference. During the night, one o'clock, two o'clock, they'd come in with the press, jump over the walls, take photographs, defame us! Even though we had shut down!"

We went back out into the yard, where workers were loading up a wooden-wheeled horse cart with piles of rawhide. A white goat with a black head wandered over, and Hafizurrahman stopped to scratch it behind the ear, composing himself.

A dozen miles or so from Kanpur, the town of Unnao has a much smaller cluster of about a dozen tanneries. It's hard for a tannery to be spotless, but Kings International, a manufacturer of high-end saddlery and a small quantity of bags and belts for the luxury export market, came close. Bougainvillea spilled over the whitewashed outer walls. A gardener was snipping away at the topiary bushes, near a sign that said,

REAL TIME EFFLUENT QUALITY MONITORING STATION
WE FIGHT POLLUTION AND SAFEGUARD THE ENVIRONMENT

The spacious reception area had black leather sofas, and bright tropical fish were darting back and forth in an aquarium. A display case of leather handbags looked ready for tags from Gucci and Hermès and Givenchy. There were framed mission statements and vision statements and no smoking signs and trade magazines to read while I waited to see the owner of the tannery, Taj Alam, who was also the president of the Uttar Pradesh Leather Industries Association.

He appeared after a few minutes, full of apologies for keeping me wait-ing. Late forties perhaps, coal-black hair, snow-white beard, beaming smile, and fluent English. He ushered me into his air-conditioned office and plunked himself down in a $500 executive chair behind a glass-topped desk. There was an ornate grandfather clock in one corner and shelves of testimonial plaques, industry awards, and equestrian-themed knickknacks. Yet for all the differ-ences in style, décor, and no doubt net worth, listening to him was like listening to Hafizurrahman in stereo.

"Okay, we are a religious minority," he said. "We cannot say whether you have to bury your dead, or throw your dead away, or burn them in a crema-torium, or burn them on the banks of the river Ganges. On that we cannot speak. But the mela, yes. They close the tanning sector for a month. You can-not process leather, you cannot make shoes, we lose billions of rupees, and how much can you store for a rainy day? But you have ten million people shit-ting in the river, urinating there, throwing stuff on the ghats. And that in it-self is a tremendous pollution thing!"

A peon brought in a tray of chai and biscuits and small bottles of water.

"Do you know how many other industrial facilities there are in Kanpur?" Alam asked.

I confessed that I didn't.

"Thirty thousand," he said. "And will you please tell me, have they imposed any treatment-plant order on any other industry?"

"So why do you think they've singled you out?" I asked, though the answer seemed obvious enough: tanning leather was one of the filthiest industries in the world.

He paused, choosing his words with care. "The logic is simple," he said. "Because the tanning sector is 99.99 percent Muslim."

Alam walked me downstairs to a large, airy workroom where men were assembling saddles and punching holes for grommets in leather belts. Out-side, we walked over to the effluent monitoring station. "It keeps you on your toes, you know exactly what you're doing," he said. "I do my primary treatment here. Then it goes to the central treatment plant. But then what happens? That water goes into the same nullah as the raw sewage, because there is no sewage treatment plant in Unnao! And that is the government's responsibility. So it all goes into the Ganga. Whatever we have done here is undone. So why bother to do it?

"People are made only to see our dark side. They are wearing the shoes, they are wearing the belts, the ladies are carrying the handbags and wearing the gloves. But what do they think would happen if we were not tanning the hides? If there's a dead body on the road, it's the eagle or the vulture that deals with it, instead of the body decaying. Hundreds of millions of Indians eat meat. And how the hell can you stop a person eating his staple food? If they close down the tanneries, the slaughtering will continue, but the skins will just be thrown on the ground or into the nullahs. You see, we are the ones who prevent diseases and epidemics! We are like the eagle or the vulture; we are the scavengers."

MOTHERS AND CHILDREN

Rakesh Jaiswal was born in Mirzapur, a carpet-making town on the Ganges between Allahabad and Varanasi, but he had devoted most of his adult life to the thankless task of ministering to the health of the river in Kanpur. He was in his late fifties now, with thick gray hair, a courtly manner, and weary eyes. "I have seen Hindus go into a sewage drain and sprinkle water on their foreheads," he said. "I have seen them dipping bodies into raw sewage and tannery effluent. I have seen Hindus who are very interested in the rituals of Ma Ganga. I haven't seen any who are very interested in cleaning it."

In 1993, he decided to change that by founding a small organization that he called Eco Friends. One of the first things he did was to go out and retrieve dead bodies from the river. Usually they were either the indigent, those whose families couldn't afford the wood for a cremation, or unidentified and unclaimed corpses dumped by the police. "We started by cleaning a ten-kilometer stretch of the river," he said. "We found a hundred and eighty bodies and got them properly buried. After that, we went out twice or thrice each year. Every time we found at least a hundred bodies in various stages of decay."

The newspapers took an interest; the government didn't.

The Manchester of the East was in rapid decline at the time, to the greater detriment of the river. The government had taken over most of the city's celebrated textile mills, which were plagued by corruption, incompetent management, labor conflicts, and sloppy maintenance. In 1992, the industry was ordered to halt all production. There were mass layoffs. As the mills decayed, the tanneries grew to become the engine of Kanpur's economy, sopping up many of the surplus workers. The central treatment plant, the object of Hafizurrahman's bitter scorn, was opened in 1994 as part of the government's so-called Ganga Action Plan to clean up the worst sources of pollution. Nominally, the plant could handle the effluent from 175 tanneries—less than half the size it would eventually need to be, and *nominally* being the operative word. The idea was to treat the waste, dilute it with treated sewage, and use the mixture to irrigate nearby villages. There was not only more tannery waste than before, it was also nastier. Old-fashioned vegetable tanning was falling out of favor; chromium salts gave a more desirable product.

Jaiswal, who by this time had acquired a Ph.D., turned to the tools of law and science. In 1998, he filed a lawsuit with the High Court in Allahabad. One hundred and twenty-seven tanneries were ordered to close until they installed their own primary treatment plants. Did they actually operate them? Well, that was a different matter. That cost money.

Over the next three years, he took his team out to the villages that were using the irrigation water from the treatment plant. They took samples of milk and other farm products and sent them to the Indian Institute of Technology in Kanpur for analysis. They found concentrations of chrome a hundred times higher than the safe level set by the government. Jaiswal's reputation spread. The Ford Foundation and the Asia Foundation opened their checkbooks. There were projects for the World Bank and the World Health Organization. He hung a testimonial on the wall of his office that said, "This is to certify that Rakesh Jaiswal, Ph.D. has been selected as one of 50 Unsung Heroes of Compassion," stamped with the gold seal of His Holiness the Dalai Lama.

We spent a hot, dreary afternoon in Jajmau. On the way to the treatment plant, we stopped at a cleared plot of land on a gentle slope less than a quarter mile from the river. "Look at how low it is," he said. "You could walk across. It's only knee-deep in places. At Haridwar, the river is bone dry. All the water goes into the Upper Ganga Canal. Then the Middle Ganga Canal, the Lower Ganga Canal. By the time the river reaches Kanpur, it's debatable whether there is even a single drop of Himalayan water."

The detritus of the industry was heaped up in piles next to an electrical substation that was painted yellow. Some were offcuts of wet blue, which gave off a faint chemical odor. Others were scraps of hide with the hair and shreds of flesh and rancid fat still attached. Dogs were sniffing at them, and they were surrounded by buzzing clouds of flies. A laborer was hacking away at some of this brown muck with a four-tined pitchfork. Once it was ground up, it would be sold to make chicken feed and glue. "This fellow will earn maybe one hundred and fifty rupees a day," Jaiswal said. That was less than two and a half dollars.

At the treatment plant, an affable engineer gave us a tour of a couple of acres of malodorous concrete structures. There were screen and grit channels, equalization tanks, mixing tanks, aeration tanks where white cattle egrets perched on the surrounding guardrail and the waste frothed and foamed like a gigantic brown milkshake. There were collection wells, pumping stations,

UASB reacters. That stood for *upflow anaerobic sludge blanket*, the engineer explained helpfully.

He reeled off some facts and figures. Each day, the plant mixed twenty-seven million liters of treated sewage with nine million of treated tannery waste, a three-to-one ratio.

"But that doesn't account for all the waste from the tanneries, does it?" I asked.

"No, they actually generate more than thirty million liters a day," he said.

"Probably more like fifty," Jaiswal interjected. "But the truth is, no one really knows."

In other words, as much as four-fifths of the waste would end up in those blue-black drainage channels, which carried it straight into the sacred river. The same applied to Kanpur's sewage; only 20 percent of that was treated.

"But the plant's been here for more than twenty years," I said. "Why was it never upgraded?"

The engineer looked helpless. "These things take a lot of time."

"And money," Jaiswal said.

"How much of the money is pocketed no one knows, no one can prove," he said as we drove away, passing a gang of laborers who were burying sludge from the treatment plant in a landfill and covering it with crushed rock. "Corruption is everywhere. It is known to everybody, but nobody talks about it. In every public service department like water or electricity or sewers, most of the work is executed by contractors who have to pay off the authorities. It's almost legal. If it's only 30 or 40 percent, it's not corruption. It's more like a right. Sometimes all the money is pocketed, 100 percent, and the work takes place only on paper."

We drove on for two or three miles to the outskirts of the city to see the irrigation canal. It ran along an elevated berm above a dusty field where workers had laid out squares of hide to dry in the blazing sun. I clambered up over the crumbling stonework onto a precarious, unguarded walkway a few inches wide. The cocktail of sewage and tannery waste came gushing out of two large rusty outflow pipes. It made its way down the canal at a fair clip. It was greenish-brown and topped with a rippling layer of black-flecked foam two feet deep. It smelled terrible.

After Jaiswal presented his study of chromium contamination, the government had installed another small plant where a portion of the spent chrome was recovered and recycled. I asked him if this had led to any improvement in the water quality. He pursed his lips and said, "No, it is just the same."

Back at his office, a sad-eyed middle-aged man served us tea. We sat quietly under the plaque from the Dalai Lama, an awkward silence. Finally, I asked Jaiswal what he had in mind to do next.

He sighed. "I don't know. The future is very bleak. Once I had a staff of ten. Now it's just Jitendra and me. I seem to have resigned and lost hope."

What about the new government, which was promising to clean up the river where all its predecessors had failed?

"Government is talking and talking and talking," he said at last. "Cow is our mother. Ganga is our mother. We will save our mother. But we will not take care of the children of the tanneries. We'll let them be killed."

PRESS ONE FOR MANGOES

Yet here and there across the endless dusty hinterland there were flickers of optimism, often signaled by the trill of cell phones. If you'd asked most Indians for a symbol of the bad old days of rigid state control of the economy and stultifying bureaucracy, they'd probably have chosen the experience of getting a telephone. You could wait years for a landline, and the only way to speed things up was who you knew and how much you were prepared to slip them in the plain brown envelope. Now there were more cell phones than people in the cities, and the service providers, offering the cheapest rates in the world, had descended on the unconnected rural areas. Uttar Pradesh, with two hundred million people—as many as Brazil, but compacted into 3 percent of the land area—was a prime target. In more and more villages, the constant soundtrack was the chirp of the Nokia ringtone.

These were not people who could afford the bells and whistles of an iPhone or a Samsung Galaxy endorsed by Bollywood celebrities. "We want to be the Southwest Airlines of the mobile industry," said one senior executive I met, whose company was locked in a cutthroat struggle for the rural market with half a dozen others. "We have thirty-five million subscribers, but that's not much. In India, everything has to have at least seven zeros." (I heard later that his company had folded, killed off by its larger competitors.)

For women especially, going mobile could mean a new life, though the freedom it gave them came with the risk of a ferocious backlash. In one village in Uttar Pradesh, the local elected council, the panchayat, had recently banned the use of phones by unmarried girls. Teenage boys were allowed to make calls, but only under adult supervision. The elders were clearly unnerved by the threat of flirtation, romance, violation of the rules of home, family, and arranged marriage. This was not a trivial matter. I'd never associated the idea of honor killings with Hinduism, but it turned out that there were three or four a week in India and that two-thirds of them were in UP. In the month leading up to the panchayat's edict, eight young people from the surrounding district had been killed after eloping; three girls were beheaded by male relatives.

The Achilles' heel of the mobile phone was the problem of keeping it charged, and most of the prospective buyers in the target market didn't have reliable access to electricity. Often the best you could hope for was to hook up to your tractor battery—but that assumed you were rich enough to own a tractor in the first place. True, the fields were crisscrossed by power lines and transmission towers. The question was whether the juice flowed through them for more than a few hours a day and at the right time; as often as not, it would happen only when you were fast asleep. One day I strolled through a village where the streets were lined with electricity poles and the houses had meters mounted on the walls. But then I noticed that there were no wires attached to the poles and that the meters were shrouded in cobwebs. Nonetheless, some bureaucrat in Lucknow or Delhi had doubtless added the place to his Potemkin quota of "newly electrified villages."

This was one reason photovoltaic panels had begun to pop up here and there on the unlikeliest of rooftops, and kids were poring over their schoolbooks in the evening by the glow of a solar lantern. Some young women had put two and two together and were making a little pocket money on the side. One morning I met a sweet-faced twenty-four-year-old named Vidyawati, who was sitting in the doorway of her house next to a shelf of bright yellow solar lanterns, waiting for customers. In a nearby storeroom, wedged in between a barrel of cooking oil and a sack of animal feed, there was a truck-size battery that drew power from the panels on the roof. Vidyawati thought of herself as an *entrepreneur*—a word that had become a kind of magical incantation in India. "I rent out the lanterns overnight for two rupees," she said. "Yesterday I rented out thirty-two of them." For charging a neighbor's cell phone, she got five rupees. In a good week, she might clear five hundred rupees, about eight dollars, which was enough to afford a few small treats like jewelry and clothes. I wondered if that accounted for the elegant sari she was wearing, which was black and silver, with Rajasthani-style mirrored embroidery.

Vidyawati—whose name, I discovered, meant "learned"—was the first member of her family to go to school. Now she was studying English literature, taking an auto-rickshaw each day to the college in a nearby town. "You have to know English to get ahead in India these days," she said. Her ambition was to join the UP police.

I asked her what kind of literature she liked best. She covered her mouth with her hand and giggled. "Love stories," she said.

Just outside Allahabad, I stopped in a desolate hamlet in the township of Phulpur, Jawaharlal Nehru's first parliamentary constituency. A man came running up to me in the street shouting, "Gulf! Gulf!" He waved a business card in my face. It was for a dry cleaning store in Abu Dhabi. He'd had it laminated. "Job!" he grinned. "Job!" He was off there on a short-term contract, and he'd be back in May or June in time to help out with the pre-monsoon harvest.

I walked over to the village hall to talk to some farmers who had bought special "green SIM cards" from another cell phone company, which took some of the guesswork out of their decisions about planting, harvesting, and marketing in a time of ever-hotter summers and ever more unpredictable monsoons. The card gave them five text messages a day, starting at 7:00 A.M.: weather reports, news alerts, helpful tips, spot prices for wheat and rice. If they found an unfamiliar pest or fungus in their crop, they could send a photograph to an expert for advice or call a help line for one rupee a minute.

One man told me his mango trees had withered; the help line told him what pesticide to use, with advice on how to handle it (wear gloves, stir with a stick, don't get it on your skin). A ten-year-old said proudly that he had picked up the seven o'clock text one morning and run to the fields to warn his father that the local market was being flooded with a useless knock-off fertilizer. Someone else's cow hadn't been responding to artificial insemination; next time, the help line expert said, feed her half a kilo of *paan*, the stimulant derived from the areca nut, then lay her down with her backside higher than her head.

"We're trying to refine the system," said the local sales manager for the cell phone company. "It's no good telling someone the weather in Kanpur if they live in Allahabad. I have this idea: press one for mangoes, two for grapes, three for guavas."

BOOKWORMS

Apart from the surviving residents of the eight neighborhoods that had been razed to the ground during the mutiny, no one seemed to miss the old Allahabad. The Anglican bishop of Calcutta, Reginald Heber, had stopped over for ten days in 1824. Apart from the massive fort of the Emperor Akbar and one or two Mughal monuments and ruins, he found the place "desolate and ruinous." He reported that the natives called it Fakeerabad, the Abode of Beggars.

Mirza Muhammad Asad-ullah Khan of Delhi, also known as Ghalib, who is described as a nobleman, poet, and letter writer, visited three years later. After a night of being tormented by bedbugs, he sat down and wrote "A Letter of Grievance from My Wanderings."

> *Oh Allahabad! May God damn that desolation. . . . How unjust to call this fearful place a city, how shameful that men should reside in this trap for fiends. If one compares this land to the plain of hell, hell would burn in anger.*

Once the clearance crews had disposed of the rubble of the burned villages, the city was transformed by a great building spree. There were two cathedrals and a slew of churches, both Anglican and Catholic, mansions, parks, bandstands, law courts and colleges, private schools, libraries, and the inevitable Victorian clock tower with a cupola that would have looked better on a mosque. Promising boys were shipped off to boarding schools like Bishop Cotton in Shimla, the most favored of the Himalayan hill stations (founded in 1859, motto "Overcome Evil with Good"). Later they could go to the Doon School in

Dehradun, which was staffed by veterans of Eton and Harrow ("Knowledge Our Light").

Mark Twain arrived by train in 1895, crossing the Yamuna on a long bridge. The river, which he called the Jumna, was pale blue and looked clean. The Ganges was muddy yellow and didn't. He was tickled by the fact that the name of the city could be translated as Godville. He described the Civil Lines, where the British had built their residences, as "comely and alluring, and full of suggestions of comfort and leisure, and of the serenity which a good conscience buttressed by a sufficient bank account gives." He didn't recall seeing the "native town," though he couldn't remember why that was. Something to do with the mutiny, he thought. But he did encounter some of its inhabitants, the manservants who lay in front of your door at night and remained there all day, motionless as statues, in case your boots needed cleaning or your drink needed topping up. He found their subservience depressing. He tried to remember the Hindi phrase that meant "come, shove along," but couldn't bring it to mind.

Although it became one of the most anglicized, anglophone, and anglophile places in all of India, it was a Frenchman named Émile Moreau who did more than anyone to make Allahabad a city of books. Moreau arrived in the city in 1857 "during the unsettling phase of the Sepoy Mutiny." A bookworm himself, he noticed that the English passengers at the new railway station always seemed to have their noses in a good book or magazine. Sometime in the 1870s, looking to prune his collection of thousands of volumes, Moreau spread out a sheet on the platform and offered some of them for sale. But having a French name was not the best marketing strategy, so he persuaded Arthur Henry Wheeler, the owner of a chain of bookstores in London, to lend his to the new enterprise.

Later, Moreau was joined by a fellow bibliophile, a young Bengali named T. K. Banerjee, or TKB. Together, they created one of the great institutions of British India, the A. H. Wheeler chain of railway bookstalls. In Calcutta's Howrah station, Wheeler was an elaborate structure made of Burma teak, manufactured in England and shipped out in sections. In smaller towns, it was usually the only place where you could buy anything to read. As part of its Indian Railway Library Series, the company was the first to publish the stories of Rudyard Kipling. Eventually, to some harrumphing from the English community, the Banerjee family took over sole ownership. Today you can buy books, magazines, newspapers, and comics at a Wheeler in more than 250 stations.

Allahabad is still the headquarters of A. H. Wheeler & Co. Pvt. Ltd., and I stopped by one day and bought an anthology of writings on the city. Anglophilia and bibliophilia were as strong among educated Indians as they were among their colonial masters. They smoked Wills Gold Flake cigarettes, sipped whiskey and soda at the Cosmopolitan Club, read Shaw and Galsworthy and Somerset Maugham, dropped phrases in French like characters out of Tolstoy. They typed essays on Royal typewriters and went to Oxford and wrote theses on *The Castle of Otranto* and the Gothic novel. After Independence, their children read Enid Blyton's adventures of the Famous Five and the Secret Seven and flew with Biggles on his intrepid missions against the beastly Hun. The boys rode Raleigh bicycles and played cricket with bats signed by the legendary Englishman Sir Len Hutton.

The editor of the collection I'd bought was a local poet named Arvind Krishna Mehrotra. Growing up in the sixties, his tastes had evolved from Rabindranath Tagore to the Penguin Modern Poets. He read Ginsberg's "America" and Corso's "Marriage" and Ferlinghetti's "Underwear" ("Women's underwear holds things up/Men's underwear holds things down"). He and his friends learned how to speak like Holden Caulfield. They got hold of an imported copy of the *Village Voice* that described a new publication called *Fuck You/a Magazine of the Arts*. On the veranda of a house at 18 Hastings Road, named for the first governor-general of India, they cranked out a local version on a dusty Gestetner mimeograph. The price was given as "Anything commensurate with your dignity—and ours." In deference to local decorum, they called it *damn you/a magazine of the arts*.

AT BARNETT'S HOTEL

George Barnett and his wife, Rose, had an exceptional talent for icing cakes, and everyone agreed that Barnetts of Allahabad, the House for Fresh Confectionery, which also sold butter toffees, "nut hardbakes," and butterscotch, was the finest in the city, if not in all of India. In the 1930s, the Barnetts turned their mansion at 14 Canning Road, with its expansive lawns, white colonnades, and elegant porte cochere, into a hotel with eight bedrooms, a convenience for passengers arriving on the new Imperial Airways flight from London to Calcutta. Allahabad was the penultimate stop, and by the time it got there, the Handley Paige airliner had hopscotched its way through Paris, Brindisi, Athens, Alexandria, Cairo, Gaza, Baghdad, Basra, Kuwait, Bahrein, Sharjah, Gwadar, Karachi, Jodhpur, Delhi, and Kanpur. The whole journey cost £122; getting off in Allahabad knocked £8 off the fare. For travelers staying overnight, Barnett's Hotel laid on a five-course dinner, veg and non-veg. For those who simply wanted a quick bite during their layover, Barnett's provided it on wheels, driving snacks out to the Allahabad aerodrome in a converted 1928 Chevrolet.

In May 1947, with India's independence three months off, the Barnetts decided they had had enough. They departed for Bombay and bought two tickets home on the Cunard Line's MV *Georgic*. The hotel was sold. The deed of sale valued the contents, including the beds, cake molds, and adjustable toffee cutters, at forty-four thousand rupees, and the goodwill at another twenty-six thousand. But Barnett's fell into decline and disrepair, reopened, closed, changed its name. By the time I made my second visit to Allahabad, it had been restored to life as the Hotel Harsh Ananda, with a website that announced "its new journey in a unique & modern avatar." Its specialty now was not butter toffees but the hosting of custom-designed weddings (Village Theme, Buddha Theme, Rajasthani Theme, Peacock Theme) for as many as two thousand people. For Muslim celebrations, it offered to provide tables segregated by gender. I decided to stay there for a few days.

Canning Road had been the heart of the Civil Lines, the British residential area. Nowadays it was M. G. Marg—Mahatma Gandhi Road—but it still had a faded grandeur, an old lady without her makeup. I walked from one end of it to the other, starting at the Gothic Revival All Saints' Cathedral. Consecrated in 1887, it had been modeled on the east end of Canterbury Cathedral, complete with stained-glass windows and flying buttresses. A man was peeing in the bushes, and a couple of teenagers got up giggling from the lawn, adjusting their clothing.

On the sidewalk nearby, in front of a handsome but derelict red-arched building, there was a small squatter colony. Kids ran up to me, saying, "*Babuji*, *babuji*," and stretching out their palms. With a long night's drinking ahead, scruffy men were jostling to press damp wads of ten-rupee bills through the metal grille of a Model Shop—sometimes known as an English Wine Shop—in exchange for bottles of cheap liquor. There were street stalls and sidewalk fires, puttering diesel generators and kerosene lamps, and the open drains were filled with gray-green sludge. Farther on there were mini-malls and pretentious but shoddily built commercial buildings with reflective blue glass façades and signs advertising the Personality Maker Unisex Saloon and Body Spa.

It was a warm and sultry evening, and I stopped for a beer at the Grand Continental Hotel on Sardar Patel Road. I was the only customer. Two waiters in striped waistcoats stood to attention against the wall, like caryatids. A short, corpulent bartender in a dark suit poured me an ice-cold Kingfisher and put a power-pop ballad on the CD player. A cricket match was playing on the flat-screen TV. In India, there is always a cricket match playing on TV, and usually on half a dozen different channels. A younger man with a notebook was taking an inventory of the Indian whiskeys lined up on the shelf. Bagpiper, Royal Stag, McDowell's, most of them made from fermented molasses and any resemblance to whiskey being purely coincidental.

There was a raised dais at the end of the room, covered in a red cloth. Some men were moving cushions around and setting up low mike stands for a harmonium and tabla drums. A sign advertised a nightly recital of ghazals, poetic songs of love and loss.

"But I'm the only person here," I said to the bartender as he brought me another Kingfisher. "How can they perform ghazals to an empty room?"

He wobbled his head. "Sir, they are starting at 7:30 only."

I looked at my watch. It was ten minutes to eight.

ALLAHABADMINTON

Edmonia Hill, known to her friends as Ted, was the dark-haired twenty-nine-year-old daughter of the Reverend R. T. Taylor, president of a Methodist women's school, Beaver College, in Pennsylvania, which, more than a hundred years later, found it necessary to transform itself into Arcadia College, a name that reflected both its ideals and its wish to avoid further sophomoric satire.

Ted met Rudyard Kipling at a dinner party in Allahabad in December 1877. Newly arrived from Lahore, he had been assigned to Allahabad as assistant editor of the weekly edition of India's leading newspaper, *The Pioneer*. She described him as "a short dark-haired man of uncertain age, with a heavy mustache and wearing very thick glasses. Mr. Kipling looks about forty, as he is beginning to be bald." In reality, he was twenty-two. She was enchanted; she decided she would call him Ruddy.

He had taken temporary rooms at the Allahabad Club, but the winter nights can get chilly in this part of India, and Ted and her husband, Samuel Alexander Hill, a science professor at Allahabad College and an enthusiastic amateur photographer, thought he would be more comfortable if he moved into their home, Belvedere House, a gracious thatched bungalow that was right next door to the Pioneer Press. It was one of the few buildings that had been left standing after General Neill's rampages in 1857.

Kipling showed up at Belvedere House in his horse trap, which he called the Pig and Whistle. They gave him the Blue Room, which had its own red sandstone veranda and caught the morning sun. He had his own bathtub, which a servant filled with water from a goatskin slung over his shoulder. He found the house ideal for his purposes. It was set a quarter mile back from the bustle of the main road, surrounded by several acres of flower gardens and greenery. Professor Hill would sit around on the veranda reading *The Pioneer* after breakfast, "clad in samite mystic wonderful." When he was done with the newspaper, he would pick up "a portentous big stick," stroll off down the long, leafy avenue of North Indian rosewood trees, and "exhort the idle labourers that life is real, life is earnest, and tapping road metal as though it were glass is not its goal."

Ted and Ruddy flirted shamelessly, though there seems to be no reason to think it ever amounted to more than that. "He was animation itself, telling his stories admirably, so that those about him were kept in gales of laughter," she wrote. "He fairly scintillated." Belvedere House had two tennis courts and six badminton courts. Kipling didn't play tennis, but he could hold his own at badminton. "If life here was to be tempered with Allahabadminton, he would begin to take comfort," Ted said.

Writing for India's leading newspaper seemed like a fine thing to Edmonia Hill. On a hot night, when it was lit by a flickering hurricane lamp, she found the press room a magical, exotic place. The "half-naked men who turn the presses look picturesque in the uncertain light as they loll against the black wall." The presses themselves "look mysterious and ghastly, and from the far end comes the tick-tick of the type being set up by white-sheeted yawners." Sometimes the workers ruined the layout by dripping wax onto it from their guttering candles. Boys slept on the tables.

Kipling, on the other hand, detested his new job. "My work on the Weekly was not legitimate journalism," he complained. He chafed at the space limitations. Everything had to be written or cut to fit. "Your poetry good, sir, just coming proper length today," the foreman told him on one occasion.

Sprawled out on cushions in front of the fireplace at Belvedere House, Kipling devoted himself to what he considered his real writing. In a single febrile year, he turned out six volumes of short stories, which Wheeler published in its Indian Railway Library Series. Professor Hill's photographs of the forests in central India inspired the settings in *The Jungle Book* where Mowgli and his companions fought Shere Khan the tiger. Kipling's stay in Allahabad gave him the backdrop for "Rikki Tiki Tavi," the trusty mongoose who protects his English owners from the snakes that live in a "large garden, only half cultivated, with bushes as big as summer houses of Marshal Niel roses, lime and orange trees, clumps of bamboos, and thickets of high grass." It was the garden of the Hills' bungalow.

I'd heard that Belvedere House was still standing, semiderelict and occupied by squatters. As far as I could tell from the descriptions, it was somewhere in a warren of small roads and open fields near Allahabad University and the Holy Trinity Church.

Kipling? Pioneer Press? Newspaper? Belvedere House? My questions elicited nothing but shrugs, blank looks.

"Printing?" one passerby said. "Here there is printing." He gestured at a narrow dirt alley, where I found an elderly Muslim man dozing in a yard outside his workshop next to a piece of antique machinery, surrounded by stacks of what looked like printed signatures, folded but unstitched. The alley came to a dead end. I retraced my steps, made a turn, and found myself in another cul-de-sac. Nothing here seemed to go anywhere. Finally, I stopped two men who frowned and debated the question and thought the word *Belvedere* rang a bell. They pointed me down a road that ended in a pair of iron gates, overhung with what I thought was a North Indian rosewood and flanked by stone pillars that had lost most of their red paint. Behind it was a three-story brick building, with laundry hung out to dry on the balconies. On a rusted yellow sign on one of the gates, there was a symbol that might have been a butterfly, or might have been the slanted eyes of the goddess Kali, and below that were a couple of mobile numbers and lettering that, being in Hindi, meant nothing to me.

Since it was a Sunday, I expected to find the place deserted, but a watchman was drowsing at the door, and he ran off smartly to find his employer, who came out a few minutes later, beaming a welcome. I apologized for disturbing him on a Sunday. "No, sir, we are working here on Sundays, there is no problem with that," he said.

He introduced himself as Anupam Agarwal and said he was the proprietor of the Belvedere Printing Works. I asked him what he knew about the great English writer.

"Ah, yes, Kipling. I came to know about Kipling only from an Australian. He spoke very fine Hindi. He told us that Kipling has lived here and he has written 'Baa Baa Black Sheep' here. This Australian was writing a biography of three writers—Amartya Sen, Rabindranath Tagore, and my great-grandfather. He said he would send me a copy of the book, but he never did so. He left me his business card, but I have lost it."

It seemed like an odd trio, a contemporary Bengali economist, India's greatest poet, and an obscure nineteenth-century writer-scholar, who was best known, I found out later, for translating *Othello*, *Romeo and Juliet*, and *The Merchant of Venice* into Urdu.

"This was he, my great-grandfather," Mr. Agarwal said. He pointed to a life-size portrait on the wall of a white-bearded old gentleman in a formal black jacket with a gold watch chain. He was standing between a red curtain and an ornamental plant in a brass pot, which made it look as if the artist had copied it from a Victorian photographer's studio shot. It was not a very good painting; the lower half seemed unfinished.

"His name was Shri Babu Baleshwar Prasad," Mr. Agarwal said. "He established the printing works, but it was called the Belvedere Steam Press in that time. Here there was a steam press, run by coal, all the machines were here, and in the back, there was a store for the paper. The residential house was just a stone-throwing from here. Pioneer building was just adjacent to this. But it has been demolished since long time.

"I was very enthusiastic to know from where our ancestors came, and I have collected data. There was a book published, in 1937, all history of Agarwals in India. All the history is there! My grandfather's brother was treasurer to Kashi Naresh, the maharaja of Benares."

I asked him what he meant by "the residential house."

"Mr. Alexander Hill's house. From him, my ancestors purchased this entire premises."

"I'd like to see the house," I said. "I heard squatters were living there now."

"Where have you heard this?"

"From a newspaper article, I think."

"Ah, newspapers. No, no, this is not true. It also was demolished. Squatters were never living there. After Partition, my grandfather was the owner of that house. He lived there actually, with his four sons and their families. It had fourteen, fifteen rooms. But then he was alone. His three daughters, all of them were married and gone. He was left there with his wife only. The house was very old, plaster was falling. So he opted to sell it to a property developer, who demolished it. Now the man has built these complexes, duplexes over there. Fourteen, fifteen families are living there. Come, let us walk and you will see."

The flower gardens and tree-lined avenues of Belvedere House had been swallowed up in modern Allahabad. Some of the houses the developer had built were ugly concrete cubes; others were ostentatious with new money. Some had engraved brass plaques on the gate giving the owner's profession and qualifications.

"These are apartments for doctors, engineers, government officials," Mr. Agarwal said. "Even people from the business class are living here."

I imagined them in the blue-glass office buildings along M. G. Marg. I imagined their wives being driven to the Personality Maker Body Spa in time for their Pilates class.

THE MOUSTACHE DANCER

Despite its Raj-inflected history, modern Allahabad was a trying place for the non-Hindi speaker. The manager of the Harsh Ananda had promised to find me an English-speaking driver the next morning, but when I went to the desk, he gave an almost Gallic shrug, as if to say, *Je suis désolé, monsieur.* But perhaps young Utkarsh could be of assistance?

Utkarsh Dwivedi, who said he was twenty and looked barely old enough to shave, had just come off duty at the front desk. He looked uncomfortable at being pressed into service, especially when I told him I wanted to visit a neighborhood called Mirganj. How long would that take in a taxi?

"Only five minutes approx," he said. "But we cannot go there."

"Why not?"

"It is a very bad place. I know this. I was born there."

"Bad in what way?"

He looked at his shoes. "It is a red-light place."

This was embarrassing. I didn't want him to misconstrue my reasons. What I wanted to see in Mirganj was the house where Jawaharlal Nehru, India's first prime minister after Independence, had been born. Utkarsh eventually agreed with some reluctance, but first he insisted on showing me the tourist sights of Allahabad, such as they are, even though I'd seen most of them the day before.

We found a decrepit, rattling Ambassador taxi. As we slalomed through the traffic, I asked Utkarsh how long he had been in the hotel business.

"Three or five years approx."

He indicated points of interest as we proceeded along M. G. Marg—the cathedral, the Big Bazaar Shopping Mall, the nineteenth-century public library with its riotous mix of Indo-Saracenic and Scottish baronial architecture, McDonald's.

"Now we will go to Chandra Shekhar Azad Park," he said. "Today there will be a special celebration there."

The park was a pleasant island of greenery and groomed walkways. Originally it was called Alfred Park, named to commemorate the visit in 1869 of Prince Alfred of Saxe-Coburg and Gotha, second son of Queen Victoria. It was the venue for the All India Lawn Tennis Championship and the annual Flower and Dog Show. After Independence, it changed its name to honor Chandra Shekhar Azad, an anti-British revolutionary and leader of the Hindustan Socialist Republican Association. (*Azad* means "the free," a name he gave himself during one of his numerous appearances before a judge.) The police cornered him in Alfred Park in 1931, and there was a shoot-out. A film called *The Legend of Bhagat Singh* features a highly colored reenactment of Chandra Shekhar's death. He is pinned down behind a tree, bleeding from gunshots to the shoulder and leg, down to his final bullet. He scoops up a handful of Indian soil, lets it slip through his cupped palms with a mournful expression, raises his steepled hands to heaven, murmurs, "So much sacrifice," and puts the gun to his head rather than allow himself to be captured. The tree is still there, and next to it is a commemorative plinth.

There was an off-key racket of tubas, trumpets, and snare drums that grew louder as we walked in through the park gates. There were eight musicians, and nearby, eight soldiers lined up in an honor guard, dressed in khaki with scarlet shakos, black-and-red belts, and white puttees, carrying colonial-era Lee-Enfield bolt-action rifles. A white Ambassador with a blue light on the roof drew up beside them, and a middle-aged man climbed out. "Chief of police of Allahabad," Utkarsh whispered.

An ancient man in a white dhoti, with a Nehru cap perched on his head, had been standing at full salute, or as much as his bent back allowed. When the brass band stopped, he raised a battered antique bugle to his lips, took a couple of shallow, labored breaths, and squeaked out a few notes. He showed me a photograph in a plastic slipcover that was pinned to his chest, next to a rusted badge with the tricolor flag of the Indian National Congress. The photograph showed him, a good deal younger, playing his bugle. The caption below it identified him as Bhagwat Prasad, a freedom fighter who had joined the struggle against the British in 1942, the year in which Gandhi issued his final call for independence and Subhash Chandra Bose formed the Indian National Army. So that made the old man ninety, at least.

A man of curious appearance was busy shepherding a group of schoolchildren, more girls than boys, into tidy rows on the steps below the statue of Chandra Shekhar Azad, which was hung with marigolds and showed the hero in pensive mode, bare-chested and resting his chin in his hand. The man led the children in a chant. "His spirit has met with God; may God bless his soul."

When the ceremony ended, the man walked over to me briskly. He was barefoot, dressed in a bright red dhoti over black pants, a waistcoat with harlequin panels of shocking pink and silver-spangled purple silk, a flat cap with alternating bands of sky blue and gold, a shock of black hair with the texture of steel wool gathered in a bun, and a beard in which several birds could have nested comfortably. His eyes somehow managed to combine kindness, ferocity, and an ethereal remoteness.

He presented me with a business card that was almost as eccentric as his appearance. It read:

R. K. TIWARI (DUKANJI)

International Moustache Dancer • Gold Medalist

India Book of World Records • Limca Book of World Records

Guinness Book of World Records

Shabash India—Zee T.V.—Civil Defense Allahabad

I wanted him to tell me more about these credentials, but there was no time; the children were calling him to duty, and to find out more about the International Moustache Dancer, I had to track down one of these books of records and do a little research.

Limca is what Indians call a "cold drink," a lemon-and-lime–flavored fizzy soda produced by the Coca-Cola Company. It sponsors the local equivalent of the *Guinness World Records*, whose editors say that by far the largest number of submissions they receive, each requiring weeks of independent verification, comes from India. The Limca book "salutes the quest for excellence" and says it is aimed at an audience of "insatiable info-buffs and quizzers."

If the insatiable quizzer were to be asked the name of the person wearing the largest-ever mantle of bees, the correct answer would be K. P. Vinodan of Kerala, who once coaxed thirty-five thousand of the creatures to settle on his body for more than twenty-four hours while he stood by the roadside sipping liquids from a glass bottle. Other examples of excellence include the largest number of saliva bubbles blown without stopping (sixteen thousand, seven hundred and twenty-two over seven hours, by Asokan Chillikadan of Madhya Pradesh); the most slices cut from a single cucumber (one hundred and twenty thousand and sixty, by Professor S. Ramesh Babu of Bangalore); the greatest distance walked while balancing a full bottle of milk on one's head (a hundred and four kilometers, almost sixty-five miles, by Milind Deshmukh of Pune). The resonantly named Yezdi F. Canteenwalla, also of Pune, had devoted thirty years of his life to the challenge of creating the largest-ever ball of rubber bands, using four hundred and twenty thousand of them to produce a bouncy sphere measuring twenty-one inches in diameter.

There were so many mustache-related records that they could have taken up a chapter of their own. The longest ever recorded belonged to seventy-year-old Kalyan Ramji Saini of Rajasthan, a place of epic facial hair. It grew to more than ten feet and trailed on the ground for some distance behind him. By Limca's account, the growth was quite accidental. After an eye operation, doctors had recommended that Mr. Saini refrain from wetting his face for three weeks. By the end of this dry spell, the prodigious mustache already reached thirty inches, more than waist-length in other words. The mustache of Naik T. Sudarsana Reddy, identified as a civilian driver from Hyderabad, was a more modest affair, not quite twenty inches, but his special skill was to use it to lift two empty cooking-gas cylinders weighing 35.4 kilos, or seventy-eight pounds.

Eventually I found the entry for R. K. Tiwari. Oddly, Limca identified him as "Rajendra Kumar of Allahabad," but it was clearly the same man. No mustache had ever achieved comparable celebrity or been put to greater public purpose. Tiwari's mustache dance involved candles, four of them nestled symmetrically in his great black beard together with an equal number of unlit objects that resembled chopsticks. He could make the candles jump around in time to music ("any musical instrument in any *rag* and *Dhun*"), one at a time, in pairs, all four in unison. Later I found an obscure blog post, which he had perhaps created himself, that described the dance as "a marvelous technique rendles [*sic*] by the controlled movement of facial muscles with Yoga, the artistry in this dance is very subtle ang uniue [*sic*]." Zipping around on a scooter painted in rainbow stripes, the international mustache dancer had taken his act to the Cricket World Cup to bring good luck to the Indian team, to the International Yoga Festival at the Hotel Ganga Resort in

Rishikesh, and to the huge crowds that assembled in Allahabad each year for the Magh Mela.

Back at the park, the crowd was dispersing, Bhagwat Prasad squeezed out a few more notes, the Ambassador whisked away the chief of police.

"Time to go to Mirganj," I told Utkarsh.

His eyes darted from side to side, looking for some deus ex machina that would spare us the ordeal of the red lights.

"But you are wanting to see the home of Nehru. It is Anand Bhavan."

The taxi driver was holding the door of the Ambassador open for us.

"Anand Bhavan," Utkarsh told him. He turned to me and hazarded a smile. "You will see, it is beautiful. And it is stone-throwing distance only."

THE ABODE OF HAPPINESS

Utkarsh was right, and he glowed when I told him so. The Anand Bhavan, the Abode of Happiness, *was* beautiful. It was a two-story building, set in immaculate gardens. The walls were cream, and the airy balcony that encircled the second floor was picked out in gray blue. Despite a pair of Mughal-style turrets, the overall effect was of an Englishman's country estate, adapted to the heat of the North Indian plains.

Motilal Nehru, the patriarch of the family dynasty, bought and remodeled the property in 1900, some years after moving from Kanpur to Allahabad to practice law at the high court. He was a deep-dyed anglophile who appeared before His Majesty's Most Honourable Privy Council in London, sent his son, Jawaharlal, there to be educated, hired English governesses, and insisted on using knives and forks at dinner. But like many upper-class Indians, he was prickly about whether anglophilia was enough to pay a man's full price of admission to the colonial elite. In 1911, he was invited to attend a reception for the Imperial Durbar in the King-Emperor's Camp. He wrote, "I have received the command of his Gracious Majesty King George V, Emperor of India, to be in attendance at Delhi . . . a funny way of inviting a gentleman."

This note was displayed in a dingy cabinet in the museum that occupies the second floor of the Anand Bhavan. Nearby was Motilal's glass tumbler, spare buttons for his clothes, his earthenware foot warmer, and a miniature travel iron.

By 1919, a year that changed the course of Indian history, Motilal had abandoned his legal practice and devoted himself full-time to politics. In February of that year, he started a newspaper in Allahabad, *The Independent*, "to wage war against autocracy." It survived for two years before the British shut it down. In April, troops commanded by Brigadier General Reginald Dyer opened fire without warning on a crowd of peaceful demonstrators in Jallianwalla Bagh, a public park in the Sikh city of Amritsar, killing 379 people and wounding more than 1,200. Dyer was rewarded with a vote of gratitude in the House of Lords and a bejeweled sword inscribed "Saviour of the Punjab." In 1920, Gandhi founded the Non-Cooperation Movement to defy the "satanic" British. Motilal Nehru, who by now was chairman of the Indian National Congress, joined Gandhi's movement and stopped wearing Western clothes.

His twenty-nine-year-old son, Jawaharlal, went to Amritsar and collected spent cartridges from the Dyer massacre. I found these in another, larger case at the museum. Also on display were his tiny spinning wheel, a collection of shoes and waistcoats, an electric toaster, an electric razor, a cyclostyle machine that he used for cranking out anti-British pamphlets, a photograph of the Samadhi Buddha that he'd kept in his prison cell in Dehradun, his first driver's license (issued in London), and a tennis racket in a canvas case. Farther along the balcony was a sign showing where Gandhi had worked when he visited the Anand Bhavan, and near that was the spartan bedroom of Jawaharlal's daughter, Indira Gandhi. It had the air of a monastic cell, with a narrow, uncomfortable-looking single bed.

Across the freshly mowed lawn was a second mansion, a long, low, colonnaded building called the Swaraj Bhavan, the Abode of Self-Rule, which Congress used as its local headquarters. Part of it had been converted into a bookstore, and the assortment of books on offer might fairly have been described as eclectic.

There were children's cartoon histories of India and popular condensed editions of the Rāmāyaṇa. There were hagiographies of Jawaharlal Nehru, Mahatma Gandhi, and Indira Gandhi. There was a copy of *Mein Kamph* [*sic*], with a photograph of Hitler on the cover.

As in any other Indian bookstore, there were also a healthy number of titles devoted to self-improvement of one kind or another. You could buy *Secrets of Mind Power*, *Seven Mantras to Excel in Exams*, *Memory Techniques for Science*, *How to Remain Ever Happy*. The writings of Biswaroop Roy Chowdhury, the owner of a company called Dynamic Memory, were especially well represented. His biography said that he, too, had made it into *The Guinness Book of World Records*, not for mustache dancing but for prodigious feats of memory, having demonstrated the ability to recall a list of fourteen randomly selected names and their accompanying birth dates, in the same order, in two minutes. That wasn't all. Despite being born with a hole in his heart, Chowdhury also held the world record for the number of push-ups in one minute: 198. It was noted that this made him the only man in history to hold a record in the categories of both mind and body.

I picked up one of the volumes on Nehru and read the celebrated passage from his last will and testament, written in 1954, ten years before his death, in which he outlined his wishes for the disposal of his ashes. Most of them were to be scattered from an airplane, "over the fields where the peasants of India toil, so that they might mingle with the dust and soil of India." A small portion was to be set aside for immersion in the Ganges. He made it clear that this was not for religious reasons. It was because *the Ganga . . . is the river of India, beloved of her people, round which are intertwined her racial memories, her hopes and fears, her songs of triumph, her victories and her defeats. She has been a symbol of India's age-long culture and civilization, ever-changing, ever-flowing, and ever the same Ganga. She reminds me of the snow-covered peaks and the deep valleys of the Himalayas, which I have loved so much, and of the rich and vast plains below, where my life and work have been cast. Smiling and dancing in the morning sunlight, and dark and gloomy and full of mystery as the evening shadows fall; a narrow, slow and graceful stream in winter, and a vast roaring thing during the monsoon, broad-bosomed almost as the sea, and with something of the sea's power to destroy, the Ganga has been to me a symbol and a memory of the past of India, running into the present, and flowing on to the great ocean of the future.*

Half a million people came to see the immersion of Nehru's ashes at the Sangam, where the Ganges meets the Yamuna. Several of them fell off an unstable platform in midstream and drowned.

THE TRAFFIC IN MIRGANJ

We entered Mirganj through the thicket of market stalls on Kamala Nehru Road, which eventually opened up onto a square that was dominated by one of the many eccentric Victorian clock towers that the British bestowed on India as emblems of home and civic dignity. The base of this one was painted Queen Anne red; it had a pair of wedding-cake balconies done up in powder blue and lemon yellow and a matching yellow onion dome that was topped with a spike like a Prussian *pickelhaube*.

Kamala Nehru Road was named after Jawaharlal's wife, but there was no monument, no sign of any kind in fact, to suggest that Jawaharlal himself had any connection to the neighborhood. I'd leafed through several of the biographies in the bookstore at Anand Bhavan, looking for references to his birthplace at 77 Mirganj, but found only euphemisms. One said that he had been born "in the old Indian part of the city in a lane which was said to be haunted." Another mentioned "a house standing in a lane in one of Allahabad's more congested localities."

Although he had grown up in Mirganj himself, Utkarsh had no idea where this lane might be or whether the neighborhood had already been a red-light district at the time of Nehru's birth in 1889. The idea of the house being in a lane at all was puzzling, since a tabletop model in the museum had shown it as a two-story house, plain in design, solid but not grand, built around a large courtyard with a partly covered roof terrace. An old, faded photograph showed it surrounded by open land. A section of the building had supposedly been demolished in 1931 in the name of urban improvement; the rest had been torn down in the 1970s.

There was a story, perhaps apocryphal, that Motilal Nehru had rented part of the house to a courtesan. In the swamps of conspiracy theory, where radical Hindu nationalist bloggers reviled Jawaharlal Nehru as a race traitor for wanting to create a multiconfessional state, this was the seed for all kinds of lurid rumors about life at 77 Mirganj. Motilal had come to Allahabad not as a lawyer but as a brothel keeper, importing Brahmin girls from Kashmir. He had fathered several children with prostitutes. Worse than that, he was secretly a Muslim himself, the son of a police official in Delhi who had concealed his true identity by adopting a Hindu name. One of Motilal's customers was a Shi'a lawyer named Mubarak Ali, the original owner of the Anand Bhavan. He had not sold the house to Motilal, as commonly reported, but given it to him as a gift for personal services rendered and a way of bolstering his image of respectability. It was not Motilal who had sired India's future prime minister, but this man Mubarak Ali, who then had his illegitimate son secretly circumcised, and had one of the prostitutes act as his wet nurse. So India's first prime minister, by these frenzied accounts, was actually a closet Muslim, raised in lies and squalor.

Now that our trip to the "red-light place" could no longer be avoided, Utkarsh had loosened up a little. "This street was famous for sweets," he said amiably. "Allahabad is a city of Brahmins, and the Brahmins always loved sweets." Now it could have been any street in any city in North India, the usual crush of rickshaws and motorbikes, fruit and vegetable sellers and fried-food stalls, decaying plasterwork, and overhead tangles of electricity wires. The sidewalks were packed with men, and only men. I did a mental count of the first hundred people we passed. Ninety-nine were male; the only exception was a little girl of seven or eight hurrying along with some groceries in a plastic bag. Most of the men were in their late teens or twenties; they seemed to have not much to do but hang out around the food stalls and gawk at girls, not that there were any girls to gawk at.

According to the 2011 census, the state of Uttar Pradesh has two hundred million people. There are nine hundred and twelve women for every thousand men. In other words, UP had almost ten million surplus males. It was hard to escape the thought that, in a country with a long history of female infanticide, an ultrasound and an abortion were much less expensive than a dowry.

UP was notorious for what Indians call "Eve-teasing." Two teenage girls, in separate recent incidents, had been doused in kerosene and set on fire for resisting their teasers. Another had been shot dead. I'd seen a small item in the newspapers a few days earlier about a company that was promoting a pistol small enough to fit into a girl's handbag, a kind of Lady Derringer.

UP was also fending off newspaper headlines that referred to it as the rape capital of India, after two teenage cousins were found hanging from a mango tree in a village in the district of Badaun, halfway between Delhi and Lucknow. The girls' bodies had been hastily buried on the banks of the Ganges, the spot marked by a red rag tied to a bamboo pole; by the time the police showed up to exhume them for DNA analysis, the monsoon was in full force, the river had burst its banks, and the graves were submerged under seven feet of water.

Five men from the village, members of a higher caste than the girls, who were *dalits*, had been accused of gang rape, and public officials were asked for comment. "Rape is a trivial incident, and it should not be blown out of proportion by the media," said the chief secretary of Uttar Pradesh, the state's highest-ranking civil servant. "Boys will be boys," said the former chief minister of UP. "Sometimes they make mistakes." "Rape?" said the CM of neighboring Madhya Pradesh. "Sometimes it's right; sometimes it's wrong."

Utkarsh and I walked from one end of the street to the other and stopped at a stall where a man was scooping samosas out of a blackened iron vat of boiling oil. The afternoon was so hot that you could have fried them right on the sidewalk. We asked for directions to 77 Mirganj, and the man gestured toward the first alleyway on the left. We'd find the house a few yards in, where the alley made a right-angled turn.

It was impossible to relate the place to the photograph in the museum or to imagine that tearing down Nehru's birthplace had had anything to do with urban improvement. The alleyway was claustrophobic, just wide enough for two motorbikes to pass, cluttered with garbage and hung with gold and silver tinsel. Pimps glared down at us from the upstairs windows. An open sewer drain ran along the front of the building, and the ground floor was painted a scabby robin's-egg blue. A row of five doorways opened onto cramped inner rooms, each with its own metal concertina gate and a bare, hanging lightbulb. Half a dozen young women were squatting on the steps on low wooden stools. As we turned the corner, they scattered indoors like birds.

The girls at 77 Mirganj were almost certainly Nepali, said Ajeet Singh, whom I met later in Varanasi. Singh ran an organization called Guria, which means "doll." Its purpose was to fight sex trafficking in UP through direct action—conducting undercover operations, staking out the railroad stations, facing down pimps and cops, raiding brothels. His first accomplishment was to clean up Varanasi's notorious red-light district, Shivdaspur, which had once been home to a thousand prostitutes.

Singh was an exuberant man in his forties with a face full of gray stubble. He looked like the kind of favorite uncle who would enjoy dressing up as a clown at a kids' party. People called him *masterji*. He said that he first sensed his mission in life when he went to a cousin's wedding and watched a sex worker dancing all night to entertain an audience of men who kept up a barrage of catcalls and lewd suggestions. He approached the woman afterward and said he wanted to adopt her children and put them through school. When he took them home, his parents thought he had taken leave of his senses, which was hardly surprising, since he was seventeen at the time.

Singh introduced me to his wife, Manju. When they married, he refused to have a priest or any kind of religious mumbo jumbo at the ceremony. All he wanted was for the local prostitutes' kids to entertain the guests with songs and dancing.

He was more than familiar with Mirganj. With the help of video that was shot clandestinely by informants disguised as street vendors, he had identified seventy girls who had been forced into prostitution with the connivance of the Allahabad police. Most of them had been kidnapped from their homes in Nepal. Some were only ten or twelve years old. There were entire villages in Nepal with no girls. Usually the traffickers, the *didis*, scooped them up in groups of four or more; three is considered an inauspicious number in Nepal. After crossing the border, the first stop was usually either Lucknow or Kanpur, where they were sold to "trainers," kept in tiny rooms, raped, and burned with cigarettes until they were broken and ready to be shipped off to places like Sonagachi in Calcutta, Falkland Road in Bombay, MG Road in Delhi, and Mirganj. Before she was finally used up, a girl might be sold or bartered half a dozen times or more.

Singh spent nine months assembling his case against the traffickers in Mirganj and finally persuaded the district magistrate to issue an order for the police to raid the brothels. The order came down first thing in the morning. "Wish we could help," said the police, "but alas, we have limited manpower and a shortage of vehicles. Perhaps we could take care of the matter this evening? Or tomorrow morning?" They showed up at 6:00 P.M. in the end, grumbling, took a handful of girls into custody, and gave several of them straight back to the brothel owners. After an hour, they looked at their watches and said that unfortunately it was time to stop; they couldn't work after seven without special permission. They did find time, however, to lock up Ajeet Singh in the Badshahi Mandi police station, a hop and a skip from the clock tower, where they threatened him with violence and trumped-up criminal charges.

Girls were not the only victims, Singh told me. Earlier that morning, in fact, volunteers from Guria had snatched a boy from traffickers at the Varanasi railway station. He was waiting to be reunited with his father and grandfather, who had just arrived from their village in Azamgarh district, seventy miles to the north. Singh went into the next room to fetch him. The boy was dressed all in white with a crocheted Muslim prayer cap. He had a deep, crescent-shaped scar that ran from his chin to his cheekbone, a smaller injury of some kind in the center of his forehead, and—as a friend said later when she saw a photograph—eyes that had seen too much. The men hugged him and wept.

"This is Abdul." Singh beamed. "He says he's nine."

THE INVISIBLE RIVER

The more time I spent in Allahabad, the more blurred the edges became between myth and reality, truth and fraud, faith and science. Like Bishop Heber, who visited this "ruinous and desolate" place in 1824, and like Mark Twain, who came here in 1895 to witness the Kumbh Mela, I needed a pocket glossary. Like the word *Ganga* itself, names here had multiple layers of meaning, both physical and meta-physical.

Prayag: a place of sacrifice, the original Hindu name of the city before it was changed by Emperor Akbar.

Tirtha: a ford, a crossing place, a place of pilgrimage.

Tirtharaja, the king of all pilgrimage places—Allahabad.

Sangam: the confluence of two rivers, a place where the faithful can wash away their sins, the confluence of the Ganges and the Yamuna being the most sacred Sangam of them all.

Triveni Sangam: the meeting place not just of two rivers but of *three*, the third being the Saraswati, named for the beloved goddess of knowledge and wisdom, who is described in the Rig Veda as "the best of mothers, the best of rivers, the best of goddesses."

Mela: a fair, festival, or gathering, secular or religious.

Kumbh: a pot or jug. During the epic struggle between the gods and demons over possession of a pot of the nectar of immortality, four drops were spilled. Each place where a drop fell became a sacred place of pilgrimage. One of the four was Allahabad.

Kumbh Mela: the greatest of all Hindu festivals, the largest human gathering on the planet, held at the Triveni Sangam at twelve-year intervals.

With these terms fixed in my mind, I took an auto-rickshaw to the confluence. The driver had a DVD player propped up on the dashboard, and he kept on eye on the movie as he drove through the crowded streets. A police-man wrapped in chains was spraying a crowd of diabolical enemies with machine-gun fire, while the disembodied head of a white-haired woman spoke to him from the clouds. Who was she? An arbiter of the battle? A tactical adviser? One of the more obscure goddesses? His mother? Or just a curious spectator? We reached Akbar's monumental fort, whose walls and turrets stretch for a couple of hundred yards along the north bank of the Yamuna. I handed the driver his fifty rupees and climbed out. I never found out how the movie ended, though I had a feeling the policeman would probably come out on top.

The Ganges came in at a ninety-degree angle from the north, narrower and shallower than the Yamuna. But where was the Saraswati? The problem was that the river was invisible, and perhaps it had never existed outside of the scriptures. The sadhus had their theories, and the scientists had theirs. This being India, it was hard to separate the two, and the government was testing a hypothesis based in faith with the tools of archaeology, geomorphology, and satellite remote sensing.

One of the bathing areas in Allahabad is called Saraswati Ghat, but that did nothing to illuminate the riddle. The ghat was fully a mile upstream from the confluence, halfway between the fort and the handsome new suspension bridge over the Yamuna. It was a steeply stepped amphitheater backed by a dozen pinkish-purplish ornamental pillars that looked like upside-down flower petals on concrete stalks. The modernist design suggested a bandshell-cum-bus-station in Brasilia.

A long, inclined walkway led up to the gate of the fort. Kipling had loathed the place, after watching British soldiers pole away the dead bodies that bumped up against the walls during high water. Inside the fort was the Saraswati Koop, a deep well that some said was the source of the mythical river. The army, which still controlled the fort and used it as a munitions depot, had just announced plans to install video cameras, slanted mirrors, halogen lamps, and an LCD screen so that the faithful could see and worship the water at the bottom of the well. The minister in charge of rivers, a saffron-robed Hindu nationalist militant named Uma Bharti, declared that "Saraswati is not a myth" and ordered the testing and carbon dating of the water in the well to see if that might shed further light on the matter.

In fact, scientists from half a dozen government agencies had been studying the mystery of the Saraswati for more than thirty years and had even come to some tentative conclusions. Yes, the river had probably once existed. It had risen somewhere in the Himalayas. Perhaps near Mount Kailash, the abode of Shiva. Perhaps in a glacier near the source of the Yamuna, about twenty miles west of Gangotri. But five or six thousand years ago, somewhere in the lowlands, it had disappeared. Perhaps this was because of changes in the climate; perhaps it was the result of tectonic shifts. Its remaining flow might have been captured by the Sutlej, which continued westward until it met the Indus.

Searching for the likeliest paleochannel of the Saraswati, the Indian Space Research Organisation had settled on the present-day Ghaggar River, which flows only during the monsoon and dries up close to the Pakistan border in the Thar Desert of Rajasthan. Those details match an account in the Mahābhārata. Satellite imagery suggested that the Ghaggar/Saraswati might eventually have reached the Arabian Sea through the great salt flats and marshes known as the Rann of Kutch. All of which was fascinating, but the larger question remained: What did any of this have to do with the Triveni Sangam at Allahabad, which was more than six hundred miles away?

But perhaps, if you were a politician, the *where* didn't matter in the end. It was enough that science and scripture should coincide. Even if the Saraswati were on the other side of India, or even in Pakistan, the faithful would still flock to Allahabad. A few months after I left the city, I checked to see if there was any update on the search for the invisible river. There was big news. In the watershed of the Ghaggar, near the small town of Mustafabad, a woman had come upon water gushing from a rock. Here finally was the true Saraswati, said the chief minister of Haryana state. Workers were digging out what they believed to be the channel, and water would be pumped into it from tube wells; worshippers were already congregating at the site. Prayag had lost its original name to the Mughal invaders, but now Mustafabad would be reclaimed for Hinduism. Henceforth it would be Saraswati Nagar. I watched a TV interview with the woman who had found the river. She was delighted at her newfound celebrity. In one of India's endless ironies, she was a Muslim.

DESOLATE AND RUINOUS

I'd been sick. I was exhausted. It was hot. I had a fever that matched the outside temperature, over one hundred degrees. The afternoon air was heavy and gray with smog, and my grasp of Hindu cosmology was fraying at the edges. The more time I spent around the Sangam, the more it felt like a low-grade acid trip.

In one of the courtyards of the fort, a flight of steps led down to the temple of Patalpuri. The name means "small city of the underworld." It was like an air-raid shelter, a huge wine cellar, the catacombs of Paris, a dark version of Madame Tussaud's. A long gallery lined with small statue niches opened up into a pillared labyrinth that Mark Twain called "subterranean ramifications stocked with shrines and idols." Countless alcoves held life-size figures of gods. A priest or a temple tout sat in front of each of them, shaking metal plates full of small coins and ten-rupee notes in my face. Perhaps it was just the effects of a sleepless night, or the roiling in my gut, but none of the deities here seemed benign.

There was Shani Dev, the most feared of all the gods, elder brother of Lord Yama, god of death and the underworld; a single glance from Shani Dev was a curse, a perverse guarantee that you would commit as many sins as possible in life so that you could be redeemed in death.

There was Bhairava, a manifestation of Shiva sculpted in black with glaring eyes, whose name means "terrifying" and is synonymous with destruction. There was also Nag Vasuki, the cobra that Shiva wears coiled around his neck.

There was Narasimha, half-man, half-lion, the fourth avatar of Vishnu, who had eviscerated the murderous demon Hiranyakashipu with his powerful claws. Even though this made him a virtuous figure, there was still something unnerving about his image.

Above the temple was the Akshaya Vat, the "indestructible banyan tree," which was sacred to Vishnu. A demon or goblin lived among its roots and branches. Lord Ram and Sita had once rested in its shade. Anyone who threw themselves off the tree to their death, no matter how greatly they have sinned in life, "shall receive a great reward in the future state and shall not be considered a suicide."

That was how the story was told by Fanny Parkes in her book *Wanderings of a Pilgrim in Search of the Picturesque*. Parkes, who was Welsh by birth, was the wife of a minor official of the East India Company and the most engaging of all the travel writers of the period. She arrived in Allahabad from Calcutta in 1832 and lived in India for twenty-four years. She had a genuine fascination with Hinduism and at the same time a sharp eye for the chicanery of its priests. She saw right through the myth of "the Holy Achibut," as she called it. It was impossible to see the tree, she wrote, because access to it had been bricked up by the British commandant of the fort. A priest took her into a room and pointed to the ceiling. "Do you not see the branch of the tree has cracked the roof in three places?" he asked. "I certainly saw three cracks, but whether from a tree or ivy I cannot say; not a leaf was visible," Parkes wrote sardonically.

From the "Achibut Room," she went to the Patalpuri temple, where she saw the same tree I had seen, its base "covered with oil, ghee, boiled rice, and flowers." A fake, she decided. "The resident Hindoos of Prag [Prayag], who know the trick the Brahmans have played, do not *pooja* the false Achibut."

A little to the north of the fort was the Bade Hanuman temple. With his crown and his bulb-headed club, Lord Hanuman, who led his monkey army against the demon king Ravan in the Rāmāyaṇa, is the embodiment of faith, loyalty, heroism, and physical strength. The Bade Hanuman had his own unique legend. A wealthy trader from the city of Kannauj, on the left bank of the Ganges, north of Kanpur, had made a huge stone statue of the god, hoping to

The Ganges—still called the Bhagirathi at this point—cuts its way through bedrock close to its source in the Gangotri glacier.

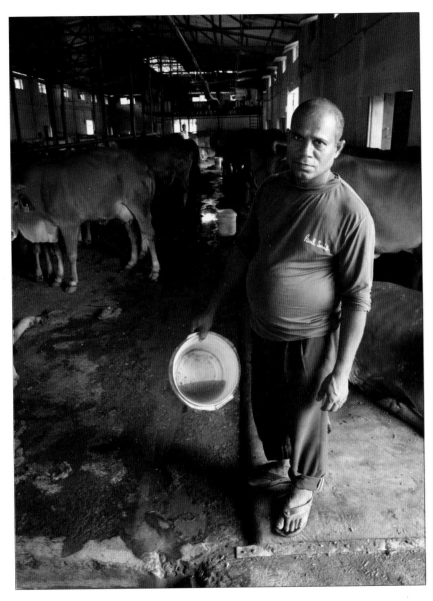

Collecting cow urine for Ayurvedic medicines and food additives at Baba Ramdev's
Patanjali Yogpeeth complex near Haridwar.

A pilgrim and a construction worker outside the home of Brij Mehra in Swargashram.

In a village near Allahabad, women thresh rice in the black carbon haze from dung and wood cooking fires.

One of the countless wandering *saddhus* on the ghats of Varanasi, a prosperous man in his earlier life.

Each day at dawn, thousands of worshippers line the ghats for their "holy dip" in the Ganges.

Alleyways near the Ganges in Varanasi are piled high with wood for the cremation pyres. (Photograph courtesy of Agnès Dherbeys)

More than a hundred bodies are burned each day at Manikarnika, the main cremation ghat.

Doms—members of the *dalit* caste who manage the cremation grounds—sift the ashes to collect any valuables left on the bodies.

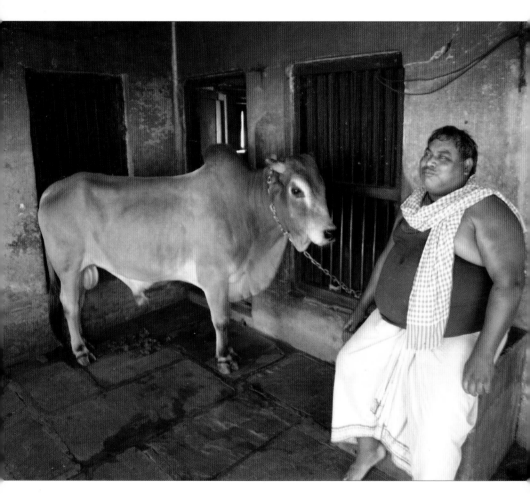

Jagdish Chowdhury, the Dom Raja, at home in the Tiger House with his Brahman bull.

Boatmen ferry customers across the river at the Saderghat ferry terminal in the Bangladeshi capital, Dhaka.

In the ruins of Rana Plaza, the factory building that collapsed in 2013, killing more than 1,100 Bangladeshi garment workers.

Dawn in the rice paddies of Khulna Division, at the edge of the Sundarbans in Bangladesh.

Stallholders from Odisha State at the Kolkata flower market, at the foot of Howrah Bridge.

Tapan Chatterjee, one of the hundreds of priests at Kolkata's Kalighat Temple, at his brother's sweetshop.

Gujarati women on their way to Gangasagar, coming to the end of a six-week tour of India's most important pilgrimage sites.

be blessed with a son, a constant theme in Hindu worship. I didn't recall ever hearing of a shrine where people prayed for the birth of a daughter. He brought the statue to the Sangam, where it sank into the sand and remained buried. Later, a visiting holy man tried to stick his *trishula*—the trident of Shiva—in the ground, but it struck some hard object. When he dug down to see what it was, he found the statue. Men tried to stand it upright, but it was too heavy. So a shrine was built around it, which became the Bade Hanuman temple.

I went inside to see the statue, which lay flat in a recessed well decorated with small blue tiles. The figure was colossal, more than twice the size of a man. But it was so laden with offerings of flowers and fruit that all that was visible of the body were two staring, disembodied eyes, so black that they looked rimmed with kohl. Here at the Sangam, even the admirable Hanuman, conqueror of evil, seemed a weird and baleful presence. Each year, when the monsoon broke and the rivers rose, India's only horizontal Hanuman was submerged under several feet of water.

I hurried to get out of the temple, feeling claustrophobic. Outside, a teenaged street vendor was selling plastic masks of Hanuman and Spider-Man.

But all I accomplished was to trade claustrophobia for agoraphobia. Not in the sense of a fear of crowds, or the contrary sense of a fear of open spaces, but somehow, strangely, of both. The whole identity of the Sangam revolved around the presence of crowds, crowds of unimaginable size, but today it was all but deserted. Nowhere could have felt lonelier. In the fact of their absence, I found it, as Bishop Heber had written, a "desolate and ruinous" place.

The pilgrims converge on these sandy flats each year in January and February, in the month of Magh, the eleventh in the Hindu calendar. The Magh Mela lasts for six weeks, becoming a city within a city. On the most auspicious day, when the sky is moonless and the most devout observe a vow of silence, as many as ten million people may bathe at the Sangam—eight times the population of Allahabad. Every twelve years, at the Kumbh Mela, the numbers may be three times as large, thirty million bathers in a single day, led by competing factions of naked and armed naga sadhus. When crowding turns to chaos, there are stampedes. The worst of these disasters was in 1954, when eight hundred died.

The Kumbh Mela has also become big business. The most recent one, in 2013, had been the subject of a study in the *International Journal of Management*. Revenues in excess of $2 billion; six hundred and thirty-five thousand temporary jobs created; three hundred and fifty-five miles of water pipelines laid, and five hundred miles of electrical wiring, to service the great tent city, which stretched over twenty square miles; thirty-five thousand public toilets; eighteen pontoon bridges across the Ganges and the Yamuna; thirty thousand police on duty and a hundred and twenty ambulances on call around the clock. Wi-Fi services courtesy of Coca-Cola India. Headsets with built-in devotional music from Vodafone. GPS-enabled apps that allowed pilgrims to locate their temporary ashrams, their sleeping quarters, and their spiritual leaders. There were luxury tents for VIPs and foreign tourists at $200 a night, with tiled bathrooms and buffet breakfasts.

But these were just the modern refinements. In the popular imagination, the festival goes back to a time before recorded history, when the four drops of nectar fell from the heavens. Or perhaps not, according to Western scholars who have studied the administrative records of the colonial period. An Australian historian, Kama Maclean, has concluded that while worshippers may always have converged on Allahabad in the month of Magh, the first Kumbh Mela in its present form, with its organized processions of sadhus, had been celebrated in 1870. For the British administrators of the city, it was a matter of public order. They wanted to avoid any repetition of the shenanigans at the great melas in Haridwar, where warring bands of sadhus had battled for spiritual dominance and control of the lucrative annual market in elephants, camels, horses, and luxury goods. Maclean quotes Mountstuart Elphinstone, the lieutenant governor of Bombay, on the notorious Haridwar Mela of 1760, where "an affray, or rather a battle, took place between the Nagas of Shiva and those of Vishnu in which it was stated on the spot that 18,000 persons were left dead on the field." At Allahabad, formalizing the role of the sadhus was a way of allowing a more rational division of influence and profit.

Now the crowds and the chaos seemed as imaginary as the Saraswati. Nowhere in the world could have felt emptier or more cheerless. Hundreds of empty boats were drawn up in the mud, hung with prayer flags. A handful of bathers were filling plastic flasks of *gangajal*, and a few boatloads of worshippers were lined up along a rope that stretched from shore to shore, marking the line of demarcation between the Ganges and the Yamuna.

I walked a mile back to the rickshaw stand, along a rough track grooved into the sand. To the west, the sun was setting behind the suspension bridge. Two boys were trying in a half-hearted way to launch kites in the stagnant evening air. They kept at it, failure after failure. There was nothing else for them to do.

By the time I reached the parking area, it was fully dark. There was noise again, drivers drumming up business, a repetitive pulse of bells, drums, and chanting from a small nearby temple, like the hammering of an alarm clock that no one would turn off.

Six of us crowded sweatily into a three-wheeler. A chaos of insects around the headlights. In the front, by the driver, another man sat with one thigh splayed across my lap. The vehicle stalled. We jumped out and pushed. The engine coughed and caught. We piled in again. A naked naga sadhu, the only one I saw all day, beetled over to us. He was rail thin, a walking anatomy lesson, no more than five feet tall with tangled hair that fell to his waist, a beard that reached to the sternum, his penis swinging like a pendulum, and a necklace of bones around his neck. He banged on the side of the auto-rickshaw with his staff, rattled the bones in my face, and spat on the ground, as if my presence at the Sangam was an affront to the natural order of the universe.

ARMPIT OF THE UNIVERSE

No one could understand why I insisted on going to Gorakhpur. I'd be robbed or shot, or if that didn't happen, I'd probably be bitten by a mosquito and die of Japanese encephalitis. Or I'd just be so bored and disgusted by the place that I would wonder what in God's name had possessed me to go there. But despite their advice, I hopscotched around the towns and villages of the Gangetic Plain, sometimes by rail and sometimes by road, and in the end, the road took me to Gorakhpur.

A city of seven hundred thousand souls on the main road from Varanasi to the Nepal border, Gorakhpur was famous for gang wars, famous for human trafficking, famous for being the home of the first Indian politician to be elected to parliament while in prison, famous for having the world's longest railway platform (eight-tenths of a mile), famous for its corrupted heart. In his novel *The Association of Small Bombs*, Karan Mahajan described Gorakhpur as "one of the armpits of the universe," and though I hadn't yet read his novel when I went there, I couldn't have put it better.

A friend and I traveled to Gorakhpur at night, a tedious four-hour drive across the darkened plains. Each time the driver punched his horn, we took bets on whether we could count to ten before he did it again. It usually happened at a count of seven or eight, even though the divided state highway was empty and lightless black except for a stretch of a couple of miles where, for unfathomable reasons of their own, the big trucks came barreling straight at us on full beam on the wrong side of the concrete median barrier.

Gorakhpur was not well provided with places to sleep. The Clarks Grand ("contemporary Hotel with all modern Facilities") was a $140-a-night slum, with cockroaches in the bathroom, stained carpets, cigarette burns on the furniture, slovenly staff, and no food in the "all-day dining venue." When I complained to the manager, he gave me a genial smile and a head wobble and said, "As long as customer is happy." I said, "But I'm not."

The Wi-Fi in my room flickered on and off, but the signal was just strong enough for me to read a bit more about the reasons for Gorakhpur's fame. I learned that the city was the hub of Purvanchal, an area that people called the Badlands of Uttar Pradesh; it was sometimes referred to as the Chicago of the East or, more obscurely, the Slice of Sicily. It owed much of this celebrity to a hit man named Shri Prakash Shukla, alias Ashok Singh, who had hired himself out to settle scores for rival politicians jostling for lucrative public works contracts like highway construction and railway upgrades. The politicians themselves drove around behind smoked glass with phalanxes of bodyguards armed with AK-47s, finding hideouts for Shukla/Singh after the police finally yawned, scratched their bellies, summoned up the energy for a manhunt, and gunned him down in what Indians call an "encounter killing" near Delhi. All this had happened a long time ago, but Gorakhpur's reputation trailed it like a tin can tied to a dog's tail.

The next morning, I came upon a group of a dozen men sitting cross-legged on a white sheet on a traffic island in the center of the city under a statue of Gandhi holding an umbrella. They had hung a gigantic red banner behind them denouncing corruption in the municipal electricity department and comparing their struggle to Gandhi's call for swaraj, self-rule. No one seemed to be paying much attention to them, being focused more on navigating the ambient scrum of rickshaws and motorbikes and wandering water buffalo.

The face of the man on the poster, with his glasses, buck teeth, and four days of black stubble, clearly belonged to the man sitting at the center of the group. I asked him who he was. He said his name was Jata Shanker Tripathi, and he spent a lot of his time protesting one thing and another, not just corruption and electricity. He also operated a toll-free hotline to report incidents of trafficking of Nepali girls, like those who had fluttered away like birds in the alleyway in Mirganj. For this work, on a trip to the United States, Tripathi said he had been awarded the prestigious title of "Arkansas Visitor." Today he was leading a weeklong sit-down protest at the government's failure to deal with the latest epidemic of Japanese encephalitis.

Gorakhpur was where the disease, which is closely related to West Nile Virus, was first detected in the 1970s. People here called it *brain fever*, he said. It causes brutal headaches and vomiting. It can lead to confusion, seizures, and hallucinations; to partial paralysis, inflammation of the heart and kidneys. If you survived an attack, it might be with permanent brain damage. The epidemics happened whenever the monsoon was unusually severe, as it had been this year. The surrounding countryside was flat and boggy, and the fields were still full of water more than a month after the rains ended. In these conditions, the *Culex tritaeniorhynchus* mosquito was in its element. But you could have said the same thing about much of Asia, where the disease was endemic. With Gorakhpur, it felt as if the explanation was karmic as well as topographic.

At least five hundred people had died so far this year, Tripathi said, and as usual, most of the victims were children. But those were just the figures from the central hospital in Gorakhpur, and who could trust numbers from the government? Out in the villages, who knew? "It doesn't happen in the cleaner and more prosperous households," he said. "It's in villages with open drains and standing water, villages of the scheduled castes."

He pulled out an iPhone from the pocket of his white kurta and swiped through some photographs that showed four small children sprawled out across a single metal-framed bed in a grimy room at the central hospital. Bare electrical wires trailed across the wall, and there were bars across the windows.

"We are making three demands to the government," he said. "One, declare a national disaster. Two, build a new hospital with four hundred beds to deal with future outbreaks. And three, fund a scientific research center to find out more about the disease." Those were his demands, but his expression said, *Dream on*. "Doctors in Gorakhpur are a very careless body. They just say, 'We have no powers, we can't make any recommendations.'" Like everyone else, the doctors fed at the trough of corruption. Just two days before our conversation, the local press had carried reports of an investigation into the recent murders of three senior health department officials in Lucknow. Were they personally involved in the corruption? Did they cross the wrong politician? Were they about to name names? Tripathi shrugged and showed his buck teeth. *Forget it, Jake, it's Chinatown.*

THE VIEW FROM THE TRAIN

Back at Lucknow Junction, I waited for my train to Varanasi. Even though there were packs of monkeys and rats playing hide-and-seek along the tracks, there was a chaotic kind of efficiency about the railway station. Train times were listed on bright LED displays. Over the loudspeakers, a clear female voice whose received pronunciation would not have disgraced the BBC in the 1950s, announced delays. "For your kind attention, please. The Shramjeevi Express, scheduled to depart at 8:30, will now depart at 10:15. The inconvenience is deeply regretted." My own train, the Kashi Vishwanath Express, named for the most important temple in Varanasi, was on schedule, though that was no guarantee it would arrive on time.

I found my reservation confirmed on a long dot-matrix printout that hung from a noticeboard like an old-fashioned galley proof. Indian trains offer twelve classes, from 1AC down to UR/GEN—unreserved general, which is as bare-bones as the name suggests. And there is always the option of riding on the roof. I had booked 2AC as usual, where each compartment has four berths, two up, two down. There were additional berths along the corridor, laid out in pairs and hung with curtains for privacy. The "AC" part failed the truth-in-advertising test because there was only a small whirring fan to cool the compartment. Next to it was a little string pouch where you could store your bottle of water. An attendant came around distributing threadbare gray sheets and scratchy brown blankets.

I slept until dawn. We were behind schedule, still a couple of hours short of Varanasi. I alternated between reading Mark Twain's account of his travels and staring out across the endless monotony of Uttar Pradesh under its permanent haze of black carbon from the mud stoves and dung fires. At the tiny halts along the way, people were asleep on the platforms with their cooking utensils spread out around them and sheets pulled over their heads. On a brick building by the trackside, someone had whitewashed the word ABANDONED.

North India was "one vast farm—one almost interminable stretch of field with mud fences between," Twain wrote. He wondered at the rivers that meandered across the plains. "Curious rivers they are; low shores a dizzy distance apart, with nothing between but an enormous acreage of sand-flats with sluggish little veins of water dribbling around amongst them; Saharas of sand, smallpox-pitted with footprints."

Bikes and motorbikes waited at crossing barriers; schoolchildren lined up behind them, dressed in neat blue-and-white uniforms and carrying small backpacks; women washed their saris in brown pools and laid them out to dry along the tracks; men urinated against a wall with torn posters showing candidates from past elections and a painted sign that said, "NOT URIN HERE." Pigs, dogs, goats, and cows explored the possibilities of piles of garbage. Here and there the landscape was broken up by clumps of neem and peepul and banyan trees.

I didn't have the compartment to myself. Outside in the corridor, a man, a woman, and a boy of five or six had been chatting on one of the lower berths when I boarded. When they were done, the man had settled into the bunk across from mine and pulled a sheet over himself without looking at me. I guessed he was in his late thirties, jowly and thick-lipped, with a fierce black mustache. The compartment filled with the heavy scent of hair oil, turmeric, aftershave, sweat, attar of roses.

As the sun rose higher, the train jolted along at a steady twenty miles an hour, and his sleeping form jogged back and forward in time with its rhythm.

I stared out of the window some more. Prayer flags waved over the pink pyramids of small temples. Elaborate cement pillars stood inexplicably in the middle of a field. The remains of something, or the abandoned start of something.

The movements of my traveling companion seemed suddenly out of sync with the rhythm of the wheels on the track. There was a rapid, regular back-and-forth of his hand beneath the blanket, and his breathing grew faster. He began to pant audibly, then let out a single long groan, scrabbled around under the sheet at his midsection for a few seconds, then rolled over onto his side and within a couple of minutes was snoring loudly again.

He woke again as we began to slow down for the approach to Varanasi Junction. He climbed down from his bunk, still without a glance in my direction, and pulled open the curtain of the berth where his wife and child were breakfasting on snacks out of a plastic bag. He began to play a game with the boy, chanting an endlessly repeated phrase that seemed to involve the threat of tickling. After a few minutes, the child grew bored and squirmed away. The man grabbed him by the shoulder, spun him around, and slapped him hard across the face, so hard that he might as well have used a cricket bat. The boy howled, and his mother stared resolutely out of the window into the brown haze.

JEWEL OF THE EAR

Gorakhpur was the armpit of the universe; India, according to scripture, was the navel of the universe, and Kashi, or Banaras, or Benares, or Varanasi, was the navel of India.

As usual in the canon of Hindu mythology, it was impossible to pin down one single version of how this came to be. By the time I got ready for my third trip to Varanasi, I'd assembled a shelfful of scholarship—hefty volumes by Western academics, popular digests of Hindu mythology I'd picked up at Wheeler railway bookstalls—and while they brought me some enlightenment, at least in an intellectual sense, they also brought an equal amount of confusion.

For early Christian mapmakers, wrote Diana Eck, a distinguished professor of comparative religion and Indian studies at Harvard, Jerusalem was the physical center of the known world, the continents fanning out around it like lotus petals. For Muslims, Mecca sits directly beneath the throne of Allah. For Hindus, Kashi, the City of Shiva, the City of Light, is where the universe was created in the first place.

In the telling of Jonathan Parry, a British scholar at the London School of Economics, Kashi is not attached to the earth. It floats suspended in the sky. It stands outside of space and time. It is where time began and where time stands still. That being so, Varanasi is immune from the ravages of time. It cannot suffer the physical degradation that afflicts the rest of the world in the age of Kali, and no one will ever go hungry there, no matter that the ebb of raw sewage, the crumbling back alleys, the crowds of emaciated and crippled beggars, the dying widows, the perpetual gray smoke of the cremation fires, and the general filth and squalor might suggest otherwise.

The fattest doorstop of all these works of scholarship was *The Hindus*, by Wendy Doniger of the University of Chicago. Fortunately, I'd bought it in New York, because all copies here, to the fury of Indian intellectuals, had just been pulped by Penguin Books India after a right-wing Hindu nationalist group brought criminal charges against the author for "deliberate and malicious acts intended to outrage religious feelings."

I was reading *The Hindus* one evening in a favorite restaurant. One of Doniger's main offenses, it seemed, was the mass of scholarly evidence she had gathered to show that the Brahmin elite had had no monopoly over the writing of the sacred texts; women and the lower castes had also played an important role in their creation. In Doniger's account, Sita, the wife of Lord Ram, who is abducted in the Rāmāyaṇa by Ravan, the demon king of Lanka, and then liberated by Hanuman and his monkey army, was anything but the usual insipid stereotype of the virtuous, submissive wife. In fact, she was a determined, independent woman with a strong sense of herself as a sexual being.

The waiter brought my food, and as I laid the book aside, I noticed that a young man at the next table was staring at me. Eventually he walked over and asked if he could join me.

"Why are you reading this book?" he asked.

"Because it's fascinating. I'm learning a lot about Hinduism."

He was still frowning. "I'm a policeman."

"That must be interesting work," I said.

He paused. "So what does it say about our religion?"

"Oh, that it's very tolerant and open to lots of opinions. You have lots of sacred texts, not just one single holy book like the Bible or the Qu'ran. No popes or bishops. The priests can't tell you what to think. You can believe anything you like."

"But the book is illegal. It has been banned in our country."

"Well, not exactly," I said, trying not to sound like the patronizing foreigner and probably failing. "It's just been withdrawn from sale because the publisher didn't want to offend people who might turn violent."

He was nodding thoughtfully now. He didn't say anything for a minute. Then he smiled shyly and laid his iPhone on the table.

"The reason I wanted to ask you these questions is that I read about all the problems with this book, and this has made me curious. So I downloaded it onto my phone. Now after we have talked, I will read it."

"Well," I said, "you might find it a bit of a challenge to read on such a small screen. It's almost eight hundred pages long."

We both laughed.

"Can we be friends on Facebook?" he asked. "My username is Smokin' Hot."

I looked him up later that night, but I never did manage to find his page.

Diana Eck gives one version of the creation myth of Kashi. After their wedding in the Himalayas, Shiva is under pressure from his new bride, Parvati, and his fussy mother-in-law to find a more permanent home. He looks down on the world from Mount Kailash, sees Kashi, where the Ganges bends auspiciously to the north, and decides this is the only place fit for their residence. But first he has to remove its ruler, King Divodasa, who has defied the gods for thousands of years. So right away that presented a cosmological conundrum: If the Himalayas already existed, and so did Kashi, how could the universe not?

An alternate version, as told by Jonathan Parry, is that Shiva and Parvati are wandering one day in the primordial forest of bliss. Again, it seems that Kashi already exists, since they decide that their main task is to bestow moksha, meaning liberation from samsara, the unending cycle of birth, death, and one of the 840,000 possible forms of reincarnation, on all those who die here, regardless of their caste or karma. In Kashi, there will be no need to fear an encounter with "the hard-hearted men of Yama"—the fearsome god of death—"terrifying, foul-smelling, with hammers and maces in their hands."

To free themselves up for this demanding task, Shiva and Parvati need help with the creation of the universe. So they bring into being a creature of astonishing beauty, Vishnu. In one of his four hands, Vishnu carries a serrated discus, a terrible weapon that he will use to vanquish evil and defend the righteous. Its first use, however, is to dig a ritual bathing tank. As usual in Hindu myth, this is slow work. It takes Vishnu fifty thousand years, and by the time he is done, he is burning with the fires of his austerity, and the tank is filled with the sweat of his labors. Parvati is so moved by the sight that she trembles with joy and one of her earrings falls off. Shiva decrees that the place will henceforth be called Manikarnika, the jewel of the ear. India is the navel of the universe, Kashi is the navel of India, and Manikarnika is the navel of Kashi. The touts and tour guides call it *the burning place*.

SACRED FIRE

On a rise of ground above Manikarnika, one of the city's innumerable temples dedicated to Shiva has a narrow balcony that looks down across the woodpiles to the cremation fires. I went up there one morning and pulled out my cell phone to take a couple of photographs. Within seconds, a villainous-looking character with unfortunate teeth materialized at my elbow.

"This is against the law. You must pay me if you want to take a photograph."

"And how much would that be?" I asked.

"Fifteen thousand dollars."

I laughed. He glared.

"The money is not for me. It will be given to the orphanage." He gestured vaguely upstream.

The orphanage, right. I turned and made a move to leave, but found that my way was blocked by a broad-shouldered boy in his late teens.

"Excuse me, please let me past," I said.

The man shook his head. "If you are not making this contribution, you must come with us."

The boy moved closer, bunching his fists. He seemed to be practicing the kind of menacing scowl he had presumably learned as a muscleman in training. The balcony was much too narrow to squeeze past them in either direction. I glanced over the edge, but decided that leaving that way would be undignified and, besides, it seemed likely to result in a broken ankle.

I pulled myself up to my full height, which was six inches taller than either of them. "Okay, I'm going down to Manikarnika now. They're expecting me. I'm planning to be there all day with two friends. One of them is a person of great influence in Benares."

This threw him. "What do you mean? Who is expecting you?"

"The Doms. It's all been arranged."

"That is impossible. I would know about it."

In fact, this being India, the impossible had become possible once an acceptable number of high-denomination bills had been transferred from one pocket to another. In this case, it had taken extended negotiations between an acquaintance of mine named Ajay, whose friends call him Pinku, a member of an old Benares Brahmin family who seemed to know everyone in the city, and someone he called "a kind of bully person" who set the terms of access to the cremation ground. The definition of *acceptable* was eventually agreed to be five thousand rupees, about eighty dollars. With that, my request was granted: unlimited time at Manikarnika, with no restrictions. My friend Agnès, a French photographer, was free to shoot wherever and whatever she wanted. I could hang out for as long as I liked with the Doms, members of the *dalit* caste that has sole authority to light the sacred fire that ignites the funeral pyre and make sure that the body is fully burned before the ashes are shoveled into the Ganges, all for a price levied on the mourners. A good chunk of my five thousand rupees would go to the Doms. A small amount would go to a couple of favored temples. Fifty percent would go to the local police. Death here was a business like any other.

I could see the man's mental wheels turning. Was I bluffing? And if so, how did I imagine I was going to get away with it, since I was outnumbered two to one?

"Look, if you don't believe me, come and see for yourself," I said. "I'll introduce you to the person who made all the arrangements."

Eventually he grunted and jerked his head at the muscleboy, and off we went, with me squeezed between the two of them like a prisoner doing the perp walk, down the steps and past the woodpiles to Manikarnika. The alleyways around the ghat were lined with small stores selling cremation goods: tinseled shrouds, bamboo for the bier, the clay water pot that the chief mourner tosses over his shoulder at the end of the ceremony, fragrant copal resin, small blocks of costly sandalwood, though sometimes these were no more than fraudulent pieces of ordinary wood splashed with perfume.

My Brahmin friend was waiting for me on the smoky arcaded balcony that the Doms use as their base of operations. He grinned at my escort and steepled his fingers and said, "Namaste!" Then he turned to me and murmured, "This is the bully person I was telling you about. But I see you have already met!"

Several fires were burning when we got to the ghat, one of them freshly set and a couple of others already collapsing into ash. Men were putting the finishing touches to another pyre, laying the pieces of wood crosswise like Lincoln Logs. A few tourists were gawking from boats. Manikarnika had its own resident menagerie. A mongoose scuttled in and out of a woodpile. Cows lay around placidly, dusted with ash, untroubled by the heat and smoke. A rib-thin goat nibbled on a discarded garland of marigolds. Monkeys squatted on the nearby rooftops, observing the human comedy. A pair of yellow dogs engaged in a sudden, vicious squabble that left one of them bleeding and whining.

I found a place to sit on the balcony among the Doms. The first corpse arrived a few minutes later, laid out on a bamboo bier that was constructed like a ladder and carried by four men who came half walking and half jogging down the steps to the chant of *Ram Nam Satya Hai*—"Truth is the name of Ram," one of the ten avatars of Vishnu. All the mourners were male. Women are considered too fainthearted to be allowed on the cremation ground; their job is to stay home to weep and grieve and try to hang on to the corpse as it's taken away to be burned. The scene looked chaotic at first, but in fact everyone had an appointed role, bustling about like waiters in a busy restaurant.

Wood sellers were weighing out logs on their ancient iron scales and making a tidy profit. Barbers were on hand to tonsure the chief mourners, who were usually the eldest sons of the deceased. Priests waited to greet the new arrivals and pocket their fees. Jonathan Parry calls them the "ritual technicians of Sanskrit Hinduism," although that doesn't imply that they have any special expertise. "The reputation of the priests for chicanery is at least as great as their reputation for scholarship," he writes, much as Fanny Parkes had written about the priests in Allahabad 150 years earlier. "The mantras they recite are learned by rote, with little idea of their real meaning, and they often mumble or talk nonsense, confident that the mourners will not know any better."

By the end of the day, more than a hundred bodies would have been brought here to burn. In the cold winter months or, like now, in the debilitating heat of early summer, it might be twice that number. Each of them would refuel the fires of creation in the place where it began, and Manikarnika was where the corpse of all creation would burn at the end of time.

I settled myself in a corner in the shade and took Parry's book out of my backpack. Not every body goes to the pyres, I learned; there are exceptions. A baby should not be cremated before its first teeth have come in and it's able to chew. Lepers can't be burned because their bodies will give off a noxious gas. People who die of snakebite are sometimes placed on a raft of banana leaves and floated downriver; the theory is that their bodies, overheated by the venom, may cool down and come back to life, and the raft will save them from drowning.

The trickiest are those who are judged to have had a "bad death," a term that seemed to have no precise definition. Parry says that burning them releases a malignant ghost in the form of shit or vomit. They have to make do with the "method of the effigy," which is an especially lucrative affair for the funeral priests. The corpse itself goes into the river. Its effigy, which will later be burned in the usual way, is constructed from fifty-six different ingredients. The blood is honey, the veins are grass, the hair is wool. The nipples are red beads, the pubic hair is coconut fiber, the penis is an eggplant. All the bodies I saw on my visits to Manikarnika appeared to have died a good death, and there was never an eggplant in sight.

A second group of mourners came jogging down the steps. They took their corpse to the river's edge, dipped it headfirst in the murk, then laid it on a fresh pyre. When they removed the shroud, it revealed a balding man in his late middle years with a gray toothbrush mustache. One of the Doms, a wraith-like figure in a loose white robe, touched a bunch of holy kusa grass to the flame that burns around the clock on the balcony, by Shiva's trident, and handed it to the chief mourner. Within minutes, they had a nice blaze going. It was all very businesslike. The mourners chatted and snapped close-ups of the dead man's face on their cell phones. Agnès took photographs of the men taking photographs. One recalcitrant leg kept springing out of the fire at a ninety-degree angle, burned and blackened but with the elastic tendons apparently still intact. A man in a Tennessee State University T-shirt hawked and spat, looking irritated, and pushed it down, but it soon sprang up again. Eventually he wrapped a protective cloth around his hand and with considerable effort managed to snap it off at the knee. He dropped the lower half, and it rolled away, but one of his companions grabbed two pieces of bamboo and, using them like chopsticks, managed to ram the leg back into the flames before one of the yellow dogs could make a lunge for it.

Even though the body was now burning furiously, it still was not dead. Death does not occur when the heart stops or the major organs fail but when the soul, the "vital breath," is released through the skull, and for that the skull has to be broken open along the suture lines that close during infancy. This part of the ceremony, the *kapal kriya*, is the most difficult for the chief mourner, and I found it hard to watch brains boil and bubble out of a fractured skull. It is the only moment when the mourner is allowed to weep. Otherwise the ghost will drink his tears. I saw the rite performed in many different ways during the time I spent on the cremation grounds. Some men went about it in a perfunctory way, jabbing at the skull once with a stick, no more than a symbolic gesture. Others were more energetic, as if they were beating a dusty carpet, making a loud *thwack* that reminded me of the washermen pounding their laundry on the flat stone slabs at the Dhobi Ghat, a little way upstream.

THE SPECTACLE OF WOOD

Sometimes, Pinku said, as the mourners wait for the flame to be lit and debate the purpose and meaning of life, you may hear a song by the sixteenth-century poet-saint Kabir.

Dekh tamasha lakri ka
Jite lakri
Marte lakri

Kabir is subject to endless subtleties of translation, but in essence this meant:

Behold the spectacle of wood
Wood when you are alive
Wood when you die

As the afternoon faded into dusk at Manikarnika, a group of men built the largest and most elaborate pyre I'd seen all day, right at the water's edge, stacking a latticework of whole logs that were almost a foot in diameter and topping it with greenery and sandalwood. It was a display of piety and also a show of the family's wealth. For reasons both spiritual, worldly, and downright venal, everyone involved in the business of death on the cremation grounds has a reason to burn as much wood as they can.

But I wanted to know where all the wood came from, now that India's Supreme Court had upheld a law that prohibited, with only a few exceptions, the cutting of any tree in an effort to conserve the country's vanishing forests. That at least was the theory.

We headed out on S-5, the state highway south of Varanasi. At the entrance to one small village, someone had strung a rope across the road. Some men were sitting around watching boys playing cricket in a dried-up irrigation canal. One of them wandered over and stuck his palm through the window of the car. The driver gave him ten rupees. The man slung a garland of marigolds over the steering wheel.

"What was that all about?" I asked Pinku.

"Oh, this village has some kind of local demigod. He's supposed to be very twisted and . . . what is the word in English? Short-tempered? So you have to give a donation to his temple."

"Or else what?"

"Or else he might make your car crash."

Thirty miles on, past the nondescript town of Ahraura, we pulled over at a chai stall. To the west of the road a small, pretty river meandered through scrubby woodland splashed with crimson blooms of Java cassia. To the east was a wildlife sanctuary where the forest was denser and there were said to be pythons and gharials—fish-eating crocodiles—as well as various rare species of deer and antelope.

We hiked upstream. The river was low and bony in the blistering heat, and it was easy to hop from one side to the other across the flat shelves of exposed bedrock. Eventually the scrub gave way to thicker forest, and after half an hour or so, the trail ended abruptly at a deep horseshoe-shaped pool. Trees grew out of the sheer, layered rock face that encircled the pool, and half a dozen bridal-veil falls dropped sixty or seventy feet into the pale green water. I stood under the cloud of spray to cool off by the roofless ruins of a hermit's hut. It was a place of great serenity, and it was easy to see why a renunciant would come here to find refuge from the turmoil of the world.

We had seen no one on the way to the waterfalls, but on the way back along the narrow forest path, we passed three woodcutters, a man and two women, carrying axes. Another man was silhouetted against the sky as he labored up a nearby hillside, balancing on his head a stack of tree limbs that looked like a miniature funeral pyre.

We stopped again at the chai stall, where the owner was tending his kettle over a mud stove. Some men were building a wall, knee-deep in muck. The *chaiwalla*'s name was Chote Lal. He was a bespectacled man with an air of resignation to the follies of the world. His little shop had been robbed seven times, although there didn't seem much to steal except for a plastic cooler with some cold drinks, a few packets of salty snacks, a cheap wall clock, and some out-of-date calendars with images of Shiva, Vishnu, and Hanuman. I doubted that there were more than a few hundred rupees in the cashbox.

Despite the heat radiating from the stove, on top of the heat of the day, Chote Lal wore a long-sleeved shirt, an undershirt, and a pink scarf. He said that his guru had lived in the ruined hermitage beneath the waterfall. He showed me a photograph of a stick insect of a man, all knees and elbows and dressed only in a white *langoti*, barely enough to cover his genitals.

"I've lived here for forty-five years," he said. "This all used to be thick forest. There were tigers and bears and leopards. Now humans are the only animals here, and the forest is almost gone."

Yes, of course the woodcutters were breaking the law, but what could you do?

"Don't the forest rangers patrol?" I asked.

That earned an indulgent half-smile at the naïveté of foreigners. "Of course they do. You see them patrolling every day, five or six of them together. But it isn't to report the woodcutters; they're looking for bribes. They can earn five or six hundred rupees a day that way. Then they let the woodcutters load their wood onto bikes and pickup trucks and take it to the markets in Ahraura, Robertsganj, Narayanpur. They get four or five rupees a kilo. In Varanasi, they can get eight. And maybe they cut fifty or sixty kilos a day. I know all about this, but I never say anything. Why ask for trouble?"

THE COMMISSION MEN

Where do you get *your* wood from?" I asked one of the wood sellers at Manikarnika. There are eight or ten dealers in the alleys around the ghat, and many of them, like this one, are members of the milkman caste, the Yadavs, who are a political force in the state of Uttar Pradesh.

"Are you going to write about this?" he asked. "If you do, tell people in America and England that I am looking for a wife." He smiled roguishly. He already had a wife, and three children.

"You want to write about our country? This is the most corrupt country in the world. Everywhere there is a commission man! If you are not using the commission man, you cannot get business. The moment they see a body coming, the brokers are looking for a way to make money."

"In Banarsi culture, when you're born, you pay a commission," another man chipped in. "When you go to a temple, you pay a commission. When you die, you pay a commission."

"But seriously," I said, "where does the wood come from?"

"Mostly from the government depots. Some is from dead trees or ones that fall down in a storm. But even then, you can't just take it. You have to inform the Forest Department, and they will come and pick it up. Then there are trees that are cut down for official purposes, like building a mine or a highway. And tribal people get special permits. I'm off to one of the tribal areas tomorrow for three days, in fact. These people still use bows and arrows! Can you imagine?"

He stopped and smiled. "And then of course there's the illegal logging."

That evening I met one of the commission men in a darkened house on a darkened street near Raj Ghat, where the logging trucks arrive at night to unload for the boats that will carry the wood upstream to the cremation grounds the next morning. Keeping the lights off was not enough for the commission man; he also insisted on setting up a blinding LED bulb in a wall niche behind his head that shone straight in my eyes and made it impossible to make out anything of his face.

"The wood is sold by auction at the government depots," he said. "My job is to match up auctioneers with buyers, and for this I am charging a commission." There was a small depot at Sarnath, a town a few miles from Varanasi where the Buddha preached his first sermon. There was a larger one at Mirzapur, thirty miles upriver. There was a lot of illegal logging around Mirzapur, he said, but it was an area he didn't like to venture into because of the Maoist Naxalite guerrillas, who were active there, still fighting the endless, futile fight they'd started half a century ago. The biggest depot of all was farther away still, in the neighboring state of Madhya Pradesh, eight or nine hours on a bad road. MP was notorious for its logging mafia, he said, and that was where most of the wood for the cremation grounds came from. Some illegal wood also came from the forests near Chote Lal's chai stall, brought into Raj Ghat at night by boat from Narayanpur.

"How can you cover up illegal logging on that scale?" I asked.

"You'd better ask the government that," he said, and I could hear his smile in the darkness of the room. "For cremation, it's a very sensitive issue, because people will always need wood. It's one requirement you can't ignore."

The forest rangers and government inspectors, the auctioneers at the depot, the brokers and middlemen, the truckers, the boatmen, the wood sellers at Manikarnika, the Doms, the funeral priests—all of them had an incentive to cut, sell, and burn as much wood as possible. Each one charged a commission to the next person in the chain, the police took their cut, and there wasn't much the mourners themselves could do to resist the final sales pitch. It was especially easy to swindle unsophisticated people who came in from the outlying villages. Wood is sold by the maund, a bit more than eighty pounds. Odd numbers are auspicious. A rich family might burn fifteen maunds, more than half a ton. You couldn't get away with less than five if you wanted to be sure of burning the body completely, and even then, some dealers might take two as their commission. Seven was better; nine better still. And it was always a good idea to throw in some sandalwood, or mango and wood apple, which are also sacred. How could you not honor the traditions of your ancestors? How would you feel if the feral dogs started chewing on the unburned parts of your mother or father? There was a time when the problem of partly burned bodies was so bad that the government decided to introduce flesh-eating turtles into the river, but the polluted waters didn't agree with them, and no one had seen one in years.

"There's a truck coming in from Mirzapur around three in the morning," the commission man said. "They'll start loading the boats before seven, so if you want to see them, you'd better get there early."

One truckload equals one boatload, a little over eight tons, and by sunrise, the team of ten porters already had the first of the wood on board. There were no steps for pilgrims or bathers at Raj Ghat, and the truck had dumped the wood at the top of a steep, rough slope. The porters loaded up and jogged down to the river, through the garbage and the shit and the discarded shrouds that had floated downstream from Manikarnika, then wobbled up a precarious gangplank to dump their wood on top of the growing pile.

"This is a skilled job, you know," one of them said to me. "You have to have special training to carry that amount of wood on your shoulders." For the heavier loads, which could weigh more than two hundred pounds, it took eight men to get all the logs and branches properly positioned. I doubted that many of the porters weighed more than a hundred and twenty. Now that it was summer, when temperatures would go up to mad-dogs-and-Englishmen levels, more people died, and dealers built up their stockpiles before the monsoon broke, the porters' pay would go up accordingly, to about two and a half dollars a day.

By a little after one o'clock, the job was done, and the men went back up the hill to sit in the shade by a tiled shrine to Hanuman and stuffed their cheeks with paan. They introduced themselves. Ramesh Sahni, Rajkumar Sahni, Chamru Sahni. Most of the ten turned out to be Sahnis, which identified them as members of the boatman caste, the Mallah. Several of them were graybeards in their fifties, though they looked even older. "I started working here in 1978," one man said, spitting out a scarlet gob of paan juice. "But I had to stop for a while because I drove a nail through my foot."

"The oldest of the porters is seventy," one of the Sahnis said. "He carries as much as he can, and everyone is kind to him because we all think about what our own lives will be like when we're old."

"And how old are you?" I asked the man sitting at the end of the row. He was bigger than the others, and his thick black beard and knotted headscarf gave him a piratical look. "Twelve," he said. "Or maybe thirteen. I can't remember." Everyone cackled.

They sat there patiently, chewing their paan and waiting for their money.

"And then you'll go home to your wives?" I said.

"No," the pirate said. "Then we'll go and get drunk."

ASHES TO ASHES

I found, tucked away behind one of the woodpiles at Manikarnika, a vermilion stone with the worn figures of a man and his wife. It marked the spot where virtuous widows had once committed sati, immolating themselves on their husbands' funeral pyres. The practice honored Sati, who may have been the first wife of Shiva, or perhaps his second, or perhaps she was the same person as Parvati, or perhaps her reincarnation. It was another of those confusing stories. I heard an expanded version later in Calcutta, in which the identity of Sati/Parvati became more confusing still.

Lord William Bentinck, governor-general of Bengal and later of all India, found a good many reasons to wrinkle his long, patrician nose at the barbaric habits he observed among the Hindoos. Nothing appalled him more than suttee, as the British called it, and in 1829 he outlawed the practice in Bengal, denouncing it as "revolting to the feelings of human nature." The City of Shiva, which also happened to be where the British had first come upon the phenomenon of female infanticide, was the most egregious offender. Sati was "a spectacle which occurred more frequently in Benares than in any other part of the [East India] Company's territories," wrote the *Asiatic Journal and Monthly Register* in 1833, the year in which the ban was extended to the rest of India. Even so, there were those who quibbled. If his lordship made sati illegal, would that not antagonize our subject people and make them harder to control? And if one form of cremation were banned, might that not implicitly endorse other kinds? After all, every good Christian was disgusted by the very idea of setting fire to a body, with its dark pagan associations.

But revulsion is a matter of culture, and attitudes can shift with time. At the Vienna Exposition of 1873, some learned gentlemen from Italy, working "in the name of public health and civilization," demonstrated Professor

Brunetti's remarkable apparatus for reducing the human body to a neat pile of white ash that you could put on your mantelpiece in a decorative urn. Sir Henry Thompson, an expert on diseases of the genitourinary tract and surgeon to Queen Victoria, empress of India, was most impressed. He invited a group of notables, including the novelist Anthony Trollope and the painter John Everett Millais, to his home at 35 Wimpole Street, where they drew up a declaration. "We the undersigned disapprove of the present custom of burying the dead, and we desire to substitute some mode which shall rapidly resolve the body into its component elements, by a process that cannot offend the living, and shall render the remains perfectly innocuous." A plot of land was bought in a discreet corner of the Surrey countryside, with help from the London Necropolis Company. Professor Paolo Gorini of Lodi was invited to give a demonstration. He tried it on a horse. Most efficacious, Sir Henry thought, although it took another six years for parliament to make cremation legal.

But the living, or at least the English living, were still offended by what went on in Benares, where the ritual was conducted in public, large numbers of partly burned bodies went into the Ganges, and the cremation grounds were located in the very heart of the city. Why the devil could they not be on the outskirts, as they were in most Indian towns, often to the south, toward the domain of Yama, the lord of death? It took another half century before British administrators bent to reality: this was where the jewel of the ear had fallen, and Kashi's conception of purity would never mesh with London's notions of hygiene. The annual municipal report for 1925 concluded with a sigh, "It is impossible to remove the burning ghats from their present location, it is not that the Manikarnika and Harishchandra ghats are there for the city, but that the city is there for the ghats."

Harishchandra is the second and smaller of Varanasi's cremation grounds. It takes its name from the story of a ruler of the kingdom of Ayodhya, an ancestor of Lord Ram. The Doms are in charge here, as they are in Manikarnika, and the story of Harishchandra is also their creation myth, the source of their authority on the burning ghats.

Indra, the god of thunder and war, was pondering a question one day. Was there, in all the world, such a thing as a truly honest man? The name of Harishchandra came up, and while he sounded promising, the gods decided that his integrity had to be put to the test. They entrusted the task to a particularly vindictive sage named Vishwamitra. First, he ordered Harishchandra to give away all his worldly possessions. Then wild beasts and a plague of insects were let loose on his kingdom. More Job-like trials followed, and when the king had nothing left to give, Vishwamitra demanded the clothes off his back, as well as those of his wife, Taramati, and their son, Rohitashwa. Still that wasn't enough, and since Harishchandra was destitute now, all that remained was to sell his wife and child, give the proceeds to Vishwamitra, and wander the land in search of menial labor. He found it at last with a *chandala,* an untouchable named Kallu Dom, a foul-breathed drunk who was the caretaker of the cremation ground in Kashi. Harishchandra agreed to become his slave and collect the fees that the Dom was allowed to charge for each cremation.

Taramati, meanwhile, was going through her own tribulations at the hands of the evil Brahmin to whom her husband had sold her. One day, while wandering in the forest, young Rohitashwa was bitten by a snake and died. Overcome with grief, she brought her son's body to Manikarnika. But Harishchandra failed to recognize either of them and demanded the usual fee. She had nothing to give, but he was implacable. "Go and pawn your *mangalsutra,*" he suggested, the necklace that identified her as a married woman.

The story continues through further trials and disasters, the details depending as usual on which of the Vedas and the Puranas you preferred. In one version, Harishchandra is even ordered to execute his wife by cutting off her head, and agrees—and only then finally realizes who she is. But since this is intended as an inspirational tale, all the variant endings are of course happy ones. Harishchandra passes the test of the gods; light streams down on the family from heaven; young Rohitashwa is restored to life. The Doms, having forced a king to do their bidding, might still occupy the lowest rung on the ladder of caste, but on the cremation grounds, they acquire their own kind of nobility. From now on, the supreme authority among them will be known as the Dom Raja.

Gandhi used to say that the story of King Harishchandra always made him weep, and it is still taught in schools as a parable of honesty and integrity. However, you will also sometimes hear Indians using the king's name as a term of derision, applied to someone who takes those qualities to a pigheaded extreme.

SLOWLY-SLOWLY

Other than a raised plinth where notable citizens are sometimes cremated, Harishchandra Ghat isn't much to look at. Usually there are only one or two fires burning there. When I strolled past the ghat one morning, a man was gearing up for the skull-breaking. "My mother!" he shouted at me, raising the stick above his head in a samurai pose. "Hundred-dollar photo only! Hundred-dollar photo!"

Behind him was a building that was a tour de force of ramshackle ugliness. It was perched on cement columns that were staggered to conform to the slope above the ghat. Snugged into the open space between the columns was the Vadav Tea Stall, with a sign that read, "Mineral Water Toilet Paper Coke Pepsi Chocolate & Sigrate." The building itself had brick walls that seemed unfinished, although one of them was painted an inexplicable lipstick pink. There were eccentric balconies and crenellations, and turret windows had been tacked onto the walls. Two spindly smokestacks rose from the roof, one metal and the other encased in a concrete base and both of them held upright with guy ropes. It was like some demented LEGO version of a cross between a medieval castle, a Mughal palace, and a power plant.

Pitting technology against cosmology, the British had argued for years for an electric crematorium, but it had been built only in the late 1980s after the death of the powerful Dom Raja of the day, Kailash Chowdhury, who had opposed it with every sinew as a threat to jobs, income, and tradition. There was a small shrine with the sacred swastika at the foot of the ramp that led up to the entrance. The iron concertina gate was half-open, and I strolled inside to take a look. The custodian and two friends were sitting cross-legged on a mat, playing cards. Above them was a poster advertising Spiritual Yoga and a Shiva calendar published by Vishwanath Associates ("A" Class Approved UP Government Electrical and Civil Works). The custodian had a few words of English. Business was slow today, so I was free to poke around. He went back to his card game.

The only sounds in the crematorium were the slap of the cards and a low-pitched electrical hum. There were cobwebs everywhere. There were two cold concrete ovens, stencil-numbered 1 and 2, and there was a simple metal slide to get the bodies inside. It was hard to avoid morbid associations, thinking of the swastika outside, how the Hindu symbol of good fortune had mutated into the Hakenkreuz.

I asked the custodian how many bodies came here on an average day. Maybe ten, he said, only about a third as many as were cremated down on the ghat. He thought that was too bad, because the electric method was a bargain for poor people—except, of course, when there were power cuts, which could have unfortunate consequences if they happened midway through the proceedings.

"The electric crematorium?" said a man I had met in a spartan office in South Delhi. "We will not say it is a success. In those days, as part of its Ganga

Action Plan, the government put in such crematoria all along the river, twenty-eight of them, in all the main cities: Rishikesh, Haridwar, Allahabad, Kanpur, Kolkata. But they were never really used except by the middle classes in Kolkata. In other places, they were just for unclaimed bodies brought in by the police. And how can they work when often there is no electric power for twelve hours a day?"

His name was Anshul Garg. He had been born into a pious Hindu family, trained as a computer engineer, studied in Bangalore, India's IT capital, and worked for a while with Microsoft. For the past fifteen years, he had been working on another solution to the problem of hygienic cremation, one that might also save a chunk of the country's vanishing forests. The name of his company was Mokshda. *Moksha* means salvation; the addition of one letter changes the meaning to "the one who gives salvation."

He did some back-of-the-envelope calculations for me. India's population was one and a quarter billion. Ten million die each year. Eighty percent of them are Hindu, and almost all are cremated. Five or seven maunds of wood each on average. By Garg's count, that translated into seven hundred and fifty square miles of forest cut down every year, just to burn bodies. And think of all the ashes dumped into Mother Ganga, which was already an open sewer.

"We have developed a system that uses a third as much wood," he said. He took me to see one of the first working units, where a cremation was already in progress. I could have watched it without leaving New York, because there was a built-in video camera that allowed for live streaming for absent relatives and NRIs—nonresident Indians.

The apparatus had perforated metal sides and an adjustable convex hood that had the effect of superheating the pyre and consuming almost all the particles that floated upward. All that emerged from the tall, tapering chimney was a faint wisp of pale gray smoke. A rack beneath the body collected the ashes. They could then be removed to cool, and the platform would be ready for the next body within three hours. Mokshda had not patented its design, Garg said, because it was a "social cause for the benefit of humanity."

However, he was unhappy with what was going on when we arrived. The corpse was almost completely burned, but several charred logs were strewn around on the ground. He glowered at a priest who was standing by. "They didn't have to use that much wood," Garg complained. "These pandits are the problem. They double as wood sellers here, and all they're interested in is making money."

It took years to fine-tune the design, he said. "In the first phase, we installed about fifty units. But there were technical, operational, social issues, questions of religion and ritual. The more religious the town, the more resistance we faced. It's a tough task, changing practices that go back to ancient times. People say, 'My forefathers did it this way and went to heaven. What about me?' I understand that it's very sensitive, and change will come only slowly-slowly. But every ritual in this society has evolved over time. The way we marry, the food we eat. Just not this one final ritual, because no one knows what will happen to them after death."

The conversations with religious authorities continued. Gradually, he said, they had come to see the virtue of Mokshda's design. It left the pyre open. Unlike the electric crematorium, it took all the ritual needs into account. You could circumambulate the body the requisite five times. You could light the fire in the mouth of the corpse. You could break open the skull.

Varanasi, not surprisingly, was the hardest sell. "It's a big threat to the wood sellers there, and they're very powerful," Garg said. "To save their bread and butter, they will go to any extent. Although, of course, it's the Doms who have the real power. Our negotiations were with the widow of Kailash Chowdhury, the old Dom Raja, and her two sons. They are the most powerful family among the Doms, and they were also the most positive. It took us seven or eight years to convince them, and now they will convince others. We will install the unit right there at Manikarnika."

The only flaw in this scheme was that the Dom Raja's widow and her family seemed totally unaware of it.

KEEPERS OF THE FLAME

There were three ways you could refer to the old lady. She was Saranga Devi, *Saranga* being her birth name and *Devi*—the mother goddess—being a term of respect often applied to a woman. She was also the Dom Rani, widow of the Dom Raja. And she was the Bari Malkin, the elder of two sisters entitled in the complex hierarchy of the Doms to preside over the cremation grounds. The dispute between Saranga and her sister, Jamuna, over where exactly each of them belonged in this hierarchy had been tied up in the courts for almost forty years in an Indian version of *Bleak House*.

Today Saranga had the *pari*, her turn in a rota system, dictated by ancient and arcane formulae that are written down in ledgers and determine the periods during which a particular Dom can sit in the prime spot on the arcaded balcony, next to the ever-burning flame, supervising the workers, making sure there is enough wood and that the bodies are thoroughly burned, and raking in the proceeds of the day. Saranga had the *pari* for three and a half days a month. She would be here until sunrise on the following day, when she'd go home and take a shower.

I found her dozing on a pile of pillows against a sky-blue wall. Next to her, some of her workers were preparing the morning puja to honor Kallu Dom, pouring country liquor into clay cups. Saranga wore a pale lilac sari with a faded floral pattern, several heavy brass bracelets, and a large nose stud. Flies were crawling around on her *dupatta*, but she ignored them. She had hard, indifferent eyes behind black-framed glasses. Her face was deeply grooved by frown lines, and her expression said, *Either peel me a grape or leave me alone*.

Saranga had married Kailash Chowdhury, the old Dom Raja, when she was fifteen. He had left her a widow in 1986, when she was still only in her thirties. Did she mind if I asked how old she was now? She said about sixty-five. One of her sons, Sanjit, was seated nearby. I asked him the same question. He said he was about fifty-five. So that made no sense, though I wasn't entirely surprised, since poorer Indians often give their ages as approximations. Sanjit had a shock of bleached-out orange hair and a bristling white beard, and the upper part of his body was an archipelago of pink-and-white scar tissue. He was swaying a little, with a strange, off-kilter smile on his face, clearly having made an early start on the country liquor.

So what did the Dom Rani think of Mokshda? She turned to her nephew, who was sitting next to her listening to the conversation, and he returned her blank look. *Mokshda?* The word meant nothing to either of them. I told them about my conversations in New Delhi, and she waved a languid hand. "Maybe someone came," she said. "It's possible. I don't remember. Many people come here to talk to us. If we did talk, I didn't take it seriously."

I described what I'd seen of Anshul Garg's method, and the frown lines deepened.

"Our traditions have come down through the centuries. How could we provide the fire for this thing? The government would bring its people in, and our workers would lose their jobs. And the wood sellers. Many families for half a kilometer around the burning ghats depend on this for their living."

Besides, where was this contraption supposed to go? She gestured at the mourners milling around the cramped and crowded ghat. It seemed a reasonable question, especially thinking of the monsoon, when the river could rise forty feet or more and lap at the balcony where we were sitting.

Saranga made it clear that she was bored by the topic. She dozed off again. I sat there with my eyes stinging from the smoke. Flecks of ash settled in my hair. Eventually she opened one eye. The annoying foreigner was still there with his questions.

I asked her when women had gained the status of *malkin*.

"In the old times, only men had this right. But then there were some problems." That was all she wanted to say.

"Many people in the Dom community have these problems," the old lady's nephew said eventually. "If the son can't take care of his duties, his mother takes over." It sounded like a general statement of principle, but there was only one son and one mother on the balcony, and her sister, Jamuna, was childless. I tried not to glance across at Sanjit, who was far away in a world of his own sozzled imagining.

Strictly speaking, there is no single Dom Raja. Whoever holds the *pari* rules for that day. But there was always one figure with charisma and connections who was regarded as the first among equals and had the right to live in the Sher Wali Kothi, the Tiger House, a garish building close to Man Mandir Ghat that was surmounted by life-size statues of a male and female tiger.

The Bari Malkin's husband, Kailash Chowdhury, had been the most powerful of all the Dom Rajas, celebrated for his phalanx of bodyguards, his briefcase bulging with cash, and his pet alligator. He was said to have become fabulously wealthy on the proceeds of the cremation grounds, with prime real estate holdings in Varanasi, other parts of Uttar Pradesh, and the neighboring state of Bihar.

Kailash and Saranga had seven children, four sons and three daughters. By the normal process of succession, the eldest son, Ranjit, should have inherited the title and the Tiger House, but he had died young—of alcoholism, it was said. That left Sanjit next in line, but while people sometimes allowed him the honorific of Dom Raja, they were only being polite. "He is dying of cancer," one of the wood sellers had told me. "He will soon go up to heaven."

I heard two stories to account for the scars on Sanjit's chest and arms. One said that a cylinder of gas had exploded at a wedding, the other that his family had thrown him out of the Tiger House because of his drinking, and his response had been to pour kerosene over his body and set himself on fire. He was in no condition to tell me which of these stories was true.

Saranga had fallen asleep again, and Sanjit had shuffled off somewhere, so I walked down through the smoke to the river's edge. Some of the Doms were collecting whatever the mourners had left behind, the perks that went with the job: shrouds, bamboo, partly burned logs that they would take home for their cooking fires. The shrouds and biers would be resold and reused. Boatmen propelled themselves along the river with bamboo-handled oars that were fashioned from the recycled frames of cremation biers.

The water was a thick black slurry of ash, and half a dozen Doms, teenage boys and young men, were waist-deep in it, sieving the muck in flat baskets like nineteenth-century miners panning for gold. A boat glided toward them. An enormously fat man, dressed all in white, sat in the boat on a pile of cushions under a sheet that had been rigged on four culms of bamboo, like the tester on a four-poster bed, to shield him from the sun. He smiled down on the workers like a beneficent Buddha, and at intervals, they reached into their pans and handed him a small coin, a jeweled nose stud, a gold earring—whatever last trinkets could be retrieved from the burned bodies of the dead. The fat man put each of them in a pouch on the seat beside him. He caught my eye, smiled, laid his palms together, and inclined his head slightly. *The divine in me honors the divine in you.*

Clearly this was where the true authority lay, not with the sad, ruined figure of Sanjit Chowdhury but with his younger brother Jagdish, who everyone on the cremation ground agreed was now the man who really merited the title of Dom Raja.

I went to a modest house in a neighborhood of Doms to see Saranga's younger sister, Jamuna Devi, the Chote Malkin. Her nephew Bahadur took me there; today he had the *pari* at Harishchandra Ghat. We sat together on a mattress in a multicolored room. On a shelf, next to the usual pictures of Shiva and Krishna, there was an ornately framed portrait of Kailash, the old Dom Raja. He had fierce, dark eyes and heavy eyebrows that swooped down like bat wings to the bridge of a large nose, and he wore his hair in a dense Afro that was parted precisely in the middle and topped with an incongruous Nehru cap.

Jamuna had an open and generous manner, quite unlike Saranga's. She must have been a great beauty as a young woman, and it was hard not to wonder, looking at the portrait of Kailash on the wall, if the acrimony between the sisters might not have been about something more than their property and *pari* rights. There were rumors.

"I was born and brought up in a village near Benares," she said. "My father was a farmer, and he conducted the cremations there, one every four or five days. I got married when I was nine, then lived with my father for another seven years. After that, I moved to my husband's house. He was Kailash's older brother, and his father lived with Kailash in the Tiger House. But I was widowed four years after coming to Benares. Saranga was hard-hearted. She said I should go back to my village and my parents. She said that I had no right to any part of the Tiger House.

"After my husband died, we all went to the Tiger House for the daily mourning rituals. When the thirteenth-day ritual was over, Kailash told my brother to take me away to his house. My brother protested. He said, 'But you're so wealthy, you have many servants, let her live here.' But Kailash refused. So my brother filed a lawsuit. That was thirty-five years ago. He said, 'At least give her one *pari* to live on.' Still Kailash said no. Finally, the court ruled that the *paris* should be divided equally between me and Saranga. After Kailash died in 1986, I got a *pari* of three and a half days in a month, the same as my sister. A police inspector came to enforce the court order."

But Saranga refused to accept the settlement, and the case still dragged on in the High Court in Allahabad, all these years later. "I have struggled all my life, and I will go on struggling until this case is settled," Jamuna said, "even though I don't know if I will live long enough to see that day."

She knew that she would never be welcome in the Tiger House, even though as many as forty people lived there—not just Saranga, Jagdish and his family, his sisters and theirs but also an assortment of menials who were given room and board. Instead, Jamuna's brother had found her these cramped rooms with their yellow walls and blue metal doors. I asked her why the portrait of Kailash still hung there on the shelf, and she glanced up as if noticing it for the first time. "The former tenants put it up there, and I've never taken it down," she said.

It was a complicated family.

IN THE TIGER HOUSE

The next time I went to Varanasi, I wrangled an invitation to visit the Dom Raja in the Tiger House. As a piece of architecture, it was almost as eccentric as the electric crematorium. Its blind brick wall reared up thirty feet or more from the ghats. The lower half was painted in horizontal stripes of ocher and brown. Above that was a tier of white cement, and above that a balustraded balcony, fancifully tricked out in yellow, maroon, and blue. There was a curious triple-arched structure in the center that jutted out into midair like a miniature Florentine loggia. The two tigers stood at the north and south corners, glaring out over the river.

Next to the Tiger House, on Man Mandir Ghat, was an imposing palace, built in 1600 by a maharaja from Rajasthan, and behind that was the eighteenth-century observatory that one of his descendants, a mathematician and astronomer, had built to study the heavens. A twisting lane led to the Kashi Vishwanath Mandir, the Golden Temple. It was the most sacred in the city, but caste considerations meant that the Doms were unwelcome there.

It had been less than a year since my previous visit, but I was shocked at the change in Jagdish. He seemed even heavier than before. Gone were the white clothes and the air of serene authority. I found him dressed in a filthy green T-shirt that was stretched tight across his sagging breasts and belly, with an orange-and-white scarf looped around his neck. For such a big man, his voice was surprisingly thin and reedy, and his cheeks were crammed so full of paan that he seemed to be speaking through a mouthful of pebbles.

The building itself gave no hint of the hereditary wealth and power of the Dom Rajas. The paint was flaking, the plaster was crumbling, and the flagstones in the courtyard were cracked and broken. Some of the inner walls appeared to have collapsed, and there were piles of rubble everywhere. Women were cooking over a fire of logs salvaged from the cremation grounds, but they scurried off indoors as we arrived. A Brahman bull was chained to the wall. It was a rare thing to see inside a city residence, but the bull Nandi was the mount of Shiva, and I took the presence of this one as a sign of piety and prestige. The animal had just deposited a huge pile of dung on the threshold, and we had to step over it to enter the house.

We passed through a darkened room full of devotional images and clutter and came out onto the balcony and into the sunlight. "One tiger is male, and the other is female," Jagdish said. Their story involved a fight with the maharaja of Benares. Though the British had direct control of the city, they had granted the maharaja a good deal of autonomy and allowed him to retain his capital at Ramnagar, on the opposite side of the river. The title still existed, but these days, the maharaja's authority was purely ceremonial. In the time of the Raj, however, his ancestors took their powers very seriously. Many years ago—Jagdish wasn't sure when exactly, but sometime before Independence—the imperious Dom Raja of the time, Laxman Chowdhury, had proposed to erect statues of two tigers on his balcony, facing Ramnagar. "Impossible," the maharaja declared. The Dom Raja retorted with the tale of Harishchandra and Kallu Dom. "And where were you at that time?" he asked the maharaja. "You may be the king of Kashi, but I am the king of the Doms. So we are equals, and if I want to put tigers on my balcony, there's nothing you can do to stop me."

Jagdish lumbered back into the room and settled onto a bed that was piled high with grubby blankets. The last time I'd seen him, he'd put me in mind of a smiling Buddha; now all I could think of was Jabba the Hutt in *Return of the Jedi*.

He told me tales of his father, Kailash.

"He was always a generous man," he said. "He would help people beyond his limits. If some poor man came with an invitation to his daughter's wedding, my father would always give him rice or dal, or even money. Once or twice a week he would organize public feasts for the poor."

I decided to say nothing of the stories I had heard from Jamuna.

The greatest of all the festivals in Varanasi is the annual Ramlila, a month-long epic folk drama, staged under the auspices of the maharaja, that tells the life story of Lord Ram. "When Lord Ram's wedding procession came to Manikarnika, my father would distribute *kir*, sweet rice pudding, to everyone," Jagdish went on. "He would also organize all kinds of sport for his pleasure—horse races on the ghats, boat races, no one could match his standard for organizing such things. He would arrange fights here on Man Mandir Ghat for the strongest male sheep. It was always hard for him to accept defeat, so whenever his sheep lost, he would immediately sacrifice it."

"Could you do such things today?" I asked.

Jagdish chuckled, and his whole body wobbled. "Inflation is the problem. A kilo of ghee used to be forty rupees. Now it's four hundred! I try to keep up the tradition with one or two things, like giving out *kir* to everyone during the Ramlila wedding ceremony. But times have changed."

One of Jagdish's nephews had been sitting on the bed, too, saying nothing, but now he said, "Kailash lived for his reputation, not for making money. To make a name for himself, that was his idea."

I decided to say nothing about the stuffed briefcase and the pet alligator.

"He behaved like a king," Jagdish said. "He used to go into the city on a horse cart, like a chariot, in a very royal way, with an assistant sitting next to him. But at other times, he would go in a rickshaw or on foot. It all depended on his mood.

"One day, Indira Gandhi came to Varanasi. She was on her way to the Kashi Vishwanath Mandir, with a large security detail as usual. No one was allowed near her. But my father went out into the street and lay down in front of her car and forced it to stop. He said, 'First you have to speak to me, or you cannot go to the temple.' Because he was the king, the Dom Raja. And Indira

Gandhi got out of the car and said a few words to him before she drove on. You see, his pride and prestige mattered so much to him."

"I am a king, so I will act like a king," the nephew said.

I asked after Sanjit's health. "Who told you he had cancer?" Jagdish asked. "He is fit and fine. He had some lung problems, but they were cured. His only problem is that he drinks too much."

To my surprise, the conversation turned to the other, deeper problems of this complicated family. They involved the older brother, Ranjit, the one who had died, and not, it seemed, from the alcoholism that had ruined Sanjit's prospects.

A man who had joined us, a family confidant, said that this brother and his young son, Jagdish's nephew, had been murdered ten or twelve years earlier. Jagdish listened and said nothing, which seemed to be his way of giving tacit permission for the story to be told. Was it robbery? I asked. The man shook his head. "We suspect that it was a family war. The eldest brother was the only one who had a son, an heir to the *pari* at Manikarnika. The boy was kidnapped and killed. Now there were no male heirs. But then Jagdish prayed to the gods and promised to make many offerings to them if they would grant his wish, and finally he was blessed with a son of his own. Now he is nine years old."

I said I'd seen the boy earlier. He was a sweet-faced child with long, dark ringlets. He had been swinging a heavy weight lifter's club to amuse himself.

"Come," Jagdish said. "I will show you the *akhara*."

The *akhara*, the family wrestling and weight lifting arena, was down a short passage between two sections of the Tiger House. The walls of the *akhara* were painted blue, and blue-and-yellow clubs like the one the boy had been swinging, some of them studded all over with nails, were stacked in a corner.

There was an orange bed of nails on a shelf and a bright vermilion shrine to Hanuman, strewn with petals of many colors. Whatever the surrounding squalor, the city always seemed to me like a child's paint box.

"Wrestlers worship Hanuman, because he is the god of strength and power," Jagdish said. "You will always find a shrine to Hanuman in any *akhara*."

The Doms were celebrated wrestlers, and the sport had been a family tradition for at least four generations. "When I was eight years old, my father started bringing me to the *akhara*," Jagdish said. "He made sure that I was well trained by my maternal uncle, who was an excellent wrestler. My uncle used to match me up against older kids, so I got much stronger. I could always beat my brothers. We used to get in a lot of fights." His body jiggled with laughter.

When Jagdish was eighteen, he switched from wrestling to weight lifting and bodybuilding. In one corner of the room, next to the clubs, there were sets of barbells and huge stone doughnuts, which weight lifters call *nals*, two feet in diameter and weighing hundreds of pounds. There was an old photograph on the wall, hung with a garland of marigolds, that showed a man lifting a *nal* with one hand. Foreign visitors to Benares had always marveled at the feats of strength that they witnessed there. One day in an antique store in Delhi, I'd found a collection of stereographs, the kind that provided Victorian families with evening entertainment. On the back of one of them was a printed note from the photographer.

I present to you here this view of Mr. Dabee Chowdray Palwan, one of Nature's athletes. Palwan is not a large man—about five feet and seven and a half inches—and weighs, if I remember correctly, a little less than one hundred and seventy pounds. He is a vegetarian; he never read a book on physical culture; he was never within the walls of a gymnasium or any place for physical training. He found he excelled in lifting weights and had a surprising strength surpassing that of most men.

You see him here as he lies on his back, with muscles not large but hard
as steel, bearing on his uplifted arms nine hundred and sixty pounds,
and thus this great stone was sustained till the camera secured for you
this negative.

As a young man, Jagdish said, he could lift almost three hundred pounds on the barbells. He could lie on his back with an eight hundred–pound *nal* on his chest and then have three or four men sit on top of it. He excelled at competitions with the clubs, the *jori*. The idea was to swing them behind your head and then back over your shoulder; the winner was the man who could complete the greatest number of swings. *Jori* contests were a special feature of the summer festival of Nag Panchami, the worship of snakes. At that time, Jagdish said, the *akhara* was whitewashed and decorated, and crowds of a hundred or more would assemble to watch men showing off their skills with the *jori* and lying on the bed of nails.

"I still try to swing the club at the Nag Panchami," Jagdish said. "Just ten or fifteen swings. But not this year."

He sat on a low wall and pulled up his dhoti to show me his grossly swollen calves. "I was very sick last year. I had medicines that made me very fat."

Steroids? I asked. But the word was unfamiliar to him.

"To keep your body fit brings peace of mind," he said. "Keep your mind on God and exercise and you will be blessed by him." He began to massage his swollen legs. "If you do not exercise, your body gets into a very bad shape, as you see me today."

I NOW FEEL I HAVE SEEN INDIA

My hotel misadventures continued. After the $140-a-night cock-roaches and cigarette-burned furniture in Gorakhpur, and a couple of overpriced tourist traps on earlier visits to Varanasi, I wanted something better, preferably close to the cremation grounds. I ended up at Scindhia Ghat, immediately to the north of Manikarnika.

Scindhia is one of the better-known bathing ghats. It takes its name from its builders, a powerful Maratha clan, originally from Maharashtra, who ruled the princely state of Gwalior under the British. I read that the ghat was built around 1850, which would have been during the reign of His Highness Ali Jah, Pillar of the Nobility, Sword of the Kingdom, Agent of the Kingdom, Chief of the Highest Authority, High in Prestige, Exalted in Dignity, Great Prince over Princes of the Brave Scindhia, Lord of Fortune, Victorious of the Age.

According to legend, it was the wealth and ambition of the builders that accounted for the most striking feature of Scindhia Ghat. The weight of its construction had been too much for its Shiva temple, the Ratneshwar Mahadev, which slid into the river, leaving one of its bullet-shaped towers tilted at a crazy angle like the Leaning Tower of Pisa. During the monsoon, this *shikhara*, or "mountain peak," was almost completely submerged.

Looking at the work of the British artists who converged on Benares in the nineteenth century, I was confused by this story. A painting by Lieutenant Colonel Charles Ramus Forrest from his popular collection, *A Picturesque Tour Along the Rivers Ganges and Jumna, in India*, showed what seemed to be the same temple, leaning at pretty much the same angle, but in the opposite direction. The mystery was that Forrest had painted the scene in 1824, long before the Scindhias had supposedly built the ghat. Later, I found an 1860 painting by Robert Montgomery Martin. In this there was not one *shikhara* but two, and they were canted at an impossible forty-five-degree angle in the Ganges like ballistic missiles waiting for the launch codes.

As so often, I felt as if I were operating in a fact-free environment. "You have to understand," a friend had told me once, only half-joking. "In India, there *are* no facts." There were only stories and experiences, and that, in its way, was fine.

The guesthouse was at the head of a narrow, garbage-choked staircase high above the ghat. As we reached the entrance, a pair of monkeys bared their teeth and lunged at us from a low rooftop. Inside, we climbed more steep stone stairs to the top floor, where we'd booked "super deluxe" rooms with a balcony and a river view. We told the manager we were hungry. He spread his hands in apology. Alas, there was no restaurant. I showed him the page I'd printed from the hotel website. "The restaurant offers sumptuous refreshments cooked under strict supervision in very hygienic conditions." He shuffled his feet. There was no restaurant.

No matter; the rooms were adequate, if not exactly super deluxe. There was a common balcony with a panoramic view of the river, and we could find a restaurant later. But when we got back after lunch, the monkeys attacked again, snatching at our hair this time, and the hotel lobby was full of uniformed soldiers with guns. We climbed the stairs to the sound of loud banging from above. We went outside onto the balcony. Men with sledgehammers were working their way along it. They had already pounded a hole large enough for a person to walk through in the wall of the room adjacent to Agnès's. Hers would be next, then mine. I went downstairs to see the manager. "Sir, please don't worry, it is not a problem," he said. I told him I begged to disagree and canceled the rest of our stay.

After we'd found a more elegant and expensive alternative, close to the Tiger House, I told Pinku about the episode. He laughed. "There are lawsuits against fifty-two buildings," he said. "Many of them are these hotels that have added illegal upper floors to give the tourists a nice view of the river." Others were prosecuted because they had been built within five hundred yards of a designated historical monument, which was also illegal. He told me about a friend who had joined the plaintiffs in one of these cases. A man threatened him with a knife one day. "Drop the matter," he said, "or you will see this knife again."

Sometimes it took years for the courts to rule, Pinku said. "You can bribe the police, you can bribe the judge, you can bribe the prosecuting lawyer to present a weak case." In the case of the hotel at Scindhia Ghat, for whatever reason, the judge seemed finally to have bestirred himself to act. The sledge-hammers had put the illegal floor out of commission. A year later, passing on a boat, I noticed that they had done the same to the lower two floors. But the website was still up, with every indication that the place was still open for business and offering delicious home-cooked food in the restaurant.

Even as the nineteenth-century British authorities were deploring the barbarism of sati, cremation, and female infanticide in Benares, artists like Forrest and Martin came here to Benares in search of the romantic, the picturesque, the sublime. They found the cramped alleys of the old city quaint and atmospheric, but their true inspiration came from being rowed along the river, preferably at dawn, much as the tourists are today.

"From passing through the streets . . . I could have formed no conception of its beauty," wrote George, Viscount Valentia, in his *Voyages and Travels to India*, published in 1809 with paintings by the Egyptologist Henry Salt.

"The immense flights of steps, called the Ghauts of Benares, form a great ornament to the river face of the city; and, in the early part of the day especially, they present a very beautiful, though, at the same time, a very awful spectacle," wrote Captain Charles Elliot in his 1833 volume, *Views in the East*. Awful, that is, in the archaic sense of the word: inspiring wonder.

For these artists, the city conjured India's most dreamlike qualities. There was *Benares Illustrated*, a collection of exquisitely detailed drawings by James

Prinsep, founding editor of *The Journal of the Asiatic Society of Bengal* in Calcutta and fellow of the Royal Society, which found a wide audience through mass-produced lithographs. There were the paintings of Thomas Daniell and the aquatints of his nephew, William, in their six-volume *Oriental Scenery*. The Daniells' images of Munshi Ghat, Shivala Ghat, Raj Ghat, and Dasaswamedh Ghat were radiant in the early morning light, with the chaos corralled into a pleasing harmony. The city, in these renderings, did indeed seem immune to the ravages of the age of Kali. Every detail of the architecture was sharply rendered. There was no crumbling stonework in the Daniells' Benares. The pilgrims and priests were exotic but orderly, dotted around the ghats in modest numbers. The boatmen rowed with perfectly synchronized strokes like oarsmen in a Greek trireme, and there were no floating corpses.

I walked north along the ghats one day as far as the great seventeenth-century mosque that was built by the Moghul emperor Aurangzeb. Its soaring minarets, a favorite subject for artists like Captain Elliot, were long gone, one lost to an earthquake and the other removed for reasons of safety. A guard unlocked the gates for me, but the interior was banal, with cheap photographs of the Kaaba and the usual clocks showing the five daily prayer times. I walked south again for three miles to the southernmost of the eighty-four ghats that line the waterfront. Ram Ghat, Mehta Ghat, Ganesh Ghat, Bhonsale Ghat, Sankatha Ghat, Scindhia Ghat, to Manikarnika, where I stopped to look at the tank that Vishnu had dug with his discus and filled with his sweat and the marble plinth that bears his footprints, on the very spot where the universe was created.

Lalita Ghat, Mir Ghat, Man Mandir Ghat, and Dasaswamedh Ghat, the focal point of activity on the riverfront and the setting for the nightly worship of the river, the Ganga Aarti. The priests, sitting cross-legged as usual on platforms under their huge concrete umbrellas, were dispensing advice to pilgrims on the proper forms of worship.

Shitala Ghat, Mansarovar Ghat, Kedar Ghat, Harishchandra Ghat, Shivala

Ghat, Prabhu Ghat, Tulsi Ghat, named for the sixteenth-century poet-saint who had made his home here. The resident herd of water buffalo was cooling off in the shallows at Jain Ghat, and nearby an old man was palming Frisbee-size dung cakes for his cooking fire. At Tulsi Ghat, a yellow dog was sprawled out on the steps, dying slowly in the heat, its entrails hanging out gray and bloody. And finally there was Assi Ghat, with its great peepul tree and its famous Shiva lingam, the excellent Harmony Bookshop, where I would browse for hours, and the last cluster of tourist hotels and guesthouses.

The river's edge was little more than a clotted soup of garbage, shit, and ashes. By the time it reached Varanasi, India's most sacred river was also its filthiest. At intervals there were pairs of squat towers, pumping stations that were built in the 1970s to keep raw sewage out of the most sensitive stretch of the bathing ghats. One pair was painted pink and decorated with Technicolor images of Shiva and Parvati in their Himalayan abode.

After Assi Ghat, there was only a broad mud flat, and then the Assi itself, once a river and now just a nullah that drained raw sewage into Ma Ganga. Later I met R. K. Dwivedi, the chief engineer for the city's sewage treatment plant, a portly man in his sixties with a Cheshire cat smile. He was proud of his pumping stations. "From Assi Ghat to Raj Ghat, you will find almost nil flow coming into Ganga!" he exclaimed. "This is expected point of appreciation!"

"But what about the Assi nullah?" I asked. "It's right at the head of the bathing ghats."

He gave a nervous smile and looked at his shoes. "Question is difficult to answer," he said.

I made a northward detour through the crush of the old city. Hundreds of pilgrims were lined up for admission to the Golden Temple, watched over by glowering soldiers in khaki fatigues who carried antique rifles and swished their bamboo lathis, nominally on the lookout for Islamist terrorists. An old woman was howling as one of the soldiers beat her around the head and shoulders. From the soldier's shouts of "Mobile! Mobile!" it seemed that her offense was not to have surrendered her cell phone before entering the shrine.

Everywhere there were hand-painted signs on the walls. Places to eat, inspirational messages, services, and souvenirs.

BOWL OF COMPASSION CAFÉ

RAGA CAFÉ, SO NICE HOME

SALON DE THÉ VISHNU

PHULWARI RESTAURANTE & SAMI CAFÉ (MULTI COCINA)
ESPECIALIDAD EN COMIDA MEDITERRÁNEA

HOTEL DIVYA/CHOICE OF BEST FOOD FROM
TRANSPARENT KITCHEN

RECONCILE YOURSELF WITH OTHERS

GANGA IS SOURCE OF LIFE THANK YOU FOR LOVING AND
RESPECTING HER

LOVE FOR EVERYONE

CLEAN MIND

NO. 1 SHOP IN TRIPADVISER/VARANASI REMEMBRANGES,
CRYSTAL, ESSENTIAL OILS, MASSAGE, TEA MASALA,
MALA'S GEM STONE, ORNAMETN

YOGA TRAINING CENTER REF: LONELY PLANET 2003, 07

Back on the ghats, boys were flying kites. Touts whispered offers of hashish. Men pissed against walls. Boatmen called up from the river, offering their services to the hordes of visitors. The tourists studiously avoided making eye contact with each other, as if they resented the obvious fact that they were not the only ones to have discovered this strange and wondrous place. The tourists in the boats held up their smartphones, framing the exotica for photographs they would post on Facebook. I thought of Charlotte, Viscountess Canning, wife of the governor general and an amateur watercolorist, who came here in 1860: "I now feel I have seen *India*," she wrote. Perhaps that was what all the tourists were feeling, and perhaps, I had to admit, it was what I was feeling myself.

THE POETS OF BENARES

Before the hippies and the jet boaters, the Israeli draftees and the bungee jumpers and the Japanese package-tour groups, there was Allen Ginsberg and his lover, Peter Orlovsky. They arrived in Varanasi in December 1962, stayed a few days in the Cantonment, the old military district, and then rented an apartment for the next five months near Dasaswamedh Ghat.

The two men had spent several months in Calcutta before boarding the train to Varanasi, and after countless hours on one of Calcutta's cremation grounds, Nimtala Ghat, Ginsberg had come away with three fascinations that bordered on obsession: naked sadhus, the various mesmerizing ways in which a human body could be turned into "blackened meat," and the steady pulse of the river. As soon as they arrived in Varanasi, he went straight to Manikarnika and spent night after night there, squatting among the sadhus, legless from ganja, breathing in the smoke from the pyres, watching the sparkling reflection of the firelight on the water, writing down the sadhus' names and their backgrounds in his journal and adding rapturous fragments about the variety of their genitals—wrinkled, pouched, or free-swinging—and their oiled and ash-smeared chests.

In the daytime, like any other visitor, he strolled for hours along the ghats. The palaces put him in mind of Venice. Looking north at the grand sweep of the river toward the Raj Ghat railway bridge, he was reminded of the Grand Canal. At other times, he wrote, he felt like an American in Paris in 1920.

They rented the apartment from a Brahmin priest, Gaurishankar Tiwari. It was on the third floor of his house, a large room with whitewashed walls and a black stone floor and a primitive toilet. There were shelves for Ginsberg's books, and Orlovsky put a red pot-bellied Ganesha in one of the niches. Ginsberg hung a portrait of William Blake. Huge doors gave on to a balcony that was vulnerable to monkeys. There were views down to the ghats and the river in one direction; in the other, you looked down on a vegetable market. I'd strolled through this market more than once myself, and I imagined it hadn't changed much over the years, with cloths laid out on the ground for the rows of vendors to display their cucumbers, eggplant, tomatoes, purple-pink carrots, beans, daikon radishes, peppers, red cabbage and red onions, spiky gourds and bitter gourds, potatoes, beets, cauliflower, garlic and ginger, coriander and turmeric. Ginsberg liked to make vegetable soup, which he cooked on the balcony over a kerosene stove.

Orlovsky spent a good amount of time tending to the starving beggars and lepers who clustered in a nearby alleyway, much as he'd done at Mother Teresa's home for the dying in Calcutta. He fed them Ginsberg's soup and brought water to the lepers, since, being unclean, they were not allowed to go down to the river. Ginsberg posed them for photographs.

He got sick a lot. Lying in bed, prostrated by bouts of diarrhea, coughing his way through the winter fogs, tormented by a kidney infection, he listened to the bright ringing of rickshaw bells and the calls of the ice vendor and the knife sharpener and the tinny clang of a sadhu with finger cymbals. When he was healthy, the nights were devoted to cremations, drugs, and sex, splayed out in bed with Orlovsky "in all this morphined ease" and then plunging into wild erotic dreams that involved women and sometimes even babies as well as the men who were his usual preference.

At Christmas, they made a side trip to visit the Taj Mahal and Vrindavan, the birthplace of Lord Krishna. Ginsberg went on his own to Bodh Gaya, where Siddhartha had attained enlightenment. But by May, things had turned sour. Ginsberg had come to India looking for answers, but India, in its usual way, had provided just as many new questions. Orlovsky had grown weary of stoned sadhus. He shaved off all his hair and moved out to a place of his own. Ginsberg, in a funk, packed up his belongings and slept on the floor with a blanket and an inflatable pillow and surrendered to a fresh round of morphine-fueled dreams. One morning, the priest's son, Vijayshankar, came to wake him. Ginsberg rolled over, went back to sleep, and dreamed that the boy was climbing all over his body before finally settling "near my loins." The boy was fourteen.

One evening, at Dasaswamedh, just after the Ganga Aarti had ended, I met Vijayshankar Tiwari, who was now a quiet, equable man in his late sixties and had long since assumed his father's role as a hereditary pilgrimage priest, a *tirth purohit*. He was sitting on his platform under his concrete umbrella as he did every day, starting at eight in the morning with his worship of the river and then attending to the death rituals and other needs of pilgrims from families his ancestors had assisted for four generations. One of his two sons would eventually succeed him, but it wasn't clear whether it would be the one who worked in a local hospital or his brother, who worked for a cell phone company. Like all the pundits, Vijayshankar had his assigned territory, and he traced its outline with his finger. The demarcation lines were strict, and there was less competition for business than there had been in the past. "In the 1920s and 1930s, there used to be bloody fights among the *tirth purohits*," he said.

He poured me a thimbleful of chai from a plastic bag, and I asked him what he thought of all the foreigners who converged on Dasaswamedh for the aarti. He glanced at a young woman, German or Dutch perhaps, who was sitting on the steps puffing on a bidi and bopping to music from someone's radio. "It is our fate," he said philosophically. "Mother Ganga, all Hindus have faith in her, and the foreigner who comes here has faith in her also. On December 25, many of them come and distribute blankets and food to the poor people. I have not studied their Christian religion, but I know this is when their saint, Jesus, was born, and they decorate their churches on that day."

"Tell me about Allen Ginsberg," I said.

He smiled. "He had a beard and long hair, like dreadlocks almost. He was the only person my father ever rented our house to. I think with Allen he felt a sameness of mind. My father was deeply religious. He used to make *shivlings* out of Ganga clay and then immerse them in the river. I know Allen was a great poet. He has written a book even. He would bring his poems to present at Banaras Hindu University. Sometimes he would read them to people sitting at the chai stall at Assi Ghat. To me, he was a religious saint, like our poets Tulsi Das and Kabir Das, who also lived in this city."

I told him that in America there had been another poet of that kind, whose name was Walt Whitman. He had poured out his emotions as if he were talking directly with God.

"Allen was a very quiet and peaceful person, a very spiritual person," Tiwari went on. "He was often busy with his writing. Peter would spend more time down on the ghats with the beggars and the lepers. They would cook their meals on the balcony."

"The famous vegetable soup," I said.

He chuckled. "Yes, I remember Allen's soup. It had no taste. But they were always so happy about it, because it was their Western food. Here in India, we don't even eat soup! But one time I noticed that they were also feeding it to the lepers at Dasaswamedh. So I think the meal was not so special if he was offering it to the beggars also."

Two shy young men in T-shirts had sidled over to sit on the edge of the platform and listen to our conversation. "I am a poet also," one of them said to me. He recited one of his poems. It concerned a rickshaw wallah, how the unceasing rotation of the three wheels of his humble vehicle was a metaphor for the cycles of his life. I found it oddly moving.

"Peter came back once, you know," Tiwari said. "It was around 1978, during one of the worst floods in the history of Benares. First level of the house was under the water; one elephant could be easily drowned."

Peter had been rowed through the streets from Godaulia Crossing, a busy commercial intersection well over a mile from the river.

"He went up to the room where he and Allen had stayed, and everything was just the same. Nothing had changed, only some new netting on the balcony that kept the monkeys away. He brought a gift for my father."

"What did he give him?" I asked.

He smiled again. "An alarm clock."

"You know they had a problem in their friendship, just before they left Benares?"

"Yes, I know Peter was upset with Allen, so Allen went to see a famous religious person, Devraha Baba. The *baba* had a theory. He said to him, 'Time will heal.'"

I imagined the *tirth purohit* as a fourteen year old, with Ginsberg and Orlovsky sprawled in bed upstairs, shooting up morphine, sated with sex. I realized that it must never have occurred to him that they were gay and certainly not that he had featured in the poet's erotic fantasies, and I wasn't going to be the one to tell him.

THE LOST BOY

Varanasi is a city of posters, leaflets, hand-painted signs, messages scrawled on walls. One day, a section of the ghats around Dasaswamedh was plastered with notices that said,

MOTHER SEARCHING FOR HER SON, MISSING SINCE 1986

There were two photographs. The first showed a young man, perhaps in his midtwenties, with an open, ingenuous expression. In the second, his hair was longer, and he was dressed in a coat and tie. Next to him was his mother, middle-aged and middle class, smiling for the camera, wearing a white jacket with black piping and a double row of pearls. Underneath the photographs, it said, "This man's mother still believes he is alive and would like to see him if possible." There was a mobile phone number and an email address that ended in .fr.

It's not uncommon to see such notices in India. You find them placed where they are most likely to yield results. If the missing person is Indian, it's more likely to be around the bus terminals and railway stations. In places like Varanasi and Rishikesh, the notices will be posted in the places where foreigners come for yoga or drugs or enlightenment or voluntary escape from their former lives.

In the Himalayas, my nomadic companion, Manto, had told me stories of the disappeared. "Most of them are low-budget tourists. They come here and they get lost with some holy man in Gangotri or Rishikesh or somewhere else in Uttarakhand. They become religious. They take a Hindu name. Sometimes they destroy their passports. Sometimes they throw away their money also. They say that now they will be on their own; nature will protect them. Sometimes their families or friends or relatives come searching for them. They put advertisements in the newspapers, but still they are never traced. Some of them are found after being lost for more than a year; they are found in the forest, or in some temple, some hut, some cave. There was a German woman who got impressed by one of the holy men, and she became pregnant and delivered a son. She tried to convince the holy man to move to Germany, but he thought his divine power would be destroyed if he crossed the ocean."

The French boy would be in his fifties now. Perhaps he was with some swami in the high peaks, robed in saffron with his head shaved and a *sikha* topknot. Perhaps he had been robbed, murdered, and dumped in a ditch when he was still young and fresh-faced. You knew that his mother would never find him.

Near Manikarnika, somebody pressed a leaflet into my hand. It was printed on flimsy yellow paper with simple drawings of a man in various yoga poses and a text that read,

PATANJALI YOGA INATITUTE

TEACHING FACILITY OF ASTANG YOGA, HATH YOGA,

RAJ YOGA, KUNDLINI YOGA, TANTRA YOGA & MASSAGE

WELCOME TO MAKE OURSELF HIGHLY CONSUSE AND

HEALTHY ALSO TEACHERS TRAINING

The owner of the school, Arun Singh, was sitting on a blue patterned mat by the door, which opened directly onto the alleyway. At the far end of the room, another door opened onto a short flight of steps that led down to the river, past a stack of logs ten feet high, ready for the funeral pyres. There was a smell of smoke from the cremation fires.

Arun had a manner that was both diffident and mischievous, and he spoke with a slight speech impediment. He was one of those people you liked immediately. He was also a man of many parts: yoga teacher, classical musician, wood seller. He handed me a *kulhar*, a tiny cup of unglazed clay, which local potters turn out by the millions, and poured me some chai. The lip of the cup tasted of earth.

He said he had taken up yoga when he was fifteen, joining an ashram in Ranchi, the capital of Jharkhand state, which borders Uttar Pradesh to the southeast. "It was run by a *baba* who lived in a small cottage. A lot of disciples came to him and offered to make a big building for the ashram, but always he refused. He spent his whole life in that cottage or on the cremation ground. After that, I came to Varanasi, which was my parents' hometown.

Here I start first the wood business, but then yoga is in my inside, and slowly-slowly I start to teach yoga here. Many foreigners come to learn, to learn the energy of India."

His next students arrived for their hour-and-a-half lesson. They were two Japanese girls who looked to be twenty at most. They were training to be geriatric nurses. We went up the narrow staircase to Arun's yoga studio. The walls were painted lime green, and the shutters, which were pulled shut against the afternoon glare, were lipstick pink. There was a pile of tabla drums against one wall, and a sitar was propped up in a corner.

"First thing of yoga, always we speak truth, always we seek truth," Arun said to the girls when they had settled comfortably on the floor mat. "First kind of truth we call outward truth. If we believe in something and we are not going to change, this is called outward truth. Many people believe in God. If someone says, 'Show me God, where is God,' you are not able to show. But you *believe*, so this is outward truth. You understand?"

The women nodded politely. His accent was quite strong, and it wasn't clear that their English was up to the challenge.

"Second truth is called behavior truth. How we are behaving in our lives, what we speak, what we taste by mouth, what we smell by nose. Third truth we call imagined truth. We believe something, but maybe with time that will change. For example, you are both very good friends here. But after five years, will you be friends or not? This is imagined truth. Understand? Any question you have about truth?"

They said nothing, and Arun motioned them to stand up straight and breathe. *First there is a mountain.* One of the girls had a natural poise and elegance. The other was plain and awkward. Now *Vrksasana*, the tree. On one leg, foot to knee, hands steepled in the namaste, then raised above the head. The awkward girl toppled; they both giggled.

"All right, now we will take a rest," Arun said after he had shown them a few more basic poses. "Second part, yoga philosophy. Just a small philosophy. If I am explaining all, it will take six, seven hours. Nonviolence is the very heart of yoga. Because more peace, more love on this earth. But how could this come, this more peace and more love? Because violence comes so easily in our minds. Sometimes we need to protect ourselves, and at that time we need energy. If we use that energy, it is not violence. But if we hurt any living creature intentionally, that is violence. Even animals, birds, insects, every creature has the right to live on this earth."

They stood up again for some simple exercises. Posture and breathing. The awkward girl looked as if she would rather be somewhere else.

"In Western lifestyle, body is stiff, always you are sitting," Arun said. "So I will explain to you what the different exercises are and for what purpose. So when you go for your job with old persons, you could use that exercise maybe. Understand? Any questions?"

Downstairs, three twentysomethings were sitting on the floor playing guitars, a man and two women. Arun greeted them. The man gave me a surly look.

I asked Arun if he thought the Japanese girls would make good students. He made a gesture that said maybe, maybe not.

"A lot of students write in my memory book, I feel like you are my father-mother, and to read that is a great feeling," Arun said. "Sometimes one, two students write bad things. Some people think yoga is gymnastic only. But that does not make me upset. I do not feel angry. Just I say better you forget yoga, learn more gymnastic."

"Your memory book?"

He delved around in a cupboard that was cluttered with old ledgers and school exercise books and pulled one out at random. It was full of testimonial messages in Dutch, Italian, Czech, English, French, German, and they all said similar things. *Thank you, Arun. You are a magic person, Arun. Arun, you changed my life.*

He leaned across to the young guitarist and said, "Do you speak Hebrew?" The man grunted and said, "Of course."

"I will tell you this story," Arun said, ignoring his rudeness. "About twelve years ago, I had one Israeli student. He came to me with three, four friends. They all say he should learn yoga, but he has only one problem. He was a fighter in the Israeli army, and he had some steel wire inside his bone, his knee, and he meet with many doctors and they say, 'No, impossible, your legs will always be like this, they will never move.' And he said to me, 'I will promise to stay longer, one month even, if you can make my legs move like your legs.' That was a challenge, and I accept that challenge. That is some creation, some new thing I can give someone, just trying to flow the good energy. And in one week, what happens? He was able to sit in a half lotus."

GANGA FUJI RAGA

On a raised platform in the Ganga Fuji restaurant, an old man was playing the sitar. He had long, snow-white hair like corn silk, and he wore it twisted up in a bun on the top of his head. The restaurant, tucked away in one of the narrow alleys of the old city, was one of the few places in Varanasi where you could order a beer, which the owner would provide under the table, sort of, for a price. There was the usual polyglot crowd of diners, and the accelerating rhythm of the raga, propelled by the tabla drummer sitting cross-legged next to the old sitarist, was just background music for their meal. The musicians reminded me of the string quartets you see sawing away at Mozart in the lobby of five-star hotels. The music was intricate and beautiful, but no one was listening to anything but their own buzz of conversation.

It was a small room with eight tables, a couple of spastic ceiling fans, and dozens of messages from satisfied customers taped to the tiled walls, some of them with quickly scribbled cartoons of sitar players, kangaroos, the Taj Mahal.

We ♥ your *chai*!
Aussie, Aussie, Aussie—love, light, and blessings to you

There were messages in even more languages than I'd seen in Arun Singh's memory book: English, Polish, Spanish, Russian, Hebrew, Chinese, Latvian, and Estonian, even Tagalog from a Filipino visitor from Zamboanga del Sur.

The owner of the Ganga Fuji was a stocky man with black-framed glasses and a thick mustache. His name was Kailash, for the Himalayan abode of Lord Shiva. The sign outside the restaurant offered "Chinese Indian Continental Japanese Food Spanish Food," but when he stopped at our table to take our order, the only options he offered were vegetable curry or chicken curry, which came with an elaborate description of his special ingredients and cooking methods. We ordered the chicken. He disappeared into the kitchen.

More than half an hour passed. We were on our second Heineken. The raga had ended, and the old sitarist was packing up to leave. Eventually Kailash returned and set two steaming plates on the table with a pile of garlic naan.

"Chicken curry." He beamed.

I looked at the plate. It was a rough puree of vegetables. "This isn't chicken," I said.

"Yes, sir, this is chicken. You will see. Inside there are pieces."

I stirred it around some more and held up a spoonful for him to inspect. It was entirely chicken-free.

"This is chicken, sir."

I took a mouthful of vegetables. It was actually delicious. Why make an issue of it?

Kailash came back later to clear away the dishes. "I hope you enjoyed your meal, sir. The chicken curry is our very famous dish."

A couple of days later, I went back to see Arun Singh. I wanted to ask him about the reverse side of the leaflet about his yoga school. It said,

LISTEN TO VERY NICE MUSIC CONCERT

SUR SARITA THE MUSIC SCHOOL—BURNING

PLACE—MANIKARNIKA GHAT

"When I came to Varanasi, I start learning music also," he said. "I learn tabla, also I know a little bit sitar. I teach yoga for a few years more, then I organize teacher for tabla and sitar, then at a small-small distance I meet Jugal Giri Baba, and I ask him to join my group. He is our sitar teacher. Thousands of people we teach, many thousands. But come, you must meet Giriji. He is upstairs."

Why was I surprised that Arun's teacher turned out to be the sitar player from the Ganga Fuji? Although it has a million and a half people, Varanasi is in many ways a small town.

The old man was slumped on a mat against the lime-green wall, apparently asleep. His bun was untied, and his white hair straggled across his shoulders. When he heard us enter the room, he opened one eye. It was impossible to judge his age. He might have been an old sixty or a young eighty, his features worn into crags and furrows by decades of austerity, musical discipline, and a diet of rice and dal.

"Giriji has a little bit English, but mind communication he has very good," Arun said. "One to one, translator he does not need, never a student has complained."

The old man came to life, tossed his hair, and laughed. "I have been learning sitar for forty years," he said in Hindi. "I am still learning."

His right eye remained closed. Perhaps it was blind.

He said he had been born in a small town in the Himalayan state of Himachal Pradesh, a few miles from Dharamsala, the home of the Dalai Lama and the Tibetan government-in-exile. "I was very religious from a young age. I was never in the worldly things. No weddings or ceremonies. I left home and went from temple to temple."

Eventually his wanderings had taken him to Allahabad. He remembered that it was the year Nehru died, 1964. At the great mela he was initiated as a *sanyasi*, a renunciant. "You meet with three gurus," he said. "One is the guru of the *langoti* [the loincloth]. One gives you the necklace. The third one whispers your mantra in your ear. I wore the *kanthi*, the double-stranded necklace of tulsi [holy basil], which shows devotion to Lord Krishna."

"If you wear the *rudraksha* beads also, when you will die you will go to the realm of Shiva," Arun added. "You will not be managed by Yama, the god of death. As on the earth you have different countries like India and England and America, so also we have different *loks*, the worlds of the gods, like Shivalok, Vishnulok, Brahmalok.

"Giriji traveled all over India, followed all the main pilgrimage routes on foot. Gangotri, Kedarnath, Badrinath. He decided to stop cutting his hair. He wore only one woolen sheet, nothing else. He would walk ten kilometers, stop, and a devotee would always bring him bread with happiness."

Giriji looked up at me and smiled. "Here in Benares, also people give free food. Perhaps it would not be possible to travel like that in your Western countries."

I asked him if he had always been a musician. "Not until I moved to Mumbai. One day I went to the Mahalakshmi temple, where there was a devotee who was the secretary of Bal Thackeray"—the incendiary leader of the right-wing Hindu nationalist movement Shiv Sena. "He had a ticket to see Ravi Shankar play. He asked me if I wanted to go, and I was so touched by the music that I began to dream of sitar. Before that, I knew nothing of music. I knew only how to chant *Hare Krishna, Hare Rama*, in the temple. But Ravi Shankar was a divine incarnation, like Mahatma Gandhi. Gandhiji used to wear just a small *langoti* and carry a stick in his hand. But he chased away the English.

"In Mumbai, they always demanded money, forty rupees for a lesson. To learn for free, you had to come to Benares."

There was just one problem: his hair.

"It was a big obstacle to playing, because it was so long. When I stood up, it touched the ground. So I used to tie it up over my head, but then my neck started hurting because of the weight. So one day I decided to cut it off and tied it in a cloth and went out on a boat into the middle of the river and immersed my hair in the water."

In Varanasi, he found a new guru and music teacher, Pandit Shivaji Rao Kevaley, a master of the *santoor*, a kind of hammered dulcimer of Persian origin that was once favored by Sufi mystics. The pandit's ashram was in the heart of the old city, in a neighborhood called Khalispura, not far from the famous Brahmeshwar temple. Giriji had lived there in a small room for more than thirty-five years.

He perfected his art, rising at three each morning and practicing until five. Finally, he felt ready to teach others.

"Plus minus fifteen years we work together here," Arun said. "Most times it's easy to teach the students, because they have a background in other instruments, like guitar. Giriji just gives them one sitar, he takes another. He plays, they copy. He doesn't know how to write, so the student writes it down.

"Ninety-seven percent of our students are foreigners; 3 percent are Indians. Some students are really serious, some are for fun only. It is divided like fifty-fifty. Sometimes it is a challenge, sometimes it is like we become magic people. Many different kinds of feelings we got in this way. Students from Germany and France, they are very serious. Some of them stay here for a long time, maybe five months. People from Russia and America, they don't take time to sit down and really learn. In India, your teacher is more like a guru; you are very respectful. In those countries, they have a different system. 'He taught me music, I paid him. The relationship is over. Bye-bye.'"

I told Giriji how much I'd enjoyed his performance at the Ganga Fuji, even though it was sometimes hard to hear him over the chatter.

He laughed. That was how it was. You had to accept reality. "Even if it is only background music for them, it is the serious music I have learned. Sometimes they are paying attention, other times they are loud, they are laughing, they are doing their own cultural thing. But I have to do this for the sake of living. I cannot survive on private lessons. So many music shops and music schools have come up. There is huge competition. At the Ganga Fuji, they used to pay me a hundred rupees, now it is a hundred and fifty."

I didn't say so, but that was less than Kailash charged for a Heineken.

"Also, in the hot months—May, June—and when monsoon starts in July, foreigners don't come, so Giriji is completely out of work," Arun said. "During that time, he must live on what he has saved. He lives all alone, makes his own food. A day living for him is sixty, seventy rupees." A dollar.

"When a person is born, everything about him is written in a book," Giriji said. "How you will live and what you will do. Your life is predefined. Play music, live a religious life, be a renouncer. This is what is written in the book of my life."

I asked if he would be playing at the Ganga Fuji again that evening.

"No, tonight it will be the Brown Bread Café and German Bakery, tomorrow again at Ganga Fuji. These two places I play, one night one place, one night the other place. I play for one hour. If audience is there, fine. If audience is not there, fine. I can't worry about a lack of respect. I am not Ravi Shankar."

Later that evening, I saw him shuffling through the darkened alleyways of Khalispura, heading for the German Bakery. His sitar was slung diagonally across his back. It was as big as he was.

THE MOTHER'S LAP

The election circus was in town, and invoking the sacred river had become a weapon in the propaganda wars. I made my way through the congested streets to Beniya Bagh, a few hundred yards north of Godaulia Crossing, where supporters of the underdog were assembling. Supporters of the favorite pelted them with eggs and black ink, and later, when the underdog appeared in person, switched to stones.

Beniya Bagh was one of the few places in Varanasi that could legitimately be called a park, although now, in the long rainless months, most of it was trampled brown dust. The perimeter was marked off by palm trees with trunks painted in the colors of the Indian flag, saffron, green, and white. The park was in a heavily Muslim neighborhood, and many of the thousands who took their seats in front of the stage, all of them men, wore the knitted skullcap of their faith, the *topi*, and the all-white *shalwar kameez*.

They fidgeted in the stupefying afternoon heat for several hours until the candidate, Arvind Kejriwal, finally arrived, well after dark. His campaign slogan was "River, Weaver, and Sewer," which conveyed his allegiance to the Ganges, his commitment to cleaning it up, and his appeal to the Muslim community, which supplies most of the labor for the city's famous silk-weaving and sari-making industry. Kejriwal's harangues against official corruption had recently gotten him elected as chief minister of Delhi, although his first administration was a firework in the night, flaming out after seven weeks. (Later he would get a second crack at the job, which went a bit more smoothly.)

Candidates for office in India can run in any parliamentary constituency they like; the idea of carpetbagging doesn't raise many eyebrows. Narendra Modi of the Hindu nationalist Bharatiya Janata Party, who was also running to be prime minister and was the strong favorite, had chosen Varanasi. "Neither BJP has sent me, nor I have come here on my own," Modi said when he made the announcement. "I am here because Ma Ganga has called me. I am a small boy come to the mother's lap."

That evening in Beniya Bagh, Kejriwal attacked Modi for practicing "the politics of hate and of division," and it was true that the campaign had its fair share of dog whistles. Campaign posters showed Modi's face, smiling and resolute, against a backdrop of ghats and temples. Some of his supporters picked up the chant of *Har Har Mahadev!*, the traditional salute to Shiva, and turned it into *Har Har Modi!*, until their candidate took to Twitter and suggested that while he respected their enthusiasm, it was probably best not to say such things out loud.

As Kejriwal was denouncing him that night in Beniya Bagh, Modi was hundreds of miles away in the town of Hiranagar, in the disputed border territory of Jammu and Kashmir, where radical Islamists had just attacked a police station, leaving six dead. Modi pointed out that the chosen instrument of the jihadis was the AK-47. So let his opponent, whom he reviled as an agent of Pakistan and an enemy of India, be known, for his initials and the pitiful length of his tenure in Delhi, as AK-49. Posters soon went up in Varanasi showing Kejriwal's face photoshopped onto a portrait of Osama bin Laden.

This was the kind of talk that can get people killed in India and frequently does, especially in Uttar Pradesh. About 20 percent of the state's two hundred million people are Muslim—the proportion is even higher in Varanasi—and UP has an especially ugly history of communal violence, in which Muslims invariably take up most of the space in the morgue. The most notorious of all the mass killings occurred in 1992, when Hindu mobs tore down the Babri Masjid, a mosque in Ayodhya, eighty miles east of Lucknow, which had been built on the putative site of the birthplace of Lord Ram, the seventh avatar of Vishnu. That triggered riots all across India in which two thousand people died. Ten years later, Hindu militants from Gujarat, where Modi was chief minister at the time, traveled to Ayodhya, where they tried and failed to lay the foundation stone of a temple on the site of the demolished mosque. When their train returned to Gujarat, it was set upon by a Muslim mob.

Fifty-nine Hindus burned to death, and more than a thousand Muslims were massacred in reprisal.

Modi had never managed to shake off the accusations of complicity in the killings or to show much regret about them. It was like being a passenger in a car that ran over a puppy, he said; what need was there to apologize?

In a back alley in one of the Muslim neighborhoods of Varanasi, I met a grave, white-bearded homeopathic doctor named Abdullah Ansari, who was regarded as a trusted elder among the weavers that Kejriwal claimed to speak for. He ushered me through a heavy steel door into a windowless office and sat down behind a desk piled high with papers. The room shook to the rhythmic whirring and slamming of power looms on the other side of the wall, which made it hard to follow his soft-spoken mix of Urdu and heavily accented English. To my surprise, he didn't show any sign of anxiety about Modi's ascent.

"Muslims are twenty-five percent of population here," he said. "Mostly they are weavers of Banarsi silk. Even in twelfth century there were some, although most came four hundred or six hundred years later. History says some Sufis came here, also soldiers from Central Asia, and this was how they found their livelihood."

By and large, the two communities rubbed along together. The rough division of labor was that the Muslims wove, while the Hindus supplied the yarn and did the sewing and ran the retail end. "And so there is an economical cohabitat," the doctor said. Keeping the peace was a matter of mutual self-interest.

Varanasi had largely escaped the horrors of Partition, he explained, and for the next quarter century "there was not any condition that any Hindu-Muslim riot takes place. Until 1972 only. Reason was the matter of Aligarh Muslim University. Government was planning to remove *Muslim* from this name. So there was some violence. But the same process was also to abolish for Banaras Hindu University." He shrugged and smiled. In the end, both universities kept their names, and things quieted down for the next five years.

"Then takes place more violence here in this neighborhood because of worship of goddess Durga by Golden Sporting Club," he said. "When puja was over, images were brought to Ganga for immersion. But some Hindus wanted to go through a route where the local Muslims opposed that. Said you should follow the old road, and this became issue of riot. It was matter of pride, turning into chanting of religious slogans, then throw stone on each other. After that there have been many more, like in '91 and '92, but not mass killing."

"Meaning what?" I asked.

"In '91, maybe sixteen, maybe thirty," he said. By Uttar Pradesh standards, this obviously didn't qualify as mass killing.

"It was Kali Puja this time, same sort of reason why riot took place, but this was worst outbreak. Again some people got overexcited in the procession, and it hurt the feelings when they were going through the Muslim areas. A lot of people were killed in the cinema halls. They were watching films; they didn't know what was happening outside. Others were killed in the barbershops while they were getting shaved. But at present, there is no such type of action and reaction as in '91. Processions now go along main roads. Same with Muslim procession of tazia in month of Muharram. This is proper."

That left something I'd been a bit hesitant to bring up. Between 2006 and 2010, there were three bombings by radical Islamists in the city. The first had left twenty-eight people dead at a celebrated temple and the Cantonment railway station. The second had killed eleven, including four lawyers, outside the Varanasi Civil Court Building. In the third attack, a day after the anniversary of the demolition of the mosque in Ayodhya, a bomb went off near Dasaswamedh Ghat during the nightly Ganga Aarti, killing a two-year-old girl.

"Were there no reprisals against your community?" I asked.

"No, no one blamed us or attacked us for this," he said quietly. "There was no type of disturbance."

The egg- and stone-throwers at the Kejriwal rally didn't bother him. "One section of Mr. Modi's party works on policy of provocation," he said, "but they are not aware of the situation here in the time of Partition. Mostly Muslim people were downtrodden, they were poor farmers and weavers, they never support Pakistan, not a single Muslim from Varanasi is transferred to Pakistan. But this fact is not known to these people. They do not know their back history, or they are mentally prepared like that. Ignorance is the biggest blunder."

Not that the Hindus had any monopoly on ignorance, he said with a sigh. "When Pakistan loses game of cricket, it is celebrated by them. But also, when India loses, some group of Muslims will celebrate by lighting the firecrackers. These things are not beneficial. But we aware them about it in the mosques."

I had to admire Dr. Ansari's equanimity when the election results came in a few weeks later. Modi was elected prime minister in a landslide. He trounced Kejriwal in Varanasi, and his party swept the board in Uttar Pradesh. Statewide, fifty-five Muslims ran for office; not a single one of them was elected.

The new prime minister's victory celebration in Varanasi was a tour de force of stagecraft and media savvy. "The man is the master guru of the photo op," said a disgruntled former cabinet minister from the Congress Party, whom I met later in New Delhi.

With camera crews in tow, Modi began by visiting the Golden Temple, where he sprinkled water from the Ganges on the *shivling*. From there, he proceeded through the alleys of the old city to the river and took his seat at Dasaswamedh Ghat for the aarti. Ganga is the goddess who cleanses all sins, and Modi promised that night that he would honor her by cleansing her in return, with a national campaign that he called *Namami Gange*: Obeisance to the Ganges.

GURU OF THE WORLD

The mayor of Varanasi, Ramgopal Mohley, was a member of Modi's ruling party and a true believer, and I thought I'd ask him whether obeisance would be enough, since Indian governments had poured billions of dollars into cleaning up the tanneries of Kanpur and the sewers of Varanasi for the past thirty years with no discernible results. The first time I went to his office, he kept me waiting in an anteroom, where I twiddled my thumbs for half an hour while six men stood around a desk yelling at each other to the point where I thought ambulances might end up being called. Eventually the mayor emerged, ignored me, strode into the street surrounded by aides and petitioners and bodyguards, climbed into an SUV, and drove off.

The next day, when I tried again, he was all smiles, gold rings, and extravagant gestures. "Since our Independence, the engine of this country has been defunct," he said, waving his arms in the air. "But Modi has put in the lubricant. Now we are in second gear. Next year it will be third gear!"

Yes, previous governments had failed, but there would be no more failures under Modi. "He is a devotee, he is determined. This is the reason! When Modiji won, he said, 'Ma Ganga has called me!' The second thing he said was that when Kashi, Benares, was guru of the nation, India was guru of the world."

It was a little like listening to a North Korean official singing the praises of the Dear Leader.

I wondered what he thought of the minister who had been put in charge of the cleanup, the veteran BJP militant Uma Bharti. She was, to put it mildly, an arresting choice. As a child, Bharti had been regarded as a religious prodigy, leaving school after sixth grade with the intention of becoming a "spiritual missionary." She was often referred to as a *saddhvi*, the female honorific equivalent of a sadhu, and like Modi himself, her involvement with the jagged edge of Hindu nationalism had begun when she joined the militant Rashtriya Swayamsevak Sangh, the RSS, as a teenager. Her incendiary speeches to the mobs in Ayodhya in 1992 had made her notorious. When a commission of inquiry later accused her of inciting violence, Bharti was defiant. "I am not apologetic at all," she said. "I am willing to be hanged for my role." Indeed, she went on, "It could be said that the demolition of Babri Masjid was a victory for the Hindu society."

When Bharti was elected to parliament in 2014, she was still facing five serious criminal charges in the Uttar Pradesh courts, including rioting, unlawful assembly, and "statements intended to cause public mischief." In a separate case before the Supreme Court, she stood charged with criminal conspiracy.

The mayor thumped his fist on the desk. "Everyone likes Umaji!"

Even the Muslims? I asked. Given her history, wouldn't they be justified in feeling a little apprehensive?

"No, no, no!" He waved away the question and brought the conversation back to the river. "Modiji has made one ministry to be in charge under her. Everyone should listen to the orders of one person; then things will get done. If ten different people are giving opinions, things will not work. Look at the determination of Modi!"

It would happen today, it would happen tomorrow, it was happening already. The promises of progress tripped over each other in wild contradiction. "By next year, you will start seeing the cleanness, up to 20 percent!" he exclaimed. "In another year, you will start seeing the real cleaning. I am telling you now that next year, Ganga will be cleaned by 50 percent. In another three years, the river will be cleaned 70 percent."

The ghats would be swept clean. You could never stop the faithful tossing flowers into the river, but now they would be collected by modern machines like oil-skimming booms and turned into incense. Garbage would be trucked to a new waste-to-energy plant, as the Canadians and Germans do. It was important to learn from such foreign examples.

"We went to Japan, both Modiji and I," the mayor said. "Kyoto and Kashi, there are similarities. Kyoto is also a city of narrow lanes and temples. Under their lanes, there are three subway lines. Over the lanes, there are flyovers."

Although, of course, he conceded, India was not Japan. Also, "Kyoto has three hundred and thirty temples, and here we have more like thirty-three thousand." Thirty-three gods, or thirty-three million. The number seemed to have a magical significance.

"But come back, you will see some result in two years," he said, looking at his watch. "Movement has started; it is like a revolution. Umaji has said if Ganga is not cleaned in three years' time, she might do samadhi." *Webster* defines the word as "a state of deep concentration resulting in union with or absorption into ultimate reality." Sometimes, Pinku added later, it involved climbing into a ditch and burying yourself alive.

THE FIELD OF FULFILLMENT

After seeing it three times, I was tired of the Ganga Aarti. It was dusk. The seven young priests had taken their places, each on his separate platform, preparing for the ceremony, which was as scrupulously choreographed as a production number by Busby Berkeley. They would chant hymns, blow conch shells, light incense, ring prayer bells, swing their heavy brass lamps in synchronized clockwise circles. All seven of them were drop-dead handsome, immaculately coiffed, dressed in identical cream-colored dhotis and kurtas. A flotilla of tourist boats had squeezed up against the river's edge, and their camera flashes were popping like strobe lights. There were Israeli kids fresh from military service, Japanese tour groups in white face masks like a posse of surgeons on their way to the operating room, back-packers on extended spring break, stolid Americans of a certain age with serious-looking telephoto lenses, superannuated hippies with dreadlocks that Shiva himself might have envied, fresh from an afternoon at the Bowl of Compassion Café or the Salon de Thé Vishnu. Temple touts were circulating among the crowd on the steps, and a little girl of six or seven was hawking lamps, *diyas*, that would become a flotilla of tiny lights in the river when the ceremony was over. A young European woman with a peaches-and-cream complexion and a diaphanous yellow dress was sucking on a joint and gazing up at one of the sadhus in a kind of erotic trance.

Pinku gave a dismissive wave of his hand. "This is the Bollywood version of aarti," he said. "If you want to see the real thing, you should go to the Shree Atma Veereshwar temple. Tell the priests I sent you."

Finding the place was neither easy nor especially pleasant. It was tucked away in the dense labyrinth of alleyways known as the Siddha Kshetra, the Field of Fulfillment, and that meant negotiating the steep steps at Scindhia Ghat, which served as a de facto open-air toilet—human, canine, and bovine. Varanasi was experiencing one of its recurrent power cuts, and the only light along the ghats came from the funeral fires at Manikarnika. I had to pick my way around a good number of recumbent cows and piles of dung before I found the cramped doorway to the temple.

After Varanasi's principal temple was torn down on the orders of the emperor Aurangzeb in 1669, Shree Atma Veereshwar served for many years as the city's most important shrine. The worship of its *shivling* is said to be the equivalent of worshipping thirty million lingams in other places. It is believed to confer special blessings, notably the gift of a son to the childless.

The inner sanctum was a small, square room, with walls and pillars painted the color of blueberry yogurt. The floor was a black-and-white tile checker-board, and the ceiling was bright yellow with a couple of fluorescent strip lights. A small electric fan barely stirred the humid air. The lingam itself, nestled in a silver-plated yoni, was enclosed in a sunken well surrounded by an ornate brass rail.

The chief priest, whose name was Munmun Maharaj, had already arrived. He was a tall, heavyset man in his thirties, with the three horizontal white stripes of the Shiva devotee daubed on his forehead and long, heavily oiled hair that was pulled back in a bun. He wore yellow-and-white robes, seamless and unstitched as a token of purity. He was already hard at work preparing the lingam for the ceremony. He cleaned it successively with water from the temple well, then with curd, then again with water, sluicing the liquid into a thin gray slop that the pious regard as *charnamrit*, nectar from the feet of the gods. After wiping down the lingam, he anointed it with sandalwood paste and attar of roses, shaping the mixture into waves and ripples like a pastry cook decorating a pie, then surrounded it with flowers, patterning them in tiger stripes intertwined with strips of tinsel, before finally placing a carmine rose and a sprig of leaves on top of the entire confection.

Three other priests joined him at intervals, filling the spaces around the lingam with candles, handbells, bananas, apples, oranges, grapes, boxes of sweets, sticks of incense, and ten-rupee bills. It was all very relaxed and businesslike. They chatted and laughed at each other's jokes as they worked. It took a full hour before everything was ready, and by that time, about twenty worshippers had shown up, all male, each of them ringing a hanging bell once as he passed through the doorway. There was a straggle-bearded sadhu in saffron, a pilgrim in white robes with the sacred thread draped across his left shoulder, a cluster of men in nondescript work clothes, and a boy who might have been eleven or twelve wearing a T-shirt that said, "BE NICE OR I'LL SEND YOU TO SCHOOL."

About half the men seemed to know all the Sanskrit verses by heart, and they joined in the rhythmic chanting as it intensified and the temple bells rang louder and faster. The room was growing hot and claustrophobic. I began to sweat, and I could feel Agnès shifting uncomfortably on the stone bench next to me. Suddenly she whispered that she needed a breath of air and slipped quietly out of the room.

Afterward, one of the priests, a stocky middle-aged man with a bristling black mustache, bore down on me.

"Come, we will talk," he said. It was less an invitation than an order. He led me into an adjoining room and motioned me to squat on the stone floor. The other three priests joined us and formed a circle, munching on leftover sweets. It was not clear to me whether they spoke English.

"Why you have brought woman here?" the stocky priest demanded.

I told him that a friend had recommended that I come to the temple. He'd said it would be all right.

The priest nodded in recognition of Pinku's name. But he was still suspicious. "But is it a bad day? If it is one of her three bad days, woman can pollute the temple."

I told him that I honestly had no idea whether today was one of her three bad days; she was just a friend. But he seemed to have lost interest in the subject. Instead he began to mutter about the injustices that foreigners like me heaped on Hindus. "An American president can kill thousands of Mohammedans in Iraq," he said, "and no one will show the finger to him." But whenever a Hindu raised a hand in self-defense against a Muslim, the world raised an outcry.

The other priests were observing us with detached curiosity. One of them gave me a finger-size banana to eat. The temple felt like the wrong place to pursue this line of conversation. Perhaps we could meet later? He thought this was a fine idea. He told me that his name was Ravindra Sand and that I could find him at his home in the old city.

TWO BROTHERS

I stopped on the way to the priest's house to buy a small courtesy gift at Rasvanti, the most famous confectionery shop in the city. India has a famously sweet tooth. *Rasgulla*, white balls of buffalo curd cheese and sugar. Deep-fried, neon-orange *jalebi*, scooped from vats of boiling oil, dripping with syrup. Creamy *rasmalai*, fragrant with pistachio. Rasvanti—Juicy Sweet—had become famous in the 1930s for its orange, white, and green creations, made in the colors of the Indian National Congress as a surreptitious protest against British rule. Men were sitting cross-legged on rush mats under a poster of Hanuman, grating coconut into large metal trays. The owner packed me up a box of lozenge-shaped green *burfi*, rich with cashews and ghee and garnished with silver leaf.

Ravindra wasn't home, but his younger brother, Arvind, invited me to come in and wait. "Sit," he said. "We will take tea, and then we will talk."

Arvind was bouncing his six-month-old daughter on his knee. He told me that she had been born at an auspicious time, on the birthday of Lord Ram. Vedic researchers had traced the birth of the god back to January 10, 5114 BC, in the town of Ayodhya, although because of the vagaries of the lunar calendar, the date varied from year to year. This year it had fallen on March 28.

"Sands are one of the oldest families in Varanasi, you know," he said. "We are Saraswat Brahmins, considered best Brahmins out of all categories."

His wife poured the tea, laid out the usual plate of biscuits, and withdrew silently.

"Right now, I am thirty-nine years," he went on. "I have always been in this custom and this religion. In America, people are not born with these things like Lord Ram in their blood. Except, of course, Christian fundamentalists brought up on Bible."

I told him how I'd met Ravindra, and he said the Shree Atma Veereshwar temple had been the focus of his brother's emotional life for twenty years. His own had taken a less spiritual direction. He was the deputy general manager of the local office of an American pharmaceutical company, Abbott India, which had a reputation for driving its workers hard, sometimes to the point of suicide. Ravindra's story was one of devotion and disappointment. He had craved a government job—for the salary, the prestige, the pension, the health insurance. Instead he was forced to toil as a humble school administrator. "He has potential above 80, 90 in any field," Arvind said. "But what he is doing now is below, say, 40 percent. On religion he would score 60, 70 at least. I am more like 30, 40 on this. Now he is married, and he is having one child also. But he doesn't want to be in this family life. He just wants to be spiritual, meditative. Even after fifty-five, after daughter's marriage, he will go from this life, he will go for *sanyas*"—the path of renunciation.

Whatever the differences between the two brothers, they seemed as interchangeable as Tweedledum and Tweedledee on the matter of Muslims. I told Arvind what Ravindra had said to me at the temple, and he reacted so strongly that his little daughter startled in his lap. "That is very correct. I also have very strong opinions. All the Muslims, they are born in India, but they are not authentically with us. Why they are not changing their roots? Why they are not participating in my country, which is India? And why the terrorist is only the Mohammedan? This is what I feel, what all Indians think."

It was apparent that by Arvind's criteria, Muslims did not qualify as Indians in good standing.

"We are having one, two kids only. And they are having six, seven, ten, like anything. After thirty years they will be in the majority, and we will be in the minority." He pointed to his daughter. Exhibit A.

Neither of us said much for a minute or two. We sipped our tea. He chucked the little girl under the chin and made little affectionate noises. Then he leaned forward, as if sensing that I might have been offended by what he'd said. There was something open and ingenuous in his manner that tempered his prejudices.

"Not 100 percent Muslims are bad," he said, before pausing again and fine-tuning the statement. "Definitely what I feel is that 1 percent of the Muslims are very good."

"What would be an example of a good Muslim?" I asked.

He considered the question.

"Aamir Khan," he said eventually. "He was an actor. He has a program, *Satyamev Jayate*, on TV every Sunday. He is giving advice. 'Don't run on the rat race,' he says. He made a film, you must see that film also. Being a Hindu, I am having the opinion he is the best person."

Ravindra was back, and he joined us, beaming. He gestured at Arvind. "My brother is a gem of a person," he said. "I am a very short-tempered person. I am not cooperative at all. Muslims? Should I be honest? I do not like Muslims at all, and Modi also is the same. I am not going to interrupt in your belief, but you are not the only ones on this earth only! I ask a Muslim a very simple question. 'Do you believe in a God?' 'Yes.' Second question. 'Does your God have any form or shape or size?' He says no. 'So why do you go to the mosque to pray to the God? You call us kaffir because we worship idols?' He says yes. So I ask him, 'Why do you go the Kaaba and circumambulate? We do it by our left hand, you do it by your right hand. And you call us idol worshippers. There are fifty-eight Muslim countries where you cannot eat pork. But you have a slaughterhouse where cows are being killed for flesh, and for us cow is like a goddess.'"

I wondered how he'd come up with the number fifty-eight. The longest list I ever found was fifty-one, and that included the French overseas department of Mayotte, which I hadn't even heard of.

Ravindra had all the symptoms of Wikipedia addiction, with a special gift for non sequiturs and free association. The war in Syria. Adolf Hitler and Germany's misappropriation of the sacred swastika. The medicinal qualities of the neem tree, also stolen, this time by foreign pharmaceutical companies. The rise of China. The decline of America. The Kennedy assassination. The preposterous wealth of the Gulf oil states. Tamerlane and the Mongol hordes. Bill and Hillary Clinton. He stopped for a moment to catch his breath. "I am not saying that all Hindus are good. Although we are God-loving and God-fearing people, we also desire toward money, toward fame, toward sex. But it is our history that we never try to conquer anybody."

Surely, I must understand that such feelings were especially justified here along the Ganges? He conceded that one might argue that Islam had arrived peacefully in the south of India or the western coast, carried on the trade routes that crisscrossed the Arabian Sea. There were also Sufis here and there; there was nothing wrong with them and their strange whirling dances. But Islam had been brought to the great Gangetic Plain with the horse and the sword, borne on waves of Mughal invaders who swept down like a pestilence from the steppes of Central Asia, leaving the wreckage of Hindu temples in their wake.

"There are three sacred places for Hindus," Ravindra said. "Ayodhya for Lord Ram, Mathura for Lord Krishna, and Varanasi for Lord Shiva. All three of these cities are in UP. And these three gods are worshipped all over India."

It had been difficult for Arvind to break into his brother's torrent of words, but he also wanted to have his say. "Have Hindus ever been involved in any crime, any explosion, any riot?" he demanded.

The last thing I'd wanted was to get dragged into a political argument, but what about the destruction of the Babri Masjid mosque in Ayodhya? Or the reprisal killings of more than a thousand Muslims in Gujarat during Narendra Modi's tenure as chief minister of the state?

Both brothers regarded me as if I were a zoological curiosity, a foreigner of the particularly obtuse variety.

"Okay, one mosque was demolished by Hindus," Arvind said. "That was not correct. What I think, God is everywhere. You are a God. I am also a God. Everybody is a God. But demolition is not the issue. Demolition is bad, but the Mohammedans have demolished each and every temple in India. Our ancient temples here they have destroyed fifteen, sixteen times. They have that feeling in their blood. They think Hindus are their enemy, as well as of course you also."

"Europe and America have their own spectacles by which they want to see the world," Ravindra said. "They are living in their make-believe world. Modi, in the eyes of America, he is a beggar, he cannot be a chooser. What happened in Gujarat? Fifty-nine Lord Ram pilgrims were returning to their native land, and they all died. Now it is known that two hundred liters of petrol were bought days before. It was cold-blooded murder, predetermined. Later, see, if a person can slap you once, and I reply him with four slaps, you are going to blame me for the fighting? It is not correct. I am sorry to say, my dear friend, these Muslims are not comfortable anywhere."

HERITAGE

One day, Pinku took me out on his battered motorbike to the Mahmoorganj district in the western part of the city to meet his friend Navneet Raman, the chairman of the Banaras Cultural Foundation. With a small number of friends, including the owner of the excellent bookstore at Assi Ghat, they organized "heritage walks" around parts of the old city that the tourists rarely visit.

We pulled over by a high wall. Behind the gates was an expanse of immaculate lawn, and behind that an immaculate white-painted building with parapets and colonnades and balconies and balustrades, all of them immaculate. This was the Raman Niwas Palace, home to eight separate subfamilies of the Raman clan, including Navneet and his German wife, Petra, who worked in marketing for Hewlett-Packard before moving to India.

Navneet was in his office. His white kurta was as immaculate as the palace.

He would sometimes call the city Varanasi if there was a technical need to do so—if he was talking, for example, about the Varanasi Municipal Authority or the local chapter of the Indian National Trust for Art and Cultural Heritage (INTACH), where he had once served as convener. Otherwise, he preferred the old name, Benares.

The Ramans are Benares aristocracy, zamindars who once owned more than fifteen hundred villages in Uttar Pradesh and neighboring Bihar. The family can trace its lineage back to an ancestor who was the finance minister of the Afghan king Sher Shah Suri. Sometime around 1540, this personage was charged by the monarch with laying out the Sarak-e-Azam, the Grand Trunk Road that runs from the Khyber Pass to Calcutta. In 1545, when the king died, the minister built an elaborate mausoleum for him in the town of Sasaram, eighty miles east of Benares.

The motto of the Raman dynasty was "Service to Humanity." According to a family history, they "considered their estate populace to be like their own children and were dearly adored and loved by the masses." For hereditary zamindars of the period, it must be said that this was not exactly typical. But whether the bond with their tenant farmers was based in fact or just family myth, the Ramans' patronage of the arts was a matter of public record.

What was remarkable about this was that in the firmament of stars around the Raman Niwas Palace, Hindu and Muslim musicians had equal standing. They included the sitarist Ravi Shankar and the master of the simple, oboe-like shehnai, Ustad Bismillah Khan.

Though his family was Bengali, Shankar was born in Benares. At ten, he left for Paris, traveling with his brother Uday's dance troupe. When he returned, he came to see Navneet's grandfather, who by then was the mayor of the city, and declared that he would like to learn the sitar. A year later, having become proficient in the instrument, Shankar came back and said he wanted to honor him with his first concert.

"My grandfather told him it must be in our family temple," Navneet said. "All the great musicians, whenever they came to Benares, they always performed there and in the house. Ravi Shankarji brought George Harrison here and told him, 'This is the house where I learned sitar.'"

Perhaps it was his Bengali origins that led the local musical elite to turn their backs on Shankar. Or perhaps they simply resented the fact that his genius so far outshone their own. Whatever the reason, Navneet went on, "They chased him out. They didn't like him because he was not part of their gang. He felt so humiliated that he vowed never again to play sitar in Benares. But then he flew in from France to play on the first death anniversary of my grandfather, to say, 'This is the man because of whom I learned to play sitar.' And that was the last time he played here."

Later, he talked about Bismillah Khan. "They have very superinflated egos, these Benares musicians, other than this great man." It was the greatest of all the city's many paradoxes: that in the spiritual center of Hinduism, the person who best incarnated its spirit was a Muslim—and one who was not even born here but in the neighboring state of Bihar.

"He was like the jewel in the crown of Benares," Navneet said. "He maintained the Qu'ran, but he transcended religious boundaries. He was so simple, yet so deep and so philosophical. Ravi Shankarji said, 'Why not move to America?' but he said, 'If you can bring my Ganga Ma to America, I will move to America. Otherwise, leave me in my Benares.' So let him be by his Ganga Ma. There is all this talk about building a big monument at the place of his burial, but let the soil be there without human intervention. No marble structure. Maybe if someone wants to do a tribute, he can bring some *gangajal* and pour it on the grave, so close to the Mother Ganga."

We walked over to the small art gallery that Navneet and Petra had opened a decade earlier. Like everything else here, it was white and sparklingly clean, and there was a small, climate-controlled archive that housed a historical collection of paintings and photographs of Benares. Small framed images were spaced evenly along the walls of the gallery: architectural details, doorways, fragments of the city's heritage. He said the novelist Geoff Dyer had visited when he was working on his book *Jeff in Venice, Death in Varanasi*, and had remarked that the gallery could hold its own with anything in London or New York. But today the room was empty. Navneet shrugged. "Maybe I have ten feetfall in a one-month exhibition," but it didn't matter. He felt the same way about the heritage walks that he and Pinku conducted. "We maybe do one walk a month. Even if we take only ten people a year, I can safely say that the ten we take will go home appreciating that Benares is more than seeing the sunrise from a boat and going to the Ganga Aarti."

One hundred thousand foreign tourists come to Varanasi each year, he said. "And we have this strange community of so-called Indian guides who themselves know nothing about the city. They think the tourists are fools, so we can make a fool out of them, we'll take a boat ride, ha-ha-ha, and we'll take their money, and they will go back to their hotel and they will have some breakfast."

"One of the agencies is offering a seven-day Varanasi-Lucknow package for $1,200," Petra said. "It's for people from the U.S., Europe, the Middle East, and Beijing."

"These are packages of stupidity," Navneet said.

The word *stupidity* came up a lot whenever he talked about the various proposals that had been made over the years to protect the city's heritage. He checked off the folly of one agency after another, accompanying each one with a roll of the eyes, a curl of the lip, or a bemused shake of the head.

"A Japanese bank proposed a road along the ghats of Benares, with seven bridges crossing to the other side.

"The World Bank proposed that all the ghats should be painted in one color! But the beauty of Benares is that in those seven kilometers you are walking through the encyclopedia of Indian architecture. Different times, different styles, different motives, different colors. If that's the level the World Bank has stooped down to, better to keep the World Bank out of India!

"In the name of heritage, the government wanted to build concrete jetties on the ghats so the boats can be organized and parked. I told them that every month the water level is different. The jetties will be too high, so you can't get into the boat, or they will be underwater. They wanted to do sound-and-light shows on the ghats. Huge amounts of money in the name of heritage! Sound-and-light shows? I said, 'This is stupidity!'"

During his tenure as chairman of the Varanasi chapter of INTACH, he grew so frustrated with this nonsense that he began writing letters to the prime minister. For this he was removed from his post without a hearing. "As a citizen of this planet, I can write to the president of America also!" he exclaimed. "You cannot say to me, 'Navneet Raman, you cannot speak a word, you are not a free man anymore!'"

And that was the end of Navneet Raman's career in the world of officialdom.

THE FOREST OF REMEMBRANCE

Navneet texted me one evening to ask if I'd meet him at six o'clock the next morning to take a boat across to Maghar, the east bank of the Ganges, and plant some trees. Maghar is a famously inauspicious place. Anyone unfortunate enough to die there will be reincarnated as a donkey.

We hailed a boatman at Assi Ghat, and as we pulled away from the steps, the sun rose and flooded the curving waterfront of ghats, temples, and palaces with the saffron glow of dawn. It was mid-May, and you could tell already that another hundred-degree day was on the way. The monsoon was still two months off, and the river was low and murky. Indeterminate objects floated by in the surface film.

I mentioned the mayor's idea of recovering the flowers that were dumped in the river and use them to manufacture incense. Navneet snorted. Turn them into incense after they'd been sitting around in a slop of shit and ashes? More stupidity.

Some years earlier, he said, he'd had the notion of asking the priests at the Kashi Vishwanath Mandir, the Golden Temple, if he and his friends, the heritage walkers, could recycle the flowers that were brought there as offerings. They could be composted. They could be used to reenergize the patches of dusty ground and stunted trees that passed for parks in Varanasi. But as the city's most important shrine, the temple was managed by the government. Written applications had to be made, meetings requested with the relevant officials. *Flowers?* The bureaucrats were mystified. If they'd offered to pave the parks over with cement, it might have been a different matter. That would have meant bringing in contractors, opportunities for kickbacks. So Navneet approached the smaller, privately owned temples. The priests there also shook their heads. The gods would take a dim view of such a project; tossing the flowers into Ma Ganga was the proper thing to do.

Our mission this morning, Navneet explained, was a good example of how the few people who cared about the health of the river had to work here. A small end-run around vested interests and the stupidity of bureaucrats. There had only ever been one person in Benares who could have been described as a professional defender of the Ganges. He was a man who was uniquely able to reconcile the physical and metaphysical concepts of purity, an engineer priest named Veer Bhadra Mishra, a professor at Banaras Hindu University and the hereditary mahant of the Sankat Mochan Temple, which is dedicated to Hanuman. Mishra was as much at home giving TEDx talks to audiences in New Delhi as he was taking his holy dip in Ma Ganga each morning. The foundation he created—although *foundation* is something of a misnomer; in truth it was closer to a one-man enterprise—collected data on fecal coliform bacteria in the river. During the lean period, when the river was at its lowest, as it was now, this could be several thousand times above safe levels. All around us, pilgrims were bobbing and ducking in the water.

"He was a great man with a great vision," Raman said. "Anyone who went to meet him at his house at Tulsi Das Ghat always brought some *laddoo* and some *channa* and some glass of water, and I have sat and had lighter moments with him. He was truly human in that sense. But isn't there a saying, fault, thy name is human? He feared that people would lose their relationship to the river if he said it was polluted. I told him, if you say that the river is your mother, and your mother is sick, you have this authority. If you could only say, at some function on the ghats with a hundred thousand people listening to your words, that until every Hindu stops throwing garbage into the river at Benares, you will fast unto death."

But Mishra was a stubborn man, and now he was gone, cremated on the plinth reserved for notables at Harishchandra Ghat in the presence of just such a crowd, his ashes consigned to the river to mingle with the rest of the black slurry. His son, Vishwambhar Nath Mishra, had inherited the priesthood, and I'd spent an hour or two with him one evening at the temple. I'd found him warm, earnest, and eloquent, with flashes of understated humor. He'd recounted the river's woes, the familiar litany. He said Modi had requested a fifteen-minute audience with him during the election campaign but had ended up staying much longer. But the younger Mishra would probably have been the first to admit that his father had left him with shoes that were too large to fill.

When we reached the far side of the river, we stepped out of the boat onto a broad expanse of dried mud. Raman reached into the bag he'd been carrying and scooped out a handful of shiny, dark purple seeds the size of pistachios. They were coastal almond, *Terminalia catappa*, known locally as the sewage tree because it has the ability to filter pollutants. Later there would also be aromatic red sandalwood and *harshingar*, night-blooming jasmine, a tree sacred to Shiva.

We walked back and forth along the narrow strip of scrubland above the flood line, scattering the seeds to the left and right. Raman had originally suggested the idea to the government forest department. No interest. More stupidity.

"Most people come to Benares to pay last respects to the memory of their near and dear ones who have passed away," he said. "So I thought that on this bank of the river we could make a *smriti*, a forest of remembrance. This is my guerrilla warfare. I am not doing it for Mr. Modi.

"So many people come here to cremate their dear ones," he continued. "Afterward, you could put some of the ashes into the river and some into the base of a nice tree. Eventually, over the years, you could put benches here, you could take a boat across in the evening, you could make a walking trail, people could exercise, elders could sit quietly with their grandchildren and talk about the city they see in front of them. Traditions would be passed on. They would sit here and say, 'See, this is a tree I planted for my wife or my father.' And in this way, we could add to the cosmic energies of Benares."

He acknowledged that this vision lay far in the future, and I found myself thinking back to Ajay Puri, the businessman priest in Uttarkashi. When would the age of Kali end, I'd asked him, this era of vice and degradation? Four hundred and thirty-two thousand years, he'd answered.

I asked Raman if he ever got discouraged by the slow pace of change, and he shrugged. "I am having faith in the great lord of our land, Shiva. When he gets annoyed, all the other gods put together cannot stop him from doing the dance of destruction. I have faith in his judgment."

We'd scattered the last of the seeds, and we walked back toward the boat.

"India is a land of discouragement," he said. "If you're not discouraged by the harsh summers, then you are discouraged by the cow eating your plant, or the motorbike or tractor or car that is running over your plant, or the neighbor who is plucking the leaves from it just for fun as he is going by. If you can't deal with discouragement, India has no place for you. You might as well leave."

PART THREE

DELTA

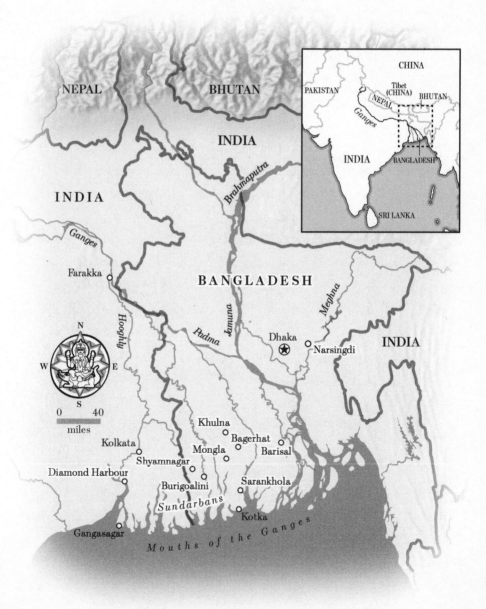

BORED IN BIHAR

A confession: I never set foot in the state of Bihar, which begins just east of Varanasi and sprawls for three hundred miles or so to the border with West Bengal. Few people do. It may be the fear of its reputation for crime and violence; it may be fear of boredom. It may be the prejudice born of years of bad publicity, that if you've seen the poverty, caste prejudice, and corruption of Uttar Pradesh, the towns and villages of the Gangetic Plain in Bihar don't have a lot to add. But avoidance of Bihar is nothing new. Even the great travel writers of the nineteenth century didn't find much to say about it; their tacit message was that apart from two or three obligatory curiosities that wouldn't have rated a *mérite un détour* in the Michelin Guide, they went there only because of the convenience, since the river ran through it.

Fanny Parkes, a twenty-eight-year-old Welshwoman, daughter of an army officer, arrived in Calcutta with her husband, Charles Crawford Parkes, a minor functionary of the East India Company, in November 1822. In her first flush of innocence, she found the climate delicious. It was the cool beginning of the short Calcutta winter, and her servants spread fine carpets from Mirzapur around her new home for warmth. For the rest of the year, when the heat blasts you in the face as if you've opened an oven door, the floors would remain bare.

Having fallen in love with the capital of the company, she began to keep a journal.

Calcutta has been styled the City of Palaces, and it well deserves the name . . .

    Dinner parties and fancy balls were numerous. . . .

    The most beautiful French furniture was to be bought in Calcutta of M. de Bast, at whose shop marble tables, fine mirrors, and luxurious couches were in abundance. . . .

    I felt very happy cantering my beautiful high-caste Arab on the racecourse at 6 A.M. or, in the evening, on the well-watered drive in front of the Government House. . . .

    We drink water from the Ganges, reckoned the most wholesome in India.

In June 1823, some friends decided to travel upriver to Lucknow, renting six boats for a family of three. "An absolute fleet!" Fanny wrote.

Ist. A very fine 16-oared pinnace, containing two excellent cabins, fitted up with glazed and Venetian windows, pankhas, and two shower baths. In this vessel our friend, his lady, and their infant, will be accommodated.

    2dly. A dinghee for the cook, and provisions.

    3rdly. An immense baggage boat, containing all their furniture.

    4thly. A vessel for the washerman, his wife, and the dog.

    5thly. A larger boat with horses.

    6thly. A ditto.

Fanny Parkes made her first journey up the Ganges four years later, when her husband was appointed to a new post in Allahabad. It was eight hundred miles by boat, two and a half months of hard rowing and sailing against the current. But it was only five hundred overland, cutting a straight line across country away from the meanders of the river, as the railway does today. Fanny and Charles sold off their horses and their furniture and sent the rest of their possessions on ahead by boat. She didn't relish the move. "The people in Calcutta abused the Upper Provinces so much, we felt little inclination to quit the city," she wrote. They jolted their way across the hot, flat monotony of Bihar. She says very little about the journey; all she wants is to get to her destination.

They arrived in Benares on Christmas Day 1826, lingered in "the high place of superstition" long enough for her to decide that "the organ of gullibility must be very strongly developed in the Hindoos," and finally reached Allahabad on January 1. She found the city pleasant enough but didn't care much for Kanpur, where Charles was transferred later, with its "bleak, dreary, sandy, dusty, treeless" hinterland. But whatever their differences, the life of a sahib and a memsahib in both places offered many of the same pleasures as Calcutta: balls, dinners, horses, dogs, billiard tables for the gentlemen, a book society for the ladies. Fanny's journal listed all the servants that a typical private family could expect to employ. It came to fifty-seven, with an outlay of two hundred and ninety rupees a month, and included a water cooler, someone to flap the punkah up and down, a torchbearer, a sweeper, a furniture duster, and a man to take care of the pigeons and rabbits. At one New Year's party, she and her friends sat up until four in the morning drinking Punch à la Romaine with ice. "The people here are icemaking mad," she wrote. "I flatter myself I understand the mystery of iceification better than anyone in India."

But Fanny's fascination with icemaking didn't mean she was an idle dilettante; it was just the kind of thing that engaged her endlessly inquisitive mind. She assembled a cabinet of curiosities with "the skulls of alligators, crocodiles, hyenas, and tigers beautifully prepared." She collected Persian and Indian proverbs and had them inscribed on seals. Regardless of her initial feelings about the organ of gullibility, she threw herself into the study of the Vedas and the Puranas. For one rupee, she bought thirty-two paintings of Hindu deities and constructed an organigram to show their hierarchy. She explored the secret, secluded lives of Indian women, which gave her the subtitle for the book she eventually published in 1850: *Wanderings of a Pilgrim in Search of the Picturesque During Four and Twenty Years in the East with Revelations of Life in the Zenana.*

People began to tease her.

1831, July 6th.—I study the customs and superstitions of the Hindoos so eagerly, that my friends laugh and say, "We expect some day to see you at pooja in the river!"

Eventually Fanny and Charles moved back to the City of Palaces, and she immersed herself more and more deeply in the life of the river. She was fully aware of the difference between the Hoogly, as she spelled it, the distributary that ran through Calcutta, and the Ganges proper, which continued to the east before hooking southward to the ocean. But she accepted the common usage; to Hindus and company officials alike, the Hooghly *was* the Ganges.

She fell under the spell of the boats in the crowded harbor, "vessels of all sorts and sizes, of the most oriental and picturesque form." Chinese ships with an eye painted on both sides of the prow for better navigation. Trading ships with sleek lines and well-trimmed sails. "Snake boats" that swarmed the river at festival time. The *mor-pankhi*, or peacock feather, "a kind of pleasure boat, with the long neck and head of a peacock, most richly gilt and painted." Low-slung budgerows, with a cabin that ran almost the full length of the deck; when she sailed upstream on one of them as far as the old Danish settlement of Serampore, curious locals waded out to it and peeked in at her through the Venetian blinds.

In March 1837, she made her first trip on the recently inaugurated paddle-steamer service to Allahabad, which was "very expensive, but . . . more agreeable." It was safer from pirates than the budgerow, although the insurance company still charged the same premium for the journey as it did for the nine thousand—mile crossing from England. It also promised to cut almost two months off the journey, but she was dismayed to find that the low water of the lean period forced the captain to make a three hundred—mile detour to the east through the Sundarbans, the vast labyrinth of mangrove forests, temporary islands, tributaries, distributaries, and side channels that is now divided between India and Bangladesh.

Fanny and her fellow passengers didn't ride on the steamer itself but on a small "flat" that was towed behind it. She was unimpressed by "these vile sundarbands [sic]. . . . A more solitary, desolate tract I never beheld." There were a few miserable huts here and there, but all the inhabitants seemed to be men. There were watchtowers, raised on poles, because "the thick jungle is full of tigers; so much so, that the Hindoos on board are not allowed to go on shore to cook their food on that account." The captain of the flat pointed out an oar stuck on end in the sand to mark the spot where someone had just been carried off and eaten. To Fanny's great relief, they eventually reached Kumarkhali, 150 miles into present-day Bangladesh, turned left onto the big river, and headed for Bihar.

She seemed less interested in seeing its few noteworthy sights than in reading about them in the *Calcutta Directory*. There was said to be a curious village where people subsisted on crocodile meat. There was the Moti Jharna waterfall, in the hills to the north of the river, but "I neither saw nor visited it." There was a mass of jumbled rocks that rose vertically out of the river at Sultanganj, the divided river rushing past it like a mill race. "They say no one lives upon these rocks; that a fakir formerly took up his abode there, but having been eaten by a snake, one of enormous size, and an eater of human flesh, the people became alarmed, and no holy or unholy person has since taken up residence."

When they reached Patna, the capital of Bihar, she consulted the *Directory* again. Noted for the production for opium, gram, and wax candles. Sole attraction: a giant dome-shaped granary built by Captain John Garstin in 1786 but presently used as a guardhouse. She gave Patna a pass. It was "a most uninteresting day among shallows and sandbanks." She sketched and read and languished in the suffocating heat. "Very gladly shall I return to the quiet and coolness of my own home."

Finally, after twenty-three days on the river, she was back in Allahabad, back to the water cooler and the *punkahwalla* and the wonders of iceification.

INDIA'S CORAL STRAND

While Fanny Parkes turned left, the Anglican Bishop of Calcutta, Reginald Heber, had turned right, deeper into the backcountry of Bengal and the Hundred Mouths of the Ganges. I'd first heard of Heber as a child, having spent an unhappy year at a Victorian redbrick primary school that bore his name—*Eebah*, as it was rendered by my South London classmates. The music teacher, a balding countertenor named Mr. Hatton, whose piercing voice made us snicker into our sleeves, had taught us some of the hymns the good clergyman had composed in the course of bringing the heathen to Jesus.

From Greenland's icy mountains,
From India's coral strand,
Where Afric's sunny fountains,
Roll down their golden sand,
From many an ancient river,
From many a palmy plain,
They call us to deliver
Their land from error's chain.

It was a time when the relics of imperial India were being disposed of at estate sales and in junk shops, when the last generation of middle-ranking servants of the Raj had retired to their modest suburban villas and were now being taken to their heavenly reward. Neighborhoods close to ours had a Dacca Street and a Bombay Street, a Kashmir Road and a Benares Road. A warehouse near my home was crammed with elephant's-foot umbrella stands, teak coffee tables, trays of chased brass, planters' chairs, exotic prints foxed with humidity, and bronze sculptures of Bengal tigers, even the odd piece of Louis Quatorze that might have been bought of M. de Bast at his shop in Calcutta.

Bishop Heber arrived in Calcutta in November 1823, less than a year after Fanny Parkes, forty years old and still baby-faced. "From Greenland's Icy Mountains" had already been translated into Bengali, not that anyone in Bengal had ever seen an icy mountain or a coral strand. Fanny thought the bishop "did not understand native character, and possessed much simplicity." He set off for Dacca the following June, a trip that involved a major detour to the east as the first stage of his visitation of the Upper Provinces. Like Fanny's friends earlier that year, he made the journey in a sixteen-oar pinnace. The crew were "all Mussulmans. . . . wild and odd-looking people, light-limbed, and lean, and very black, but strong and muscular . . . with a fiercer eye and far less civil manner than the Hindoos of Calcutta."

He packed James Rennell's map of Bengal, and I tried to use it myself as a guide to his route. But it was almost impossible to decipher; most of the place-names had changed, and the bishop himself was often confused because the rivers of the delta were such constant shape-shifters, even in the half century since Rennell had completed his survey. It was even harder to trace Heber's path on a modern map, which made the waterways of the delta look like a CAT scan of the central nervous system.

Some Englishmen in India clung on to their Englishness more fiercely than others, and "our own dear England" was Heber's constant point of reference.

The countryside around the Hooghly was not unlike parts of Oxfordshire and Buckinghamshire along the Thames, although the Hooghly was wider, and the Thames is not known for rice paddies and palm trees. The tumbledown governor's mansion at Chandernagore put him in mind of Moreton Corbet, a ruined Elizabethan manor house in Shropshire.

About forty miles north of Calcutta, the boatmen struck off to the east, following a small, winding distributary of the Mathabhanga, itself a distributary of the Ganges. They were now in "a part of the country I am told not many Europeans traverse." The river they were on was "about as wide as the Dee a little below Chester."

Bearing north, he reached the town of Shibnibash and stopped to inspect its objects of interest. On the jetty, he saw men carrying large kedgeree pots full of *gangajal* from Benares, bound for a cluster of local temples, where he examined a shiny black *shivling* and a statue of Ram and Sita. The priest declined his offering, saying he could accept money only from a fellow Brahmin. Nearby were the overgrown ruins of a Mughal palace. They reminded the bishop of Conway Castle, or Bolton Abbey. Or perhaps Carnarvon Castle was closer to the mark?

After Shibnibash, the pinnace appeared to meander westward. Dacca lay in the opposite direction, and the bishop felt "some perplexity about our further progress." One morning, he woke to find the river choked in "stinking fog." There were sudden squalls of rain. His mood declined. He tried chewing paan and was shocked to find that it turned his tongue and lips bright orange (though he "thought it not unpleasant"). "Rennell . . . is indeed nearly useless here," he grumbled, and looking at the map, I had to agree.

"Dear, dear England!" the bishop wrote. "There is now less danger than ever of my forgetting her, since I now, in fact, first feel the bitterness of banishment."

Eventually they found a navigable channel that led due east to the main stem of the Ganges, and beyond that was Dacca. Despite his frustrations, Heber had never lost faith in his Muslim oarsmen. "Though they may sometimes be over-cautious, they always know their own rivers, and the state of the weather, better than we can do. Most, if not all the accidents which occur to Europeans on the Ganges, arise from their making their crews proceed against their wishes and judgment."

They passed a pretty tributary that made him think of the Cherwell at Oxford, and then, quite suddenly, he found himself looking across a vast sheet of water dotted with sandy islands. The landscape spread out before them was "not unlike the coast of Lancashire, as seen trending away from the mouth of the Mersey." It was, in fact, "Gunga in her greatest pride and glory." Five days later, he was in Dacca, exhausted and sunburned but eager to preach his first sermon.

It was a ruinous place. Its glory had been the production of fine muslin, but the local handloom weavers were no match for the cheap mass-produced cotton goods that had begun to flood in from the mills of Manchester. Most people lived in squalid huts, and many of the better houses had been ravaged by floods. The city was surrounded by impenetrable jungle. "Much place for elephant," said the bishop's servant, Abdullah, who had converted to Christianity.

The local magistrate guided Heber around and gave him a breakdown of the population. A few Armenians, several of them quite wealthy; a handful of Portuguese, "very poor and degraded"; a fair number of Greeks, "industrious and intelligent people." The only English civilians were a couple of indigo planters, although ten companies of infantry were also stationed in Dacca to defend the city against Burmese raiders.

The population of "Hindoos and Mussulmans" numbered about three hundred thousand. By the time I got there, almost two hundred years after Bishop Heber, East Bengal was Bangladesh, the city's name had changed to Dhaka, and the population was more than fifteen million. All that remained the same was that the great majority of them still lived in squalid huts.

EASY LIKE WATER

In the Mirpur neighborhood of Dhaka, Mostafizur Rahman Jewel, a bright and personable young man who was eager to show a visitor all possible points of interest in the People's Republic of Bangladesh, took me to see the rickshaw graveyard.

"How many are there?" I asked, trying to take in the scale of the place.

Jewel said that the common estimate was fifteen thousand.

They were jammed into a field that covered a couple of acres, flanked by palm trees and utilitarian five-story apartment buildings stained with damp. The frames and handlebars were pitted with rust, the bamboo-frame canopies were tattered, the chains were lost or scavenged. There were also a few deceased trucks and buses, half strangled by weeds.

The rickshaws were lined up in rows, stacked in pyramids, strewn randomly upside down with their wheels silhouetted against the sky like a conceptual art exhibit. There was a towering scrap heap of orphaned plastic seat cushions in a riot of primary colors. The rear panels of the rickshaws were a vivid gallery of painted scenes, with the artists favoring a range of stock motifs. Heartthrobs from Dhallywood, Bangladesh's junior cousin to Bollywood, with fearsome mustaches and impressive guns, rescuing sloe-eyed damsels in distress. Technicolor renderings of the Taj Mahal. Roosters, spotted deer, crocodiles, and Bengal tigers locked in mortal combat. More oddly, there were rhinos (which disappeared from Bangladesh more than a hundred years ago) and zebras (which were never there in the first place). Many of the rickshaws were ornamented with bright, wistful fantasies of the rural homeland the pullers had left behind, a world of limpid lakes, brightly painted cottages, tropical flowers, swans and peacocks. One bold spirit had broken from chaste local convention and depicted a man pressing himself between the thighs of a half-naked woman with a sari pulled up around her hips.

But the fifteen thousand wrecks in the rickshaw graveyard were only a retired fraction of the fleet. Dhaka is the rickshaw capital of the world. The common estimate is that there are at least six hundred thousand and maybe as many as eight hundred thousand—and that includes only the pedal-powered variety, not the motorized three-wheelers. Someone told me later that when Google Earth came to map Dhaka with their Streetview cameras, they found the gridlock so atrocious that they could only get any work done before dawn or late at night. It can take an hour to drive a mile, yet the rickshaws somehow shimmy their way through the chaos like shoaling fish, in a racket of bells and car horns, avoiding oncoming buses by inches. Dhaka traffic calls for the same reflexes that passengers are taught in a plane that's about to crash. Brace for impact.

On the way back into the city center, after one near collision, Jewel raised an eyebrow in amusement as I relaxed my death grip on the dashboard of our vehicle and exhaled.

"No problem," I said, trying to appear nonchalant. "Piece of cake."

"Piece of cake?" Jewel's English was good, but not that good.

"Slang expression. Something really easy, no sweat. Like not killing that rickshaw walla. How do you say that in Bengali?"

"*Panir moto shohoj*," he answered. "Means 'easy like water.'"

Easy like water. That seemed like a strange choice of words, because water is Bangladesh's existential curse.

The Ganges presents its passport at the Bangladesh border and changes its name and identity. It becomes the Padma, and except to the country's small minority of Hindus, it is no longer considered to be a goddess. A short way south of Dhaka, the Padma meets the Meghna. This is a smaller river, but from the confluence to the ocean, Meghna is the name that sticks. The country it flows through is as flat as a pool table. Almost 160 million people are crammed into an area the size of Iowa, or, if you prefer, a fraction more than England.

The flow of the Padma and the Meghna is sluggish in the extreme. The massive load of silt and mud it transports from the Himalayas and the North Indian plains forms islands that come and go, form, disperse, re-form somewhere else. Some of these *chars* are solid enough that people take up residence there, farm rice, and hope their new home survives longer than the previous one. From June to November, Bangladesh reels under the force of the monsoon. The rivers bully their way into the fields, the banks erode, and farms, sometimes whole villages, are swallowed up in the current. Rivers can break through the lowlands and change their course entirely. In a fortunate year, a third of Bangladesh is flooded. In a bad year it's half; in the worst, it can be two-thirds.

However, try asking the millions who live in the delta of the Ganges if they have enough water, at least of a kind that is of any use to them. Over the past few centuries, the natural course of the river has shifted eastward, redirecting the surge of freshwater that used to dilute the inflow of salt from the Bay of Bengal. Major rivers that once helped to channel the Ganges to the Indian Ocean have dried up or been blocked by silt. The Mathabhanga, the Bhairab, the Sialmari are now little more than names in a history book.

Bangladesh is also synonymous with man-made calamities. In 1970, a year before it fought its war of independence from Pakistan at the cost of three million dead, Indian engineers built a barrage across the Ganges at Farakka, a few miles short of the border, to divert the flow to the thirsty megacity of Calcutta and flush out the silt that threatened to clog up its harbor. So for much of the year, parts of Bangladesh have too little water, not too much.

Those who live in the delta are further tormented by the cyclones and tidal surges that sweep in from the Bay of Bengal. One cyclone in 1970 killed 300,000 people; in 1991, another 138,000 died. The early-warning systems are better now, keeping the body count down, but disaster still feeds on disaster. Bangladesh built a huge web of dikes and embankments to shield themselves from future floods. Dutch experts came to help, having long experience of such things. But the solid walls of earth had a perverse effect. They held the rivers back, but at the same time they blocked drainage on the land side. The fields remained waterlogged for months. Already cursed by topography, the delta now has to cope with a warming and rising ocean, which will make the storm surges fiercer, the fields saltier, the monsoons more unpredictable.

How bad will it be? From the rickshaw graveyard, Jewel took me to see one of the legion of experts in Dhaka who are trying to answer that question. Mohazarul Alam—Babu to his friends—is one of Bangladesh's leading climate scientists. A dapper, good-natured man with a neatly trimmed mustache, he chose his words with care.

"We will permanently lose between 12 and 15 percent of our surface area," he said.

He registered my shocked expression and smiled.

"Oh, you have to understand, this is under the most benign scenario."

THE IMPOSSIBLE CITY

Even in the upscale neighborhoods of Gulshan and Banani, where diplomats and garment buyers and earnest foreign humanitarians congregate, a misstep in the dark can drop you through a pothole into an open sewer. I went to a guesthouse in Gulshan the next morning to meet another of Dhaka's legion of outgunned experts over a cup of nasty instant coffee.

Professor Haroon ur Rashid was a professor at Dhaka's North South University, a specialist in urban planning. He was a small, owlish man, inclined toward gallows humor. His English was impeccable.

"Amartya Sen grew up in Dhaka," he said. "You know, the economist who won the Nobel Prize. He once told an interviewer from the BBC that his children saw him as a man without taste, because he had said he liked every place he had ever visited and could happily live anywhere. There was only one exception: Dhaka. *That* was unlivable."

Rashid grinned. The city was his home. He lived the unlivable.

In 1953, he said, the population of Dhaka was half a million—not much more than it had been in the days of Bishop Heber. The big leap came in 1971, after the War of Liberation, when people could choose between living in Pakistan, now reduced to its western portion, or in newly independent Bangladesh. People in the east spoke Bengali, not Urdu. Bengali Muslims practiced a form of Islam that was quiet and conciliatory. They had lost three million of their citizens to the Pakistani Army and Air Force. So most opted to stay put in Bangladesh.

"Now the population of Dhaka is growing at 6 percent a year," Rashid said. "Most of the newcomers are from the countryside. These are people with no skills. They work in low-wage, marginal occupations. The city has grown by accretion, not by planning. In terms of infrastructure, water, services, sanitation, Dhaka is a total disaster. God only knows what it will be like in the future."

It was fifteen million now, maybe sixteen. No one knew exactly. I did the 6 percent math in my head. Four hundred thousand rural migrants a year. The population would reach twenty million by 2020. Maybe twenty-five million by 2030. And Babu Alam's best-case scenario meant another seven million or more being driven from their homes by the ocean.

"What is the government doing about it?" I asked.

Rashid just looked at me with an eyebrow raised as if I'd asked a particularly stupid question.

The migrants come to Dhaka, a thousand or more of them every day, from flooded coastal divisions like Barisal and Khulna, or from the drought-stricken northwest border areas that have lost out to the Farakka barrage and the demands of Calcutta. Their flight has a powerful cascade effect on the city. Once they arrive, they face a new version of the very thing they were trying to escape, trading one water emergency for another, and making matters worse by the simple fact of their own presence.

Generally, it's the main breadwinner who comes first. As likely as not, he'll start off as a pavement dweller. Then, tracking opportunities by word of mouth, he may find work as a day laborer or a garbage picker, a seller of scraps from the tanneries of Hazaribagh, a place every bit as dismal as Kanpur, or as a brick breaker or a security guard, sitting all night on a plastic chair in the dark outside a parking garage or an ATM booth. Many will join the ranks of the rickshaw pullers, earning two hundred taka a day, two dollars and fifty cents.

The migrant will eventually find a place to live in a *basti*, one of Dhaka's hundreds of slum areas. Some of these are no more than a straggle of stilt houses along a polluted canal. Others are virtual townships of a hundred thousand or more, each with its own complex internal economy and social hierarchy. He'll sleep in a room that measures six feet by eight, perhaps sharing his bed with other men working rotating shifts, paying his monthly seven hundred taka to the local slumlord. "It's like the Godfather or Al Capone," said Babar Kabir, another of the city's experts and an especially overburdened one, since his portfolio at BRAC, a giant nongovernmental organization that occupies a twenty-one-story building and has a half-billion-dollar budget, includes disasters, the environment, and climate change. "There's a whole invisible pyramid of lieutenants and sublieutenants and rent collectors. And if you fall behind on payments, you'll get a visit from the *mastaan*, the muscleman." As for potable water, unless some kindly NGO has installed a tap, the migrant may have nowhere to turn but to the "gray business" that controls its sale in the slums. Often he'll pay fifty times more for a liter of drinking water than people in a middle-class neighborhood like Kabir's, who simply need to turn on the faucet.

As the new migrant puts down tenuous roots, his family will join him. Sometimes they come one at a time, sometimes all at once. The sons will follow his pursuit of menial jobs; the wives and daughters will gravitate toward domestic service, manual labor, or a sewing machine. More and more these days, women were also leaving their families behind to find work in the apparel industry. Sometimes they came alone or with a friend from the same village. "These are often adventurous young women," Kabir said, "and they need to find an honest middleman, because there are plenty of others out there who will take them for a ride, sell them into brothels, or traffic them across the border into commercial sex work in India." Sometimes they will even be drawn into the booming black market in human organs, cajoled into selling a kidney for the equivalent of a year of minimum wages. Once a young woman finds a job, the engine of kinship kicks in: she does well, she recommends her sister, who calls a cousin, and so on until a half dozen members of the family may be working in the garment factories.

The next expert on my list was Iftekhar Mahmud, a reporter for *The Daily Prothom Alo* (First Light), the leading Bangla-language newspaper, who spent most of his time writing and fretting about the havoc that climate change would wreak on a city that was already unlivable. We met in a fashionable teashop-cum-art-gallery that would not have been out of place in New York or London or Berlin. "The rains are now more concentrated in the peak months of the monsoon season," he said. "They have more than doubled in volume in August alone over the past twenty years. The city's drainage system is equipped to deal with ten millimeters of rain, but we often get ten or twenty times that much in a single day." Much of the city is only a couple of meters above sea level, and it didn't surprise me to learn that the poorest *bastis* occupy the lowest and most flood-prone sections, which are inundated constantly with sewage-tainted water that brings disease in its wake. To make matters worse, the natural drainage areas that buffer the floods have been steadily encroached upon by land grabbers who pump them dry to throw up new housing, much of it illegal. One new development I had seen on drained land next to the Buriganga covered nearly four hundred acres, more than half a square mile. Bangladeshis, ever a poetic people, call it *sandfill*.

WHERE YOU ARE FROM?

There were times, walking or driving around Dhaka, when it seemed that the city was dissolving into its constituent elements. If it was made of iron, it was rusting; if it was vegetable, it was rotting; if it was brick, it was reverting to mud, to river sediment.

Jewel and I made our way through the clog of rickshaws to the old city. At every stop—and there were many more stops than starts—street children, bird-thin old women, blind men, people with deformities out of a horror movie tapped their nails on the windows of our car and put their fingers to their mouths. Vendors offered pirated copies of *The Da Vinci Code*, *Harry Potter*, and the *Lonely Planet* guide to Bangladesh.

The waterways along the road were lined with stilt shacks made of tin, tar paper, and dead palm fronds. The residents clustered on the banks, washing their clothes and cooking utensils, soaping themselves up, and brushing their teeth with twigs. Naked children splashed around in scummy ponds choked by water hyacinths. The city had a single sewage treatment plant; located on the southern outskirts of Dhaka, it could cope with less than 10 percent of what the city produced. The rest, more than a thousand tons of untreated human waste each day, went straight into the rivers, ponds, canals, and gutters.

We stopped near a fish market to chat with some brick breakers in lungis, the sarong-like garment that many Bangladeshi men wear in preference to trousers. They were using hammers to reduce the bricks to pebble-sized fragments. On the left side of the canal twenty feet below us was a precarious outhouse, propped above the black water on culms of bamboo. On the right, raw sewage was pouring in through a concrete pipe. I lost my footing on the muddy slope and careened down it like a kid on a playground slide. A mat of weeds and garbage broke my fall, just short of the water. A small crowd of men had assembled for the spectacle. There was great hilarity among the brick breakers. One of them asked, "Where you are from?" Bangladesh was off the beaten tourist track.

In the narrow streets of the old city, there were signs for the Oxford International Academy; the Pathway English Club—Results Guaranteed— Expert Teachers; and the Benchmark Academy—O/A Levels All Subjects. On one building there was a faded notice referring to a property dispute that quite likely dated back to the days of Partition, when countless homes were abandoned, squatted, and mired in decades of litigation. The English-language portion of it said,

IN THE MEAN TIME DEFENDANTS ARE RESTRAINED
BY AN ORDER OF AD INTERIM-INJUNCTION FROM
DISPOSSING THE PLAITEFF FROM THE SUET PROPERTY
DESCRIBED IN THE SCHE DULE OF THE PLAENT

There were alleys that sold only bicycles, others that sold only musical in-struments, others that sold only burkas. The exposed eyes of the mannequins followed you down the street. Overhead was a tangle of power lines, a cat's cradle of black spaghetti. Buildings seemed to remain vertical by sheer force of will. Muezzins called from minarets. Bloodstained butchers with henna-dyed beards hacked away at carcasses for the upcoming feast of the Shab-e-Barat, the "night of deliverance." Heavily rouged groups of *hijra*—whether they were transgender or eunuchs was impossible to tell—lounged on the street corners, pouting and flirting with their eyes.

Finally, we reached the Buriganga, the Old Ganga, which curls around the western edge of the city. The reason it has this name is that many centu-ries ago, before the Ganges changed its course, silting up old channels and carving out new ones, the Buriganga had been connected to the big river. Now it was forty miles away.

The Buriganga was the color of a moonless night, coated with a sheen of oil and floating debris. At the boat terminal known as Saderghat, the wharf was lined with decrepit triple-decker ferries. I saw one of those headlines that appear from time to time on the inside pages of the newspaper. OVERCROWDED FERRY CAPSIZES IN BANGLADESH: 300 FEARED DEAD, SEARCH CONTINUES FOR SURVIVORS.

We climbed aboard one rusted hulk and watched small, sharp-prowed boats laden with baskets, jute sacks, and piles of green coconuts weave in and out among the larger vessels. After a few minutes, there was the sound of footsteps on the deck behind us. It was a group of young men. My camera seemed to be of interest to their leader. My stomach muscles clenched. Camera, cell phone, passport, wallet, cash freshly withdrawn from an ATM. He advanced on us slowly, staring. Then he gave a timid, sweet smile and said, "Where you are from?"

The next time we went to Saderghat, a boatman rowed us across to the other side for a few takas, and we climbed a staircase to a fifth-floor rooftop to take in the view. We held on to the corner of a colossal billboard that said, "BE AN INVESTMENT PHILOSOPHER."

The ramshackle building was a warren of tiny sweatshops making saris, lungis, and T-shirts for the local market. Girls of eleven or twelve sat on the floor, cutting up bolts of fabric or sewing on buttons. I asked one of them where she was from, and she said Barisal, in the coastal southwest. A boy of the same age was sitting at a sewing machine, stitching something red. His round head was shaved to the point of baldness. One of the men laughed, pointed to his own head, and said something to Jewel.

"He says they call the boy Watermelon," Jewel said.

Later, we drove out beyond the city limits to the northeast. It was mango season, and we'd stopped to buy a bagful from one of the wharf-side fruit vendors at Saderghat. "The mangoes in Bangladesh are the best in the world," Jewel said, patriotically but also accurately, and we feasted on them until the juice ran down our arms. The monsoon had finally broken. A fierce rain drummed on the roof of the car, and the windshield wipers beat time. The fields were already waterlogged. For mile upon mile, they had been staked out for drainage and development by real-estate speculators, whose signs were planted at intervals in the knee-deep water. This is where Dhaka would grow in the future to accommodate the twenty-five million that the experts feared would push the city to the tipping point.

Textile mills and dyeworks were strung out along the road leading to the town of Narsingdi, which sits on the left bank of the Meghna just short of its confluence with the Padma, where the Ganges begins its final slow lap to the ocean. We talked our way into one of the mills, where a twelve-year-old boy named Mainul Islam stood up from his labors in the packing room to show off his new cell phone, a pink Chinese-made Sunny model that he could never have afforded if he'd stayed in school. No one else in his family worked; he was their sole support. He posed for a photograph under a large red sign that said, in English and in Bangla,

WE DO NOT EMPLOY WORKERS LESS THAN 18 YEARS OF AGE

The highway back to the city was lined with lengths of dyed cloth, orange, yellow, red, purple, green, and blue, hung out on clotheslines to dry like some roadside version of Christo's Central Park project, *The Gates*. In the labyrinth of narrow, muddy lanes, whole families were dedicated to the business of turning out low-quality fabric for the sweatshops on the Buriganga. Their rickety homes vibrated to the clatter of cast-iron looms that looked as if they dated back to the Industrial Revolution. In their earth yards, men and boys were sloshing cloth around in zinc bathtubs, up to their armpits in dye, hands and wrists stained permanently indigo and crimson. One man told me that he scrubbed his arms every night with scouring powder and bleach, but it didn't make much difference. "Don't worry," he grinned. "This is good water. It doesn't harm you." He upended his tub and poured some of the liquid into a drain hole. From there it would run into a nearby sewer, which ran into a canal, which ran into a stream, which ran into the Meghna, which ran into the Bay of Bengal.

WOMEN OF THE DELTA

Down in the hole that had once been Rana Plaza, there were mountains of sodden, half-sewn clothing, spools and bobbins of thread, and bolts of brightly patterned cloth. The crushed remains of half a dozen cars were still waiting for removal, and next to them was a broken plaster mannequin. She was lying on her back in a puddle of early monsoon rain. She wore a pair of tight purple knee-length pants, but she was naked above the waist. Her torso had been severed in a neat diagonal below the right breast, but her head was intact. She had ivory skin, a pink rosebud mouth, ash-blond hair brushed straight back off her forehead, and piercing blue eyes. You wanted to read an expression into them, one that said, "What happened?" But there was no expression; they were just fixed on the sky.

What happened was that Rana Plaza, seven stories high, had pancaked in upon itself. It was worse than the fire at the Tazreen factory five months earlier. One hundred and twelve garment workers had died at Tazreen. In Rana Plaza, it was almost exactly ten times that number, this time not burned alive but flattened and dismembered by concrete pillars with unattended cracks and third-rate rebar. With the exception of the World Trade Center, it was the worst structural collapse of a building in human history, only this one was the result of negligence, greed, and corruption, not murderous intent.

The thing I found hardest to absorb about the shallow pit was how small it was. The site of the Twin Towers covered sixteen acres. The footprint of Rana Plaza was not much larger than a basketball court. The building next door was still under construction. It reminded me of the shoddy new office buildings I'd seen in Allahabad, its façade a thin veneer of blue reflective glass that seemed to have been slapped on like a Post-it note. The interior was just a raw skeleton of brick and mortar walls. This being Dhaka, there was every reason to assume that its building plans had involved the same unholy collusion between venal developers and corrupt politicians.

I hopped the security barrier. A couple of cops in neatly pressed blue shirts were sitting on plastic chairs a few yards away, and they yelled at me. But this seemed to be something they had been told to do in their training manual rather than something that actually called for further action, so I climbed over a heap of bricks and took the unfinished stairway to the top floor.

The upper levels of the building had suffered a good deal of collateral damage. Great sections of ceiling had bellied downward and were propped up in a tentative way with single stalks of bamboo. Whole walls had been blown out by the force of the collapse, and papers from the upper floors of Rana Plaza had floated in. Many were still strewn about in the wreckage. There were cards with samples of buttons and zippers, and pattern forms and order books and cutting instructions and packaging for shirts that said, "Blue Side: Quality Never Goes out of Style."

The Tazreen fire had created a scandal for Walmart because one of its suppliers had been making nightgowns in the factory. The company was called International Intimates. This was known because of documents that workers had uncovered in the ruins. At Rana Plaza, many of the dusty papers I found in the rubble related to contracts with the United Colors of Benetton, headquartered in Treviso, Italy. They were shakily translated from the Italian. *Regolare bene le tensione delle macchine. Adjuste better the tension machine.* Outside Babar Kabir's office at BRAC, I'd seen an elegantly dressed woman sitting in the waiting area. She was tall, blond, and somewhat resembled the mannequin. "She's from Benetton," he'd said.

The journalists who flocked to Rana Plaza in the days after the disaster poked at the raw nerve of our moral culpability, the hidden cost of our trips to the mall. For the most part, they hewed to the usual narrative conventions of the tragedy in a poor country: evil owner (which he was), innocent victims (which they were), the one miraculous survivor (there invariably is one in these stories; in this case, it was a woman who somehow made it out alive after being trapped in the wreckage for seventeen days). None of the reporters, as far as I could tell, ever asked where the women of Rana Plaza were from or what had brought them here in the first place.

Rana Plaza was a long way from the sweatshops on the Buriganga and the dyeworks on the road to Narsingdi, which served the humbler end of the domestic market. It was part of a globalized industry where the buyers cared about things like the precise angle at which their logos were sewn on, an industry that brought Bangladesh 80 percent of its export earnings and employed three and a half million people, most of them poor and uneducated women.

In Dhaka, the majority of the garment workers lived in two neighborhoods on the northwestern outskirts of the city: Savar, where Rana Plaza was located, and Mirpur, the most rapidly growing area of the city, where Jewel had taken me to see the rickshaw graveyard. Most of them were recent migrants from the countryside. In Mirpur, I met a longtime advocate for their rights named Shirin Akhter. "Work is the pull, and water is the push," she said. "We are a country of rivers, but we have no water to drink."

If the women work in Savar, they're likely to be from the northwest. There, the enemy is drought and the drying up of the Ganges watershed. If they work in Mirpur, they will more likely be from the southwest, from the Hundred Mouths of the Ganges, where the enemy is floods, and the rivers are turning to salt. In both areas, it was a tale of failing farms.

Akhter had a theory that explained the difference between Savar and Mirpur. She pulled out a map and pointed to two bus terminals on the west side of the city. If you were coming from the north, the bus dropped you near Savar; if you were coming from the delta, you got off at the terminal that was a little way to the south, closer to Mirpur.

In Savar, I went to a housing development called Jamgora. It was one of Dhaka's biggest slums, home to more than a hundred thousand people. But they were not the poorest of the poor. The garment workers may start off in the bamboo, tin, and palm-frond huts of the *bastis*, but once they get a little money, they tend to graduate to places like Jamgora, where rents are two or three times higher.

Jamgora was a complex of grim, water-stained concrete tenements connected by underlit corridors. Each block was divided up into cheerless cement-walled rooms, with heavy metal doors and windows secured by padlocks against theft. In one room, two young women in their late teens were sprawled on the bed watching a soap opera. I asked one of them where she was from. She answered in a shy whisper that her home was a village in the northwest, just across the border from India's Farakka dam, in the water-starved triangle of land between the Padma and the Brahmaputra rivers. It was her day off. Like many, she worked for ten hours a day, six days a week, but she was no longer on minimum wage, which at the time of the Rana Plaza disaster was less than forty dollars a month.

A young man wandered over to join us. He was from the same area. The family's crops had failed once too often; now his mother, a brother, and three sisters were all working the sewing machines.

Bleak though it was, Jamgora was about a limited kind of upward mobility. The wages were low, there was no sick leave, you could be dismissed on a whim, the supervisors had advanced degrees in sexual harassment, you didn't even have the right to ask for a toilet break. And there was the constant unspoken fear of another Tazreen fire, another Rana Plaza. But at least the women in Jamgora had also broken free of the suffocating taboos of village life. If they'd remained, they would have faced the prospect of an early and unwanted marriage, arranged by a father desperate to keep down the cost of his daughter's dowry, which would only increase as she got older. But here they could chat with friends on their cell phones, go out at night for a soda or an ice cream if they weren't too tired, perhaps dare to put on a little lipstick. If they were hard-pressed to pay the rent, some might even split the cost with a male roommate (usually platonic), hoping that rumors wouldn't reach their parents.

———

The following evening, Shirin Akhter took me down a darkened back street in Mirpur to meet a group of about a dozen women. Confirming her bus-station theory, all but one were from the delta, nine of them from the division of Barisal. They gathered in a circle on the floor and recounted the stories of their migration. The causes were a mix of what the experts called "extreme" and "slow-onset" changes in their circumstances. The stories varied from one woman to the next, but water was their common thread.

Rokeya said she had come to Dhaka from her home on the edge of the Sundarbans, the great coastal mangrove forests, because a tiger, driven from its customary habitat and deprived of its usual prey as the land grew saltier, was menacing her village. Nasima got a call on her mobile from a neighbor, warning that the riverbank by her home was slipping into the water; by the time she got there, her house, garden, and trees were all on their way to the Bay of Bengal. Nargis, who was from a village near the mouth of the Meghna, had left after the great cyclone of 2007 with four siblings, all of whom now worked in the garment factories. But her parents had refused to leave, and the remittances that the kids sent home had helped them rebuild their small farm. Jesmin, who was also from southern Barisal, had come to the city as a teenager with her brother after their father died of leukemia. Another brother followed, and soon all three were sewing clothes. A decade later, after the cyclone struck, village life became so precarious that Jesmin's mother and two remaining siblings concluded they could no longer survive in Barisal, and they headed for the city, too.

Jesmin was thirty now. She wore a graceful red sari with brocaded sleeves and a tiny gold nose stud. She had high, sculpted cheekbones and dark, deep-set eyes, and while some of the other women stared at the ground and told their stories in almost inaudible monosyllables, Jesmin had a calm and direct gaze, a poise, a natural charisma. She spoke about the hardships of life in the garment factories and the nostalgia she and her friends sometimes felt for their villages, their resentment of official indifference. But when the conversation turned to Rana Plaza, I told her that well-intentioned consumers in the West were asking whether it was right to buy clothes from a place that permitted

such things to happen. I said I'd heard about a store in Canada that had posted a notice in the window that said, "We Sell Nothing from Bangladesh." She looked at me in disbelief and then began to laugh, and soon most of the women in the room were chuckling and shaking their heads. It was as if they'd never met anyone with such a preposterous sense of humor.

When the laughter finally subsided, Jesmin looked me straight in the eye and said with a smile, "But if you stopped buying the clothes we make, what do you think we would do? We'd die."

THE WILL OF ALLAH

The road south from Dhaka was lined for miles with tall, tapering smokestacks trailing black plumes from the brick kilns. Each of the chimneys was marked with letters identifying its owner: NGN, NBM, AG, KAS. Children squatted by long, low walls of mud, pressing it into rectangular molds and stamping it with the same initials. Workers with long beards and embroidered skullcaps carried heavy loads of freshly fired bricks yoked to their shoulders, a dozen in each basket, and arranged them in neat stacks. Others dozed in tarpaulin shelters. Wives tended to the surrounding rice fields or sorted lumps of coal for their cooking fires. The sun beat down through a gray-brown haze.

The brickworks extended all the way to the Mawa ferry point on the right bank of the Padma, the main stem of the Ganges, just above its junction with the Meghna. Dredgers were at work on the riverbed, and there were a handful of one-room corrugated metal stilt houses. One of them had collapsed onto the beach, but the structure remained intact, and a man had somehow con-

trived to rope the whole thing onto a bicycle cart, canted at a forty-five-degree angle. Otherwise, there was little in the way of facilities, just a short pier to accommodate the larger ferries. The foreshore was lined with smaller vessels and fiberglass speedboats that could hold a dozen people. You could reach them on narrow bamboo gangplanks or by wading. We chose the gangplank, and one of the speedboats zipped us across the river, which was quite narrow here, not much more than a mile or two wide. Sandy flats stretched away in both directions, fringed by a low wall of trees.

On the other side, we climbed aboard an aged blue Land Rover with no air-conditioning and not much in the way of suspension. We drove for a couple of hours until we reached the town of Bagerhat, where we stopped to take a look at the fifteenth-century Shait Gumbad Masjid. People call it the sixty-dome mosque, although in fact it has seventy-seven of them, and the interior had the chambered coolness of an equal number of pillars. The black-bearded imam bustled over toward me as I came out into the sunshine, and he shooed away a crowd of pilgrims, most of them women in burkas. "No talk for you," he chided. "Only for people from America." They retreated a few feet and formed a semicircle, straining to follow the conversation. "Where you are from?" a woman asked.

The imam introduced himself as Mohammed Helal Uddin. His English was fractured, my Bengali was nonexistent, and my translator had gone tempo-rarily AWOL, so it wasn't the most fluid of exchanges. I could get as far as the *as-salaam o alaikum*, but even that made me nervous, knowing that some Muslims believe that the Prophet, Peace Be Upon Him, had instructed them not to offer the *walaikum as-salaam* in return to an unbeliever. But the imam did so courteously and seemed anxious to allay any misgivings or prejudices I might have, even though I hadn't expressed any. "Islam is very peaceful religion," he said earnestly. "Holy Qu'ran says all people created equal, no difference. Ladies and gentlemen, different prayers, but also same, equal. Islam is always speaking truthful, no bad word."

He told me about the last great cyclone—or, to give it its proper technical name, Extremely Severe Cyclonic Storm Sidr, 06B—which had struck in November 2007. It raged for five days, and the winds reached 160 miles an hour. The mosque had come through it unscathed, although huge palm trees had crashed down across the outer brick walls. "Is very difficult for us," he said. "People come here to mosque to be shelter."

We talked about the changes in the weather, the ferocity of the storms, the rising seas, the salt that came surging into the fields from the Bay of Bengal. I asked him what he thought accounted for them.

"We see the will of Allah," he replied. "We see as *da'wah*"—a summons to piety.

The great cyclone had smashed directly into Sarankhola, a cluster of five villages on the broad and sluggish Baleshwari River, thirty miles or so south of Barisal and another thirty from the open ocean. The Baleshwari was typical of the rivers of the delta in its chaotic topography. Again, my maps weren't of much help. The river appeared to emerge as a side channel of the Meghna. But which one? Did it begin life as the Naya Vangani? The Arial Khan? The Kalabadar? It meandered for many miles in a series of sloppy loops, braids, and oxbows, picking up tributaries, sliding around *chars*, changing its name to the Katcha, joining forces with the Kaliganga. Secondary streams seemed to leave one river only to empty into another a few miles away. Some curled back on themselves like a snake eating its tail. Some seemed to flow in two directions at once. By the time it reached the ocean, the Baleshwari had become one of the largest of the Hundred Mouths of the Ganges, a good five or six miles wide. Or perhaps by the time it got there it was the Bhola. It was impossible to tell.

Most of the people of Sarankhola were Muslim; maybe 10 percent were Hindus. Despite the bitter conflicts of the past, the two communities appeared to coexist in striking harmony. The Muslim homes were simpler, with neat, muffin-shaped haystacks in their yards. The homes of the Hindus were sturdier and more ornate, painted in vivid primary colors. Some were decorated with patterns that looked like henna stencils on a woman's hand. They had fenced vegetable gardens and flattened yarels to winnow their rice and scrupulously tended shrines in adjacent huts. Every house, regardless of religion, brought offers of biscuits, fruit, and small cups of sweet black tea.

A group of villagers walked with me along a narrow, elevated path, a shoelace of doughy, yielding gray mud raised six or eight feet above parallel rows of fishponds that were coated with emerald-green algae. They grew two rice crops a year and a few vegetables. They ventured into the forest to cut timber and firewood, though the tigers made them anxious. A fifteen-year-old boy from the neighboring village of Khuriakhali had been eaten a few weeks earlier while he was out fishing.

One man was old enough to remember the catastrophic cyclones of 1970 and 1991. The early-warning systems were much better these days, he said. From the radio, people knew that Sidr was on its way two full days in advance. A three-tier system of red flags in the main population centers predicted its likely strength. Government officials and village volunteers spread the word via handheld bullhorns and loudspeakers mounted on bicycles. Right up to the last minute, however, no one knew exactly where the storm would hit. In the end, it made landfall around 10:30 at night. Most people in Sarankhola made it to the shelters, which were raised ten feet above the ground on concrete pillars. But in Khuriakhali, fourteen were trapped in their homes, reluctant to abandon their meager possessions, or swept away and drowned. "The water came up to here," the man said, indicating his collarbone. "But only four thousand died."

The winter that followed had felt like a long, slow-motion aftershock. For months, the fields were tainted by salt. The rice and vegetable crops failed. The wells stayed brackish. The fishing boats were reduced to kindling. The weather continued strange throughout the dry season, which lasted a month longer than usual, punctuated by sudden freakish downpours. At ten in the morning, people were still shivering in sweaters. They were plagued by familiar ailments—headaches, vomiting, diarrhea, fatigue, the raging fevers and bone-numbing chills of malaria—but they came at unaccustomed times.

As we walked back through the village, a young woman named Mukhti, which means "salvation," sang me a Bengali folksong in a clear, sweet soprano. A farmer asked if I would be interested in buying his daughter, who was of marriageable age. A wizened old man greeted me outside his home, leaning on a stick. I asked how old he was, and he said one hundred.

FIELDS OF SALT

B angladesh's third-largest city, Khulna, lay on the sluggish Rupsha River, which ends up in the Bay of Bengal as another of the Hundred Mouths of the Ganges, one of the largest. It was a ramshackle place, but mercifully decongested, at least in relative terms, after the bedlam of Dhaka.

Finding a decent bed for the night proved to be every bit as challenging in Khulna as it usually was in India. We chose a mid-price establishment with murals on the walls of the dining room that depicted teddy bears and cartoon characters larking around in a snowstorm. Next to them was a VW Beetle with holiday suitcases lashed to the roof, and the words "Go Baby."

There was a large framed painting of flowers on the wall of my dark, cavernous room, and something was moving behind it, which turned out to be a splay-footed lizard fully eighteen inches long. I called the front desk to ask if they could send someone up to remove it, and a few minutes later two men arrived with cricket bats, a large, rusty, pump-operated spray can of insecticide, and an English vocabulary that consisted entirely of the words "no problem." I tried to convey through frantic sign language that there was no need for all the weaponry. If they could just remove the creature gently and put it back in the garden? "No problem," they said, yanking the picture from the wall, spraying the lizard in the face at point-blank range with insecticide until it tumbled to the floor, and then commencing to beat it with their bats. When it finally stopped twitching, they carried it out by the tail.

Even in Uttar Pradesh, with its two hundred million people, there had been some respite from the press of population. A small patch of forest, a stretch of empty road. But driving deeper into the delta toward the Sundarbans induced a strange kind of open-air claustrophobia, with no break either from people or from land under one form of cultivation or another. Every mile was a white-knuckled battle between overburdened trucks adorned with wooden folk art carvings and buses with their headlights on full beam despite the bright sunshine and with passengers clinging to the roof. Rickshaws, bicycles, and motorbikes engaged in their own adventures and misadventures as if they were auditioning for NASCAR. Flatbed cycle carts were heaped high with firewood, twenty-foot culms of bamboo, sacks of rice, cooking pots, hay bales, teetering pyramids of cooking oil tins, and people. The imbalance of weight was too much for one small cart, which abruptly tipped over, catapulting the driver backward like a circus performer shot from a cannon and sending his ten passengers, including a frail elderly woman, sprawling onto the highway and into the path of the oncoming traffic. The old lady picked herself up, dusted herself off, and started all over again, reattaching herself to the crush of humanity and livestock wandering randomly along and across the blacktop: scrawny goats, undernourished cattle, chicken, geese, dogs, children, old men with white beards hobbling along on canes, women in saris and burkas, day laborers in their checkered lungis. Life on the road was a crude Darwinian contest that the trucks and buses would always win.

We drove on, cutting due west across the endless rice fields before looping back to the south until we reached the busy little town of Shyamnagar at the edge of the Sundarbans, just a few miles from the Indian border. Shyamnagar merited a line or two in the histories of Hindu-Muslim conflict because of Pratapaditya, a sixteenth-century zamindar and maharaja who resisted the navy, the artillery, and the formidable war elephants of the Mughal emperor Jahangir until he finally surrendered and was transported to Varanasi, where he died in captivity. The redbrick ruin of one of his palaces was still standing, just barely, in Shyamnagar, at the edge of a field where some boys were playing cricket. Trees grew out of the windows, and squatters had hung their laundry to dry in the derelict rooms that they shared with a healthy population of cobras.

Another bicycle cart meandered past. Behind the driver, on the wooden flatbed, a bearded man was shouting into a deafening pair of loudspeakers.

"What was that all about?" I asked Benedict, a young man who worked for an NGO called Uttaran, which busied itself with the concerns of the poorest communities in this part of Bangladesh, giving them advice on everything from drinking water to domestic violence.

"He says if you give money to the madrassa, you will go straight to heaven."

A few hundred yards on, another loudspeaker was blasting invitations to an Islamic gathering. A crowd of teenage boys blocked the roadway, collecting funds.

"They're also from the madrassa," Benedict complained. "It's only for boys, of course. There are many more of these schools than before, more all the time. The main thing they do is read and memorize the Qu'ran. In Arabic. The government encourages them to teach modern and general education, too. But . . ." He threw his hands up; what could you do?

In the past, rural Bangladesh had never been ruled by the dictates of the imam, whose role were generally restricted to the rituals of birth, marriage, death, and burial. The cultural lines between Hindu and Muslim were blurred. Communities had gathered without regard to religion to hear the epic tales of the Sufi master Gazi Kalu, who had enjoyed the favor of both Allah and the goddess Ganga, or to debate local issues to the accompaniment of songs and poetry and stylized performances by traveling troupes of actors. Now those things were slipping away in favor of the *Wa'azi*, prayer gatherings that sometimes edged toward militancy. Saudi money was pouring into the country.

At dawn, vague figures moved in and out of the mist on mud paths dotted with date palms and windowless thatched huts, as if Monet had set up his studio in Bengal. The sun was a pale tangerine ball over the horizon, a glittering reflection between the half-submerged stalks of rice, and the landscape was cut up into sharp rectangles. The rice fields were broken up here and there by shrimp farms, and then the shrimp farms took over, interrupted only by the occasional square of emerald paddy. English words began to appear next to the florid Bengali script on the roadside signboards. Prawn Hatchery; Gold Coin Aquaculture. The water in the ponds was mildly salty to the taste. In this part of Bangladesh, the salinity of the soil was eighty times higher than it had been forty years ago. Much of the land was no longer fit for grazing, and the competition between rice and shrimp was as unequal as the contest between a bus and a bicycle cart.

Benedict told me how the big shrimp companies had come by all this farmland. They started by leasing it: maybe twenty thousand takas, $250, for a two-year lease on half an acre of land. Then they renewed it. Shrimp farming was not a labor-intensive industry. You lost your land, you lost your job. If a farmer had a problem with that, the companies would bring in their musclemen, the *mastaans*. The shrimp were on their way to Japan, the United States, and Europe with lucrative price tags attached, so there was never much doubt which side the government would be on.

Benedict's boss, Shahidul Islam, whom I'd met earlier in Dhaka, had found this out the hard way by asking awkward questions. One day two soldiers dragged him from his office and took him to a nearby army base, where he was blindfolded and beaten. He had the impression that they used a field hockey stick. They broke his foot, and he still walked with a slight limp. He spent seven months in jail under Bangladesh's Special Powers Act, charged with "organizing landless people against the state."

Burigoalini, Tatinakhali, Kolbari. We had run out of road, and the last villages on the edge of the Sundarbans were at the end of earthen embankments and bicycle paths. Burigoalini was an old name. It paid homage to a local woman who once had pastures here for milk cows, a paddy for rice, and thriving freshwater fishponds. The economy she embodied was a thing of the past. The checkerboard of shrimp ponds extended to the horizon, and eels, bound for China and Japan, were hung up to dry on ropes along the muddy banks of the Kholpetua, a tributary of the Arpangasia, yet another of the Hundred Mouths of the Ganges. Sluice gates flushed the brackish water from the river into the shrimp ponds. On the other side, a hundred yards away, was a solid wall of forest, the beginning of the Sundarbans, a place where no one lived.

In Tatinakhali, the villagers were trying to raise crops on the dikes, above the salt line. They were experimenting with floating vegetable gardens and raising crabs in small ponds fenced off with reed matting. Researchers were at work on saline-tolerant rice. The experts in Dhaka called this the economy of resilience, and *resilience* was a word that might have been invented with Bangladesh in mind.

"Ninety percent of the people would leave if they could," a man said. But it was hard. The young ones dreamed of city life, but they had no money and no connections to make it happen. The older you got, the more powerful the ties that bound you to the village. Building a home and a fishpond, taking care of a patch of cultivable field, clearing a yard to dry and winnow your rice—that was a twenty-year investment of time, labor, and emotions.

The groundwater in Tatinakhali had become so salty that it was undrinkable, and the mud paths were crowded with women and girls in plastic flip-flops on their way to the sand-filter well in Kolbari, the next village, which purified water from the muddy fishponds. It was a mile and a half in each direction, three times a day, carrying home enough in your battered aluminum pot to supply your family's daily needs. Nine miles altogether, under a stupefying sun. A round-faced woman named Shajida said that sometimes, if you were hot or tired or got a late start, you were late putting dinner on the table, so your husband took the back of his hand to you. A neighbor's three small children were wide-eyed in the doorway behind her. Shajida told me that their father had been eaten by a tiger three weeks earlier.

"What happens when your husband does that?" I asked Shajida. "Is there a remedy?"

She gave me a tiny smile. "Crying," she said.

THE TIGER OF CHANDPAI

Mongla was a scruffy river port with a harborful of rusted freighters, and there were murals on the main road to the jetty that told you what to do in the event of a cyclone. A cow was floating away in the flood. A man was clinging onto a wooden bed frame. Another was halfway up a palm tree, strapping his naked baby to the trunk. I boarded a small riverboat, the MV *Bonbibi*, and set off southward into the Sundarbans, looking for tigers.

One of the garment workers in Dhaka had left her village at the edge of the great mangrove forest because it was being menaced by a tiger. The teenage fisherman in Khuriakhali had been eaten by one. The three children in Tatinakhali had just lost their father. Now there was a problem tiger in the village of Chandpai. It had begun by killing goats, dogs, and cattle, sixty animals in the course of a few months. Then it had killed an old woman, breaking into her hut through the thatch roof and dragging her from her bed in the middle of the night. The most recent victim was a man gathering fodder for his livestock at the edge of the forest.

Long before dawn, I was awakened in my narrow bunk by the grating clank of the anchor chain being raised. I rolled over, lifted the flap of the mosquito net, and squinted at the illuminated dial of my watch. Four fifteen. On the shore half a mile away, Chandpai was beginning to stir. The first lights were flickering on, accompanied by the soft *putt putt* of a generator. Then the *Bonbibi*'s engine kicked into life, coughing once or twice before it settled into a loud, steady throb.

Chandpai occupied the tip of a narrow promontory only a couple of feet above the mean tide level, encircled by the dense green wall of the Sundarbans. The name is a matter of dispute. Some say it means "beautiful forest," but most people say it's the forest of the sundari trees, which yield a reddish timber that is greatly prized for making the hulls of fishing boats. Two-thirds of the Sundarbans are in Bangladesh, and a third in India. Together they cover more than 2,300 square miles, the largest contiguous expanse of mangroves in the world. Three and a half million people live on the fringes of the Sundarbans, in villages like Chandpai, but the forest itself is free of human habitation except for a few scattered outposts where government guards stand watch for illegal loggers, fishermen without permits, river pirates, and tigers.

A sea-level rise of twenty-six inches—now almost certain to occur within the next few decades—will obliterate the Sundarbans, destroying the buffer that shields the Ganges delta from the fury of future cyclones. It will also wipe out one of the richest natural gene pools in the world: 334 plant species; 186 birds; 53 reptiles; 222 finfish; 100 shellfish. The rarest creatures of all are the gigantic, endangered estuarine crocodile, of which fewer than two hundred survive, and the Bengal tiger, which numbers around four hundred.

The tiger has always been an object of terror. The male can weigh up to five hundred pounds and reach ten feet in length. During the spring tides, it is capable of picking a fight with a crocodile, a favorite scene on Dhaka's painted rickshaws. It can swim as far as five miles in search of prey, and it can climb into fishing boats. And one of them was now frightening the wits out of the people of Chandpai.

———

The *Bonbibi* chugged slowly down the broad Passur River as the sun rose above the treetops. There were two other passengers, friends of mine, two forest guards in brown uniforms, and a crew of nine. The cook laid out our breakfast at a long table, an aromatic selection of curries, rice, and steaming flatbreads.

"What kind of curry is this?" I asked him.

"Green wegetable, sir."

At 10:30, he returned and loaded up the table again.

"Snack, sir?"

The second round of "green wegetable" gave me a furious thirst, but there was only bottled water. Bangladesh was officially alcohol-free. In Dhaka, rumor had it that you could find it if you knew where to look and whom to ask. Supposedly it was smuggled in across the border from Myanmar. But I'd never figured out the right code words. One day when I was eating lunch in a white-tablecloth restaurant, an obsequious waiter had delivered a bottle dripping with condensation to a smartly dressed middle-aged man at the next table.

Next time the waiter passed, I told him I'd like one, too.

"Sir," he said, "we are having no beer."

"But you just gave him one." I pointed.

He considered how to break the news of social niceties in Dhaka. "Sir, he is VIP."

The *Bonbibi* had turned off into a narrow channel, fifty or sixty feet wide, and I went up on deck and picked up my book. I was rereading *Heart of Darkness*. Chugging along through the mud-brown water and the thick tangle of forest, we might have been in Conrad's Congo. A troop of rhesus macaque monkeys cavorted on a narrow strip of beach. Spotted deer and wild boar browsed in the shadows. Several species of kingfisher—blue-eared, black-capped, brown-winged, white-collared—made sudden flashes of movement and color. Endangered adjutant storks prowled the shoreline on their spindly legs, and Brahmini kites and sea eagles glided overhead. At the junction of two larger rivers, a pod of rare Gangetic dolphins broke surface. Nearby, fishermen were setting sky-blue nets to capture fry for the shrimp farms.

We passed a couple of crocodiles sunbathing on a mudbank, twenty feet long and brutally armored. As the boat drew closer, they disappeared into the water in a great swirl of mud. In the idle warmth of the morning, my friends and I debated which would be the worst way to die: crocodile, tiger, grizzly bear, or shark. The tiger severs your spinal column with a single bite to the neck. With a grizzly, there would be the stinking meat-breath, the claws that could rip open the side of a car. With a shark, the silent, invisible attack from below, a chunk of your thigh gone suddenly, blood in the water, the helpless flailing. But the crocodile seemed the worst: the double horror of being clamped in those terrible jaws and then being dragged under to drown.

The cook called up from below. "Lunch is ready, sir."

It was another spread in varied shades of green, and he stood nearby as we picked at it without appetite.

"Sir, you would like tourist thing?" He gestured at a storage locker. I imagined cheap souvenirs, bangles, T-shirts, bamboo flutes. I shook my head.

He paused. "I have *very special* tourist thing. I can show you."

He opened the locker. Inside was a cooler, and in the cooler were a dozen bottles of Heineken, well chilled.

The *Bonbibi* was named for the goddess of the Sundarbans, who is believed to control the movements of the tiger. *Bon*, from the Bengali, the forest; *Bibi*, from the Urdu, the lady. Lady of the Forest. She is a syncretic deity, typical of the traditions of Bengal. In certain village shrines on the margins of the forest, she is depicted as a Hindu goddess wearing a green or blue sari and seated on a howling tiger, her countenance peaceful and serene. Her brother, Shajangali, carries a club to drive away the beast. He is dressed, in one scholar's description, "like a member of the Muslim gentry."

Many of those who venture into the forest to make their tenuous living— the fishermen, woodcutters, and honey collectors—will conduct elaborate rituals before they leave home, imploring Bonbibi to protect them. Anthropologists have documented ceremonies in which a variety of objects are offered to the goddess—conch-shell bangles, vermilion, scraps of red cloth, green coconuts, earthen pots, decorated figurines, sweetmeats, hemp, and incense. In the Indian section of the Sundarbans, there was a brief experiment in which forest workers tried wearing a mask on the back of the head to confuse the tiger, which attacks from behind. There is no evidence that this made any difference, any more than the prayers to Bonbibi.

Official reports say that about one person a week falls victim to the tigers. But many more deaths go unreported. The honey collectors, the *mowalis*, are especially vulnerable. They work for two months each year, in April and May, pursuing the rock bees that swarm south from the Himalayas in search of the nectar-bearing flowers of the holly mangrove, *Acanthus ilicifolius*, and the river mangrove, *Aegiceras corniculatum*. A skilled collector can bring back two hundred pounds or more. Once he has paid the forest service for his permit and given the forest guards and government officials their cut, this may bring him the equivalent of about seventy-five dollars for two months of unimaginably hazardous work. The *mowalis* work singly or in pairs, and their presence is disruptive at this time of year, since the tiger cubs are only a couple of months old and are still in their dens. The first attacks are likely to be defensive, but the kill will convert the tiger from a "circumstantial" to a "dedicated" man-eater.

Later that day, we sat idle at anchor for an hour or two. There were bangs and grunts from the engine room, and a member of the crew emerged at intervals, grasping a monkey wrench and smeared with black grease, and muttered anxious mechanical reports to the captain. A small boat pulled over beside us, and the boatman tossed a rope across the gap and tied up. A fresh-faced young man in a green polo shirt climbed aboard the *Bonbibi*, and I was startled to see another Western face in this remote place. His name was Adam Barlow. He was English-born and had written his thesis on the Bengal tiger at the University of Minnesota. Now he was living in Dhaka. He said he was on his way to Chandpai, with the aim of teaching villagers how to anesthetize their problem tiger, put a radio collar on it, and return it to another part of the forest, far from their homes.

I asked him how they usually dealt with the problem.

"Normally they put out bait for the tiger," he answered. "Then, when they've lured it into the village, they gather by the hundreds, arm themselves with sticks, and form a circle around it. Then they beat the tiger to death."

ON THE BEACH

One of the forest guards took up position behind me and the other walked in front, and they carried their rifles slung across their shoulders as we crossed an unstable wooden gangplank at the mouth of a tidal channel called Kotka Khal.

The outpost at Kotka was where Bangladesh finally dissolved into the ocean. There was not much here but a forest department sign, a couple of concrete buildings, one of them reduced to a broken shell by the most recent cyclone, and a watchtower on the far side of the channel. To the west, the beach stretched for three miles of gray-brown sand, strewn with coconuts and palm fronds, until it ended at the mouth of the broad Betmore Gang, which sounded like a Mafia casino operation but was still another of the Hundred Mouths of the Ganges. In many parts of the world, you might have expected to find a Club Med or an expensive eco-resort on a beach like this, but here you had the tigers to worry about.

The edge of the beach was carpeted with the spiky knee roots of the mangroves, and beyond them a narrow trail led into the forest. The guards' rifles had bayonets and chipped wooden stocks, and they looked as if they belonged in a museum. The problem was not so much the age of the guns, one of them said, as the age of the bullets. They were forty years old. But he told me not to worry; if we encountered a tiger in the forest, they fired correctly at least one time out of four.

We found day-old scat on the trail, there were claw marks gouged deep into the bark of a sundari tree, six feet off the ground, and a male had left fresh pugmarks in the sand, as broad as the spread of my hand. But there were no tigers to be seen, and we went back to the beach. "You were unlucky," the guard said.

I stood at the water's edge, letting the tide slap gently at the soles of my hiking boots. The Indian Ocean stretched away to the horizon, vast and brown and thick with silt, and if you sailed in a straight line due south, your next landfall would be at Mikhaylov Island, off the West Ice Shelf of Antarctica, five thousand miles away.

HOLI ON THE HOOGHLY

Once, in Varanasi, I'd seen a banner strung up on one of the ghats warning visitors of the perils of Holi, the spring festival of colors. It said, "For your Information it is Dangerous Festival for the girls. All Man will be totaly Drunk. Don't give any hug this day! Nobody keep control so don't take any Risk."

In Calcutta, meanwhile, hugs were actively encouraged. On the concrete pillars of the flyover that makes a feeble attempt to speed traffic along Chowringhee Road, there were giant billboards that showed a woman in a wet sari wrapping herself around a Bollywood-style hunk with three-day stubble. The text said, "Holi Gets Wild." I think it was an ad for deodorant.

A friend took me to a Holi party in the garden of a small gated apartment complex in a quiet middle-class neighborhood. I exchanged greetings and holiday wishes with the hosts. She was a molecular biologist, he was an engineer, and they had a small organic farm on the banks of the Hooghly. The engineer fixed me a vodka mojito, complete with a sprig of mint, and one of the guests came lurching toward me with a plate of pakoras laced with bhang. She thrust it into my hand and told me I had some catching up to do. Looking around at the crowd, it was clear what she meant. There was a lot of lurching and swaying going on, and several of the dancers seemed to have passed out in armchairs. Kids were running amok, and two of them came running up and showered me with the obligatory colored powder, green, red, yellow, and purple. "I think the colors symbolize triumph," somebody slurred. "Maybe triumph in war, or something." Another of the ads we'd seen on the way to the party, from a construction company, urged people to use organic colors this year.

Most of the guests seemed to be in their forties or early fifties. When I asked them what they did, that typical American question, most answered with something vague about being semiretired or freelance or some kind of a consultant—teaching or college administration or IT, which is big in Calcutta. All of them spoke flawless English, lightly accented in a way that hinted at an English or American education. One man said he was digitizing the vast art collection at the Victoria Memorial, the Taj of the Raj, as people sometimes call it, and played a little jazz on the side. "Count Basie makes my heart skip a beat," he said. We agreed that the Count's recordings of blues numbers with Jimmy Rushing were particularly fine.

"Calcutta has always been a wonderful place," a woman said. "This is where I have got to see people like Jacques Derrida, Edward Said, Sasha Waltz, Herbie Hancock. They all come here. It's wonderful."

Everyone seemed to refer to the city as Calcutta, not Kolkata. For reasons no one can fully explain, some of India's postcolonial name changes have stuck, and some haven't. Most people these days seemed to say Chennai, not Madras, but hardly anyone referred to Bangalore as Bengaluru. Mumbai versus Bombay was a more even split, like Varanasi and Benares.

Debating the relative merits of Calcutta and Kolkata, and the possible origins of the name, called for another round of pakoras and mojitos. The most common theory was that the city had been named for the goddess Kali, its most important deity, whose celebrated temple was at Kalighat. A more outlandish idea was that Christian missionaries had been so appalled by the pestilential swamps along the Hooghly, and the speed with which they carried off foreign residents, that they compared the area to Golgotha, the Place of the Skull. The story I liked best told of an early British visitor who asked a passing grass cutter what the place was called. Misunderstanding the question, the man said, in Bengali, *kal kata*. It was cut yesterday.

"Kolkata has the long Bengali *O*, of course, but they sound almost the same, so what does it matter," a woman said.

"There were public opinion polls," a man chimed in. "Most people preferred Calcutta."

"Calcutta, Kolkata. It's a matter of identity. This is our cultural schizophrenia," said a third person.

While no one seemed to be losing any sleep over the problem, there was always that slight cultural uncertainty in Calcutta. Use the Bengali name and you were affirming a proud and distinctive heritage, filled with song and poetry and nostalgia for an ancestral homeland that was now divided in two, east and west. Use the anglicized version, and you might be implicitly endorsing the idea that Calcutta's deepest identity was to have been the second city of the empire, the pinkest part of Queen Victoria's map, with all its splendors and all its cruelties. But if you were a jazz-loving IT consultant, *Calcutta* also marked you as a sophisticate, a citizen of the larger world; if you said *Kolkata*, did it mark you out as a modernizer or a bumpkin?

We left the matter unresolved, piled into a rattletrap Ambassador taxi, mildly stoned, and headed for the ghats, where so many people were soaping the Holi powder off their bodies that the river had turned a deep purple.

THE WORLD OF APU

Hovering below the surface of this talk of Derrida and Basie, there were always the shades of Bengal's two greatest artists: Rabindranath Tagore, the white-bearded poet-novelist-composer-polymath who cemented a distinct idea of Bengali culture at the turn of the twentieth century and became the first non-European to win the Nobel Prize for literature; and the incomparable filmmaker Satyajit Ray.

Calcutta was a riddle, Tagore wrote in a recollection of his childhood. "Something undreamt of was lurking everywhere, and every day the uppermost question was: where, oh where would I come across it?"

Ray, who was born into the city's cosmopolitan elite, struggled mightily over his feelings for Bengal, the emotional push and pull between village and city, aspiration and disappointment, idealism and failure, the desire for change and the desire for continuity.

What should you put into your films? What can you leave out? Would you leave the city behind and go to the village where cows graze in the endless fields and the shepherd plays his flute? You could make a film here that would be pure and fresh and have the flowing rhythms of a boatman's song. . . .

Or would you rather stay where you are, right in the present, in the heart of this monstrous, teeming, bewildering city, and try to orchestrate its dizzying contrasts of sight and sound and milieu?

The two most celebrated scenes Ray ever shot are in *Pather Panchali*, the first of his *Apu Trilogy*. One is of rain, the other a train. The enduring rhythms of the village, and the surging energy of escape.

In the first of these scenes, dark clouds build up over the fields, thunder rumbles in the distance, lily pads stir in the wind, Apu's mother takes in her drying laundry, his father looks up at the sky and unfurls his umbrella, the first drops of the monsoon pock the surface of a pond. Apu, who is six, takes shelter under a tree, bare-chested and shivering, then breaks into a smile as he sees his sister, Durga—named for the goddess revered by Bengalis—tossing her long hair as the water streams off it in the downpour.

In the second scene, they press their ears to an electricity pole, listening to the hum in the wires, crouch in the long grass where Apu turns to his sister and asks, "Where are we?" and she says nothing in reply, then they sprint across the field to a raised embankment where a train thunders past them, trailing black smoke.

At the start of the sequel, *Aparajito*, Apu is nine. In blurry black and white, right after the certificate of approval from the Central Board of Film Censors, we see the Ganges through his eyes, flashing through the struts of the Malviya Bridge in Varanasi, just above Raj Ghat, where the porters load wood for the cremation grounds. His father prays and preaches on the ghats but soon falls sick. "Here it is not as good as it is in our native place, isn't it?" he asks Apu. After being blessed with a last mouthful of *gangajal*, he dies.

Halfway through the film, another train whistle blows. The train clatters across the river again, this time in the opposite direction, headed back to Bengal, and Apu watches the ghats recede into the distance. He dozes with his head on his mother's lap as she stares out at the passing landscape. A boy poles a boat along a canal; a man leads a bullock cart along a mud embankment.

Back in the village, there have been subtle changes. A horse-drawn tonga arrives one day, with a man who wears a *topi* and a white suit with a rosette in his buttonhole and introduces Apu to "the tender leaf of literature."

"In which land are the trees and plants the most green?" the man asks. "In which land are all equally welcome? Where is it that golden vegetables and lotus are grown? It is our Bengal. Our land called Bengal."

In school, Apu is given two books. One is *Livingstone in Africa*. The other tells the lives of the great scientists: Archimedes, Galileo, Newton, Faraday. At sixteen, he places second in the district exams. He tells his mother that he has been offered a scholarship to study science in Calcutta, worth ten rupees a month. He begs her permission. "Will I not go? Everyone goes there," he tells her.

They argue.

"What's wrong with being a priest like your father?" she demands. "What will happen to me?"

He shows her a globe, a gift from his headmaster. The blue oceans. He studies it in the third-class carriage. The train steams into Howrah Station, along a converging web of tracks. On the platform, Apu is pushed and jostled in the crowd of other passengers. Outside in the street, he is startled by a motor car. His reaction suggests that he has never seen one before.

He takes a job in a printshop on Patuatola Lane, near the University of Calcutta and the bookstalls of College Street, and studies at night. He learns the meaning of the word *synecdoche*. He becomes familiar with the great sights of the city: the Victoria Memorial, the Kalighat Temple, the Keoratala cremation grounds. He sits on the riverbank, gazes at the ships, and dreams of the blue oceans.

His mother sends him plaintive messages. "Why do you never write or come home?" He shuttles back and forth on the three-hour train ride to his village, stricken by guilt and ambivalence. A letter comes from a neighbor to say that his mother has fallen ill. He hurries back but finds the house empty. He mourns her death with an old man who wears the sacred thread across his left shoulder.

"Where will you go?" the man asks.

"Calcutta."

"Why to Calcutta?"

"I have college."

"What about your mother's last rites?"

"I'll perform them in Calcutta, at Kalighat."

The old man touches Apu's forehead in blessing. Apu heads off barefoot along the muddy path, away from the camera, and never looks back.

THE AGING PROSTITUTE

I f the undreamt of was lurking everywhere in Calcutta, as Tagore believed, the only way to find it was on foot. No matter how suffocating the heat and humidity, I rarely tired of walking the streets of the city, and somehow I always found myself drawn back to the claustrophobic neighborhood around Howrah Bridge—now renamed Rabindra Setu in honor of Tagore. It was one of those places that seemed to distill something of the essence of India within its narrow, chaotic confines, although you knew, of course, that whenever you thought you had found the essence of India, you had probably just ensnared yourself in clichés.

Half a mile from the bridge, on BBD Bagh, which was once Dalhousie Square and is still the political heart of Calcutta, there were digital displays from the city government that said, "KEEP KOLKATA POLLUTION FREE and KEEP YOUR VEHICLE'S POLLUTION WITHIN LIMITS." There was no indication of how this was to be accomplished in practice. Across the Hooghly, the red-brick towers of Howrah Station and the fishing boats and ferries chugging along the far side of the river were usually no more than dim shapes in the smog.

The cantilever bridge, which is five hundred yards long, was a masterpiece of British engineering, built in 1943 as part of the war effort—the same war effort, and in the same year, that led to a famine that killed three million people, fully 5 percent of the population of Bengal. They were victims of the triage of wartime. Singapore had fallen to the Japanese in 1942, and now they were rampaging through Burma. London stockpiled a large percentage of Bengal's rice crop and diverted potential relief supplies to feed the troops and compensate for shortages in Britain. Colonial police destroyed warehouses full of rice in the coastal areas to prevent them falling into the hands of the enemy. Only the speculators thrived. Churchill's view was that the Bengalis had brought the catastrophe on themselves because "they breed like rabbits." He had never concealed his feelings about where India belonged in the hierarchy of eugenics. "I hate Indians," he once said, wishing that he could arrange for Gandhi to be trampled to death by a large elephant. "They are a beastly people with a beastly religion."

Two million people cross the Rabindra Setu every day. This is said to be the heaviest volume of foot traffic carried by any bridge in the world. The crowd is almost entirely male, a crush of busy men with briefcases and cell phones, porters in lungis with impossible loads on their heads, schoolboys with satchels and book bags.

Close to the base of the bridge are the neoclassical pillars of the Armenian Ghat. One of the oldest on the Hooghly, it was built in 1734 by economic migrants from Persia. They thrived in Calcutta as the city's first moneylenders, bent with the political winds, and served the interests of the East India Company as faithfully as they had previously served the Mughal nawabs. An Armenian merchant named Catchick Arrakiel put on a fireworks display to celebrate George III's recovery from madness, though he was no doubt saddened when this proved to be only a temporary remission.

Near the Armenian Ghat is a small Shiva temple that Allen Ginsberg liked to visit. Drunks are usually sprawled on the steps outside the Country Spirit Shop (Opening Hours 11:00 a.m. to 9:00 p.m., Closed Thursdays). Other men soap themselves down at a tap where a poster gives a toll-free number for those who are interested in finding out more about how to prevent HIV-AIDS. Others pay a visit to the Pay and Toilet Complex, which is maintained by the White Welfare Society, whatever that might be. If you're too poor to pay the admission charge, you can squat and do your morning business at the neighboring Ram Chandra Goenka Zenana Bathing Ghat. The building at the top of the steps has a Mughal-style dome and turrets overgrown with foliage; all over Calcutta, trees and shrubs and aerial roots shoulder their way out of windows, walls, and rotted rooftops. The interior is a maze of pillars and archways that suggest a Romanesque crypt. The ghat was designed for women to bathe in privacy, but that distinction was lost long ago, and nowadays people of both genders and all ages gather there to take their dip and shit on the steps. A sign would be useful at the Zenana Bathing Ghat: watch where you tread.

One morning, I had breakfast with my friend Damayanti, the one who had invited me to the Holi party. Her many friends called her Dodo.

We went to the Indian Coffee House, just off College Street, where students were eating fifty-cent mutton cutlets under a life-size painting of Tagore, arguing and flirting and chatting on cell phones and pickling themselves in caffeine and nicotine. Upstairs, in small rooms off scuffed and shabby hallways, men were clacking away at manual typewriters, writing letters that would end, "Kindly revert," or "Please do the needful." Hole-in-the-wall printing presses were cranking out literary newsletters and pamphlets analyzing the role of the Bengali proletariat in the coming world revolution.

Dodo, who called herself a "freelance dissident," had grown up in the world of Apu and Tagore, with all its complexities. "My parent eloped and got married, simply because of caste," she said. "My father was from a big family of landowners, zamindars, in East Bengal. He gave up his sacred thread when I was fifteen, and that was my proudest moment. My mother was from this side. My father's family was always into music and the classical arts. The tabla player Zakir Hussain, the great sitarist Nikhil Banerjee, so many other musicians. They all used to stay in our home. On my mother's side, they were writers and artists and painters and dancers. Majumdars, who are considered one of the foremost families of Calcutta. So it was a very privileged upbringing. I grew up watching Satyajit Ray films, hearing those stories. My eldest uncle designed many of the sets for his films."

Her mother sounded like the most interesting of all of them. She had made her name as a painter by encouraging her students to create murals that would cover up the revolutionary graffiti that disfigured the walls of Calcutta in the 1960s and 1970s. "She thought it should be replaced with work that was easier on the eye for schoolchildren, since this is not a good thing to see when walking to school," Dodo said. Many of her mother's own paintings were reimaginings of Calcutta's two great goddesses, Kali and Durga, in which she mixed classical iconography with elements drawn from Bengali folk art.

After we'd finished breakfast, Dodo wanted to show me more of the waterfront, and we ended up back at Howrah Bridge, where the monumental relics of the Raj rubbed shoulders with the clamor of the modern city. "I always remember something that was once said by an urban planner," she said as we walked along Strand Bank Road, past the derelict shells of the old warehouses and godowns, which were now being bought up by developers. "Calcutta is like an aging prostitute. She's covered in open sores, but she can still show you a trick or two."

A train lumbered past on the local track that encircles the city. It was lined with crumbling shacks, built so close that the residents could have reached out and shaken hands with the passengers. We stopped at a stall that was selling a round, spiky fruit I didn't recognize. Dodo said it was thorn apple, or jimsonweed, a member of the nightshade family. Poisonous, aphrodisiac, and hallucinogenic. "That's why we use it for Shiva's puja," she said. "Because he was our first marijuana-smoking god."

Next door was a bicycle and rickshaw repair shop with the usual posters of Shiva and Krishna and Ganesha and Lakshmi, the goddess of prosperity, but also another of a mustachioed deity I'd never seen before. He was surrounded by an abstract design of wrenches, sickles, pincers, axes, and trowels. Dodo identified him as Vishwakarma, the god of tools and crafts, who gives his name to a caste that includes metalworkers, blacksmiths, carpenters, and stonemasons. One of the employees was using a hammer and a cold chisel to dislodge a heavy cast-iron grating, stamped with the name of its British manufacturer. I asked him what he was doing. "The authorities don't clear the drains unless there's an emergency," he said. "So we have to take precautions before the monsoon starts." The previous year, the river had risen so high that it flooded the railway tracks behind the shop, shutting down train service for the whole day. All it takes for Calcutta to flood, people say, is for a frog to pee.

At Mullick Ghat, a long line of trucks was unloading bundles for the flower market, which is reputed to be the biggest in the world. Porters prodded me and jostled me and barged me aside without an ounce of hostile intent, just going about their business.

It turned out that quite a few of the flower sellers were from Orissa state, to the south of Calcutta—or Odisha, as it is known now, another of those name changes that keep people off balance. "We are licensed by the port authority," one of them said. "But people still consider us as outsiders. The locals start ganging up on us, and then life becomes difficult. We complain to the authorities, but they won't listen."

"Do you have to pay them bribes?" I asked.

"No, we would never do that."

"Well, obviously that's what he's going to tell you," Dodo muttered to me in English.

The man from Odisha had opened for business at three in the morning. He would close up shop at nine in the evening. He sat in the middle of a mountain range of flowers: prodigious garlands of orange and yellow marigolds; white roses from Bangalore for funeral arrangements; chrysanthemums dyed in rainbow colors; small pink korobi; bright gerbera daisies; bluish-purple *aparajita—Clitoria ternatea*, so-named because of their resemblance to the female genitalia—sacred to Shiva and said to be good for urinary tract infections; hibiscus threaded so tightly together in strands that they looked like scarlet firecrackers; clusters of *rajanighanda*, "the fragrance of the night." An old lady was squatting at the head of the steps, separating the waxy white *rajanighanda* flowers from their stems with her long arthritic fingers to make necklaces. Her bangles jingled. I asked her how long she'd been doing this, and she said sixty years.

The vendor was still expecting another shipment that day, but the truck was running late. "Maybe the driver had an accident," he said.

"More likely he's drunk," said another man.

Since most of the business was in marigolds, I asked the man from Odisha how much they sold for. He said he charged two hundred rupees for twenty garlands, a little over three dollars, but people usually bargained him down. The problem was that nothing seemed to be selling, and though it was only midmorning, the temperature was already well into the nineties, and the sweat was dripping off me. He shrugged. "If they don't sell by the end of the day, we'll pack them up and ship them to Bihar or Bombay." He pointed to a couple of young men who were filling bags of ice. "They will stay fine. I won't let anything spoil."

The economics of the flower market defeated me. Ten rupees, fifteen cents, for a garland four or five feet long. How much did the growers earn? The pickers? The truckers? The middlemen? The porters? The vendors? The shippers? The ice packers? The buyer in Bihar? The seller in Bombay? How did any of them make enough to stay alive? Dodo said these were questions to which she had no answer.

A WALK IN THE PARK

We Bengalis are a lazy lot," Dodo said one day as we sat in a sweltering Ambassador in stalled traffic on our way to Prinsep Ghat. "Unlike the immigrants who come here from Rajasthan, like the Birlas, who make these cars." The Ambassador, modeled on a British workhorse called the Morris Oxford, had been manufactured continuously in the Birlas' Hindustan Motors plant in Calcutta since the 1950s, resisting all design changes and shifting fashions.

"Same thing with the taxi drivers," she went on. "Most of them are from

Bihar; they're very hardworking." The driver was pounding his hand on the horn, which was doing nothing to relieve the gridlock, and she snapped at him to stop. The Biharis might be industrious, but they were also noisy.

"It's psychological," said Pradeep Kakkar, who was on his way to the river with us along with his wife, Bonani. Pradeep had earned his Ph.D. in management from UCLA and worked all over Asia as a consultant. "It's their way of making social contact with other people. 'Here I am, recognize me.'" He meant it sympathetically, but still, he said, "Noise is India's number-one problem." He and Bonani, who was an expert on public health, had organized anti-honking rallies with a small citizen's group they'd founded on Earth Day in 1990. They called it People United for Better Living in Calcutta, which gave them a handy acronym: PUBLIC.

The Kakkars, who were in their late middle age, had a formal manner of speaking that was very English, beautifully modulated but slightly stilted. They would have made a good choice as readers of audiobooks on serious subjects. "PUBLIC started out of anger," Pradeep said. "We were all a bit younger, at a stage of our careers where we were trying to make it to the next notch." Calcutta had become synonymous with decay and dysfunction, and middle-class Calcuttans were abandoning the city in droves. "Voting by caste and religion had made a mockery of democracy," he said. "We were going through power outages every day that might last six, seven, eight hours without any warning. So we organized a night march against power cuts. Everyone dressed in black. We carried lanterns and signs in black with luminous paint. We also started a campaign against noise near hospitals and schools. What kept us here was that we loved the city. We thought this was one of the greatest cities in the world, and it should continue to be so. We decided that what was needed was middle-class activism. Before us, the emphasis was always on social welfare, helping the needy and the poor. We were the first group to come together and say, we want a better city, with a certain minimum standard of living which other cities in India already have."

We arrived at Prinsep Ghat. It was a Palladian arcade. It looked like one of those follies that you might find on a strategic hilltop at an English stately home, and it raised the familiar question: What was it exactly that made Calcutta one of the world's great cities—its Bengali culture or its British heritage? The monument had been built in 1843 to honor James Prinsep, secretary of the Asiatic Society, an artist who created a beautiful series of sketches and lithographs of the waterfront at Varanasi. The ghat was still used at the time for the execution of pirates, who were not hanged but put to death by drowning. It was also the embarkation and disembarkation point for visiting royalty.

"We were doing a river cleanup one day," Bonani said, "and I told people lunch would be served. There would be a van waiting with sandwiches at Prinsep Ghat. But there was scaffolding all around it, twenty feet high, and a circular fence covered with creepers. This magnificent monument! You couldn't see the river. I couldn't believe it. I said, 'There *is* no ghat.' So we convinced the government to restore it as a valuable relic of the Raj era."

That was in 1993. Now Prinsep Ghat, with its Ionic columns, was the southernmost end of a new park that stretched as far as Babu Ghat, where the columns were Doric. That still left it some way short of Motilal Seal Ghat, where they were Corinthian, with handsome fluted pilasters.

The restoration of the waterfront was far from complete. There were still abandoned boats rusting away at the water's edge, strangled in vegetation, like a slow-motion chemistry experiment to demonstrate the effects of water and sunlight on iron. "They look like Angkor Wat before it was cleaned up for the tourists," Dodo said.

But the completed parts of the park were pleasant. There were garbage cans in the shape of kangaroos, alligators, and dolphins. Each of them had a sign that said, "Use Me," which, to be honest, was not something you saw often in India. There were large topiary elephants behind blue-and-white railings. There were blue-and-white public toilets. Police patrolled the park in modified golf carts, also painted blue and white. Whoever had the contract to supply blue and white paint had to be making a fortune. "Oh, that's Didi's brother," Dodo said, referring to the chief minister.

"This government is the first of a different color in thirty years," Pradeep said. "Before that, it was a left government that was labeled 'Communist' but made no difference to life on the street. These new people have come into power because of the stupidity of the previous government. People like me were terribly upset, so we voted against it. But it was a case of frying pan into the fire. A lot of what they are doing is cosmetics. My personal psychological insight into this is that the leadership comes from a fairly deprived background, so having bright lights on the street and fresh paint on the sidewalks is in their view an expression of achievement. Although in some cases that's not a bad thing, like this riverside improvement, because that has long been needed."

To be fair, it was the previous government that had created Millennium Park in the first place—in the year 2000, as the name implied. But even then, under "Communist" rule, you couldn't escape the fact that the British were embedded in the bone and sinew of Calcutta.

"George Nicholson of London Rivers was here for a conference," Bonani said. "He took a walk along the Hooghly and told the authorities that Calcutta had come up in the first place because of the river, but now it had turned its back on it. You couldn't even approach the river because of all the shanties. The view was blocked. All connection to the river was lost. The only time you were reminded that there even *was* a river was when you drove across the bridge to the Howrah railway station. George was insistent, and so was the British deputy high commissioner. So government officials went to London to see the redevelopment of the Thames, how the river there had become alive with all sorts of art galleries and restaurants. Seeing that, the government started focusing on the river here and what it could become. That was in 1999."

"Clearing the squatters was the toughest part," Pradeep said.

"We went there one morning and saw fire engines and police and payloaders. They just came and smashed into everything," Bonani said.

Her husband thought it was important to clarify. "But not the people who were living there, just the people who had started illegal businesses. There were even boats that were being used as brothels. We've always taken pride in the fact that Calcutta, unlike Delhi or Bombay, has never sent in bulldozers.

Even in the 1970s, during the Emergency. We always say that people are living on the streets because we've failed. The fact that they're in our face is a reminder that there are human beings who are living in such conditions, and we shouldn't brush them under the carpet."

"When we were kids, it used to be a Sunday treat to come down to the river," Bonani said. "It was cool here. There were balloons, ice cream sellers."

"All you need to do is give people unencumbered access," Pradeep said. "We've seen riversides like that even in poorer countries, like Cambodia, so we should be able to do it here."

Babu Ghat, with its Doric columns, was a confusion of priests and bathers. One of the priests was sitting quietly on a platform on a rush mat, reading from the scriptures. He lived on the platform, he said: worked there, ate there, slept there. It was about eight feet long and four feet wide; more than big enough. His name was Balaram Panda, and he'd been here for fifty-eight years. He was the fifth generation of his family to occupy the spot, the descendants of eleven Brahmins who came to Calcutta in 1830, the same year the ghat was built. Like the flower sellers I'd met at Mullick Ghat, they were natives of Odisha.

"What do you do all day?" I asked.

"Any kind of puja people ask for," he said. "When a child first has solid food, weddings, the sacred thread ceremony, funeral rites, the blessing of a house."

"He's a one-stop puja shop," Dodo said.

With a little imagination, you might have thought you were in Varanasi. There, heritage was about Hindu temples and palaces and gardens of remembrance; here, it was neoclassical columns and ice cream carts. A walk along the ghats couldn't have been more different in the two cities, but the underlying message seemed the same: bring people closer to the river, and honor its heritage, even if you couldn't agree exactly what that was.

GOING NATIVE

P
ark Street was originally called Burial Ground Road, and in the old colonial cemetery, there were more Ionic, Doric, and Corinthian columns than you could count. I took a circuitous route to get there, looking for somewhere to grab an early lunch first. I skipped Domino's Pizza and Pizza Hut ("Cheesiest Pizza in India") and McDonald's, which was offering a special on its McSpicy Paneer. Finally, I spotted a restaurant called Kwality, which served something that approximated Indian food.

A loud party of English tourists with a South London twang had already settled in around a long table near the entrance and were reviewing the options on the menu.

"You know you can get cornflakes and porridge here for breakfast?"

"*Dosa*. That's the long one, isn't it?"

"Oh, I'm not all that hungry. I think I might just have pudding."

"Let's get some Kingfishers, though."

You could never entirely escape the English in Calcutta, and I was already planning to spend the afternoon among English people who had been dead for two hundred years. I wasn't in the mood for the tourists' chatter, so I got up and walked on a little farther down Park Street to the Au Bon Pain at the corner of Sir William Jones Sarani. It had all manner of muffins—blueberry, carrot and chocolate chunk, and raisin bran—as well as Greek yogurt with granola, pain au chocolat, cheese danish, and various kinds of croissants. I opted for an everything bagel with cream cheese and a cappuccino. I might have been in New York, although all the other customers seemed to be upwardly mobile Bengalis.

Sir William Jones was the most celebrated of the Orientalists, the founder of the Asiatic Society, which held its meetings and kept its library at 1 Park

Street. "Asiatic Jones" was a judge, a philologist, and something of an archaeologist, a man of scholarship and tolerance, especially in matters of religion. "I hold the doctrines of the Hindoos concerning a future state to be incomparably more rational, more pious, and more likely to deter men from vice than the horrid opinions inculcated by the Christians on punishment without end," he wrote. He mastered thirteen languages and had a working knowledge of another twenty-eight. The joke was that he knew every language in the world except his own; like Fanny Parkes, he was Welsh. Jones died in 1794, at the age of forty-seven, of "a common complaint in Bengal, an inflammation of the liver." He was buried in the South Park Street Cemetery.

At the gatehouse, I signed the visitors' book and paid the caretaker a few rupees for a skinny booklet printed by the British Association for Cemeteries in South Asia and the Association for the Preservation of Historic Cemeteries in India. The caretaker was a small, trim man in his sixties with a toothbrush mustache and a bald head, dapper in slacks and a polo shirt. He was obviously European, but he was burned as dark as any Bengali. He took a piece of paper and wrote down his name for me: Kenneth Fernandes. I wondered if he might be a descendant of one of the Portuguese traders who had been among the earliest settlers on the Hooghly, and he smiled.

"No," he said, "nothing like that. My father came here from Portugal in 1939 to join the police."

"And your mother?"

"She was English, from London."

"What brought her to Calcutta?"

"Believe it or not, she came out originally to play for a hockey team, in 1943."

He told me that there was no obligation, but if I wished I could also make a donation to the "adopt-a-tomb" scheme to sponsor the repair and upkeep of a particular grave. It was obvious why this was necessary. The marble and stonework had been savaged by 250 years of monsoon rains, and for decades the cemetery had been left to decay, degenerating into a small, walled jungle that was home to refugees from East Bengal, drug addicts, feral dogs, and poisonous snakes. Now its restoration was half-complete, which created an odd effect, like a head of hair left shaggy on one side and shaved bald on the other. The restored section was crisscrossed by neat, grassy pathways and shaded by mango trees; the other was still an overgrown House of Usher where the inscriptions were obscured by moss and lichen.

With the help of the booklet, I quickly found the grave of Asiatic Jones. It was a towering Cleopatra's Needle, flanked by four urns in high relief and the symbol of two crossed spades in tribute to his archaeological talents. His epitaph, self-composed, said, "Here was deposited the mortal part of a man who feared God, but not Death, who thought none below him but the base and unjust, none above him but the wise and virtuous."

In summertime especially, the stonecutters and chiselers had had more work than they could handle. In the decades before the first grave was dug at South Park Street, in 1767, more than half the employees of the East India Company died of disease, and most of them died young. "A man can be talking to you at breakfast and be dead in the afternoon," said one Anglo-Indian. In Calcutta, there was no end to the things that could put you in a coffin: cholera (which originated in the Ganges Delta and killed with terrifying speed), malaria (the cause of which was eventually discovered in Calcutta in the 1890s by Sir Ronald Ross), typhoid, dysentery, tick fever, blackwater fever, "jungle fever," smallpox, snakebite, sunstroke, drowning, polo and riding accidents, rabies, venereal disease, an infected cut. Alcoholism was usually camouflaged beneath euphemisms, but it was also a killer; in the glory days of the Hon'ble Company, a man thought nothing of putting away three bottles of claret over lunch.

For the "Fishing Fleet," the women who made the six-month voyage to Calcutta on an East Indiaman to find a husband, childbirth was often lethal.

ELIZA, THE AFFECTIONATE WIFE OF W. G. GRIELEY.

DIED IN CHILD-BED

1ST AUGUST 1827 AGED 22 YEARS 7 MONTHS & 26 DAYS.

SACRED TO THE MEMORY OF ISABEL MATILDA,

WIFE OF MR. WM. J. SHULDHAM,

WHO DEPARTED THIS LIFE ON THE 23RD APRIL 1854

AT THE EARLY AGE OF 15 YEARS 5 MONTHS

DAYS AFTER GIVING BIRTH TO A BOY WHO SURVIVED

ONLY 11 HOURS

Many of the gravestones had poetic epitaphs, in the sentimental language of the period.

IN MEMORY OF HENRY PATRICK WILSON ESQ.

WHO DEPARTED THIS LIFE ON 11TH OF MAY 1793 AGED 42 YEARS

IN MANNERS GENTLE AND IN TEMPER MILD

IN WIT A MAN, SIMPLICITY A CHILD

ROSE AYLMER, WHOM THESE WAKEFUL EYES

MAY WEEP, BUT NEVER SEE,

A NIGHT OF MEMORIES AND OF SIGHS

I CONSECRATE TO THEE

Rose had gone to meet her maker in 1820, as the consequence of "a most severe bowel complaint brought on entirely by indulging too much in that mischievous and dangerous fruit, the pineapple."

I finally found one or two people who had survived into old age. A dark, ponderous mausoleum housed Maj. Gen. William Hopper of the Bengal Artillery:

(SERVED EAST INDIA COMPANY FOR 60 YEARS, DIED AGED 77,

SINCERELY LAMENTED, AND HIS WIFE MARGARET,

HIS RELICT, AGED 74)

Nearby was the tomb of another high-ranking military officer.

MAJOR GENERAL CHARLES STUART

(KNOWN AS HINDOO STUART)

1758——1.4.1828

QUARTER MASTER OF THE 1ST BENGAL

EUROPEAN REGIMENT & LATER COMMANDED

THE 10TH ANDIS REGIMENT

This was the one I'd been looking for.

"I see you found him, then," said a voice behind me. I turned around. It was Mr. Fernandes.

"Well, it wasn't exactly difficult," I said. After all, among the dozens of classical plinths and pedestals, columns and cupolas, Grecian urns, pyramids, and obelisks, it was the only tomb that looked like a Hindu temple, complete with carvings of gods or holy men—it was hard to tell which, because the features had been eroded by time, weather, and pollution.

Hindoo Stuart, who was born in Ireland and came to India in his teens, had the same inquisitive and enlightened spirit as Sir William Jones. "The chief purpose of travelling into foreign countries [is] to study the manners, customs, policy etc. of their inhabitants," he wrote. But he was more pamphleteer than scholar. In a paper called "A Vindication of the Hindoos," he railed against "obnoxious" Christian missionaries. "As far as I can rely on my judgment," he declared, "[Hinduism] appears the most complete and ample system of Moral Allegory that the world has ever produced."

This was more than an expression of respect; it was a statement of personal allegiance. Stuart considered himself a convert, although formal conversion to Hinduism wasn't technically possible. He wore pointed slippers and furnished his home with spittoons for paan juice and a priceless collection of statues of the gods, some of which ended up in the British Museum. He refused to eat beef, which must have drastically limited his options at regimental dinners. He went to Allahabad to take part in the Kumbh Mela. Eventually he took up residence on Wood Street in Calcutta, half a mile from the cemetery, and strolled down to the Hooghly every morning to take his holy dip.

His preference was for bathing at a ghat where women gathered. "He has the *Itch* beyond any man I ever knew," a friend said.

British women had been coming out to Calcutta since the 1670s, but until the arrival of the Fishing Fleet, which began in earnest around 1820, the numbers were tiny. If they failed to find a husband within a year, the Hon'ble Company shipped them back home as "returned empties." Since there were four thousand British men in the city in 1790, and only two hundred and fifty women, this was the worst ignominy a woman could bear. If he couldn't find someone to his taste, an unmarried man always had the option of his bibi, who had the additional virtue of acting as a "sleeping dictionary" to help a chap master the tricky native language. In return for her services, she could expect a couple of servants of her own and a modest allowance for clothes, shoes, paan, tobacco, and jewelry.

Job Charnock, founder of the city and administrator of the East India Company, had three children by a beautiful Hindu woman after snatching her from her husband's funeral pyre on the banks of the Ganges in Bihar. She was fifteen at the time. Her name was Rani, although he preferred to call her Maria. The attorney William Hickey buried his wife, Charlotte, at South Park Street. After her death, at the age of twenty-one, he had a servant procure him a bibi named Jemdanee, "as gentle and affectionately attached a girl as ever man was blessed with."

Some felt more of an itch for Muslim women. General Sir David Ochterlony, also known as Loony Akhtar, who is honored by a column that stands across from the Victoria Memorial in Calcutta, had a harem of thirteen and once shocked Bishop Heber by receiving him dressed in a Muslim gown and a green turban. One eighteenth-century Calcutta Resident had himself circumcised to add to his appeal.

Stuart stuck to Hindus and shared his feelings with the readers of the *Cal-*

cutta Telegraph. "The new-mown hay is not sweeter than their breath. . . . so exquisitely formed, with limbs so divinely turned, and such expression in their eyes, that you must acknowledge them not inferior to the most celebrated beauties of Europe . . . the dazzling brightness of a copper-colored face, infinitely preferable to the pallid and sickly hue of the European fair." He urged Englishwomen to wear the sari, whose virtues became apparent to him whenever he took his holy dip. Since a Hindu woman bathes fully clothed, he wrote, she "necessarily rises with wet drapery from the stream. Had I despotic power, our British fair ones should soon follow the example; being fully persuaded that it would eminently contribute to keep the bridal torch for ever in a blaze."

His pet hate was the corset, and Fanny Parkes, who at times comes across as something of a protofeminist, felt the same way. "In Europe, how very rarely does a woman walk gracefully!" she wrote in *Wanderings of a Pilgrim.* "Bound up in stays, the body is as stiff as a lobster in a shell."

Stuart inveighed against unflattering underwear in an anonymous series of publications called *A Ladies' Monitor.* It had the impressive subtitle, *Being a series of letters first published in Bengal on the subject of FEMALE APPAREL Tending to favour a regulated adoption of Indian Costume; and a rejection of SUPERFLUOUS VESTURE By the ladies of this country: with Incidental remarks on Hindoo beauty; whale-bone stays; iron busks; Indian corsets; man-milliners; idle bachelors, hair powder, side saddles, waiting maids, and footmen.*

It was not just a matter of sensuality and aesthetics, he pointed out. There were also practical considerations. All those iron stays in an Englishwoman's corsets could be better used to help poor farmers by strengthening the wheels of their bullock carts. Worse yet, they posed the constant risk of attracting lightning strikes.

The army seems never quite to have known what to make of Hindoo Stuart's eccentricities, but they allowed him to climb the ladder of promotions until he eventually retired as a major general. They denied him only one thing: his wish, as a good Hindu, to be cremated. It was another half century before polite society agreed that was the proper end for an Englishman.

LAST JEWEL IN THE CROWN

A *sadar* was a local court of appeal in Calcutta, and over time, *sadar* morphed under British influence into *sudder*, and on a Sunday morning of blistering sun and paralyzing humidity, Sudder Street was as dense as always with human activity. Calcutta is the last bastion of the hand-pulled rickshaw, and half a dozen skeletal men were offering their services to tourists while others were napping. Backpackers were checking out the ten-dollar-a-night guesthouses to see if the price included bedbugs. Young men whispered, "You want hash?" as I passed. A homeless family was bedded down on the sidewalk outside the Indian Museum, cooking up a pot of dal over a kerosene stove, while one of Calcutta's ubiquitous blue-headed crows tugged with its beak at a roll of rusted baling wire as if it were intent on dragging it across the street. A sign said, "Mass Feeding of the Poor, Every Sunday at 9:00 a.m.," and the sound of hymn-singing drifted from the open door of the Wesleyan Church.

Down the block at the Fairlawn Hotel, I ordered the full English breakfast. Fried eggs, bacon, fried mushrooms, fried tomatoes, and baked beans. The toast came with imported marmalade. The teapot was kept warm with an embroidered cozy. Glass-fronted cabinets held a collection of chinoiserie and matchboxes and ornamental teaspoons from around the world. On the wall by the reception desk there was a portrait of Queen Elizabeth II on her Golden Jubilee, a photograph of Kate Middleton and Prince William kissing on the balcony of Buckingham Palace, and a sticker that said, "I GAVE UP DRINKING, SMOKING, AND SEX. WORST 15 MINUTES OF MY LIFE."

Outside on the patio, Violet Smith, the Duchess of Sudder Street, was holding court, surrounded by tropical greenery. She was short and wide, with thick-lensed, tinted glasses in heavy black frames and pancake makeup and hair so massively lacquered that its weight seemed to be pressing her down deeper into the chair. She was ninety-three years old. She patted the seat next to her and said, "Come and sit here. I need a new toy boy."

She told me her maiden name had been Sarkies, which was Armenian. "After the 1915 genocide by the Turks, my grandmother carried my mother, Rosie, on her back all the way from the Khyber Pass to Dhaka. But my parents never spoke about it. We Armenians always mind our own business. My family went into the jute business in Dhaka. I was born there. But if you're born in a stable, it doesn't make you a horse. If they ask me where I was born, I say I come from the Planet of the Apes."

In the 1930s, Vi's father lost his job in Dhaka, and the family fell on hard times. "One rupee meant a lot to them," she said. They came to Calcutta and blended in with the local Armenian community, which had been here for more than three hundred years.

"There are hardly any Armenians left today," said Jennifer Fowler, Vi's daughter, who was sitting on the other side of the table, going over the accounts. "They all sold up in the late fifties and sixties. They still bring poor children here from Armenia to be educated, but then they send them back. There's one old lady who lives down the road in absolute squalor. There's still the Armenian Home, but she refuses to go and live there."

The Fairlawn was built in 1783, at the height of the Orientalist era, by an Englishman named William Ford. The deeds defined it as a pukka building, meaning that it was built of brick, a right to which only Europeans were entitled. For Bengalis, construction materials were restricted to coconut palm and mud. It passed through various sets of English hands, including a pair of nineteenth-century naval officers who were rumored to be opium smugglers and two spinster ladies, a Miss Clarke and a Miss Barrett, who owned it from 1900 to 1936, when they sold it to Rosie Sarkies, who turned it into a hotel.

During the Second World War, the Fairlawn was requisitioned by the Canadian Air Force. That was also when Vi met her husband, Ted Smith. He was British, an officer in the Northamptonshire Regiment. "So I feel English, I feel Armenian, I feel cosmopolitan," she said.

Another guest strolled over from the breakfast room to say good morning, an English expatriate. "How are you today?" Vi asked him as he bent over for a powdery kiss. "Have you been a good boy or a naughty boy?"

Vi and Ted married at a fearsome time, when the only ones getting fat in Calcutta were the crows and the vultures and the black marketeers. It seemed wise not to raise the issue of Winston Churchill and the famine, so instead I asked how life in Calcutta had changed for them after Independence in 1947.

"Not very much," Jennifer answered. "They went to the clubs every night, dinner dances, their own little circle of friends. It took time for things to change, you know, apart from the skirmishes that were going on within the Indian community."

"As I said, we Armenians mind our business," Vi said.

Skirmishes. Well, that was one way of putting it. There was the constant stream of refugees from East Bengal after Partition, and another mass influx during Bangladesh's war of independence in 1971. There were the communal riots of 1964, after a hair of the prophet disappeared from a shrine in Kashmir, and Hindus in some parts of Muslim-majority East Bengal were forbidden to wear shoes, carry an umbrella, or ride in a rickshaw. That was before several thousand of them were slaughtered, and a hundred Muslims in Calcutta were killed in reprisal. Then there was the Maoist-influenced Naxalite rebellion, which began in 1967 and still dragged on in various parts of northeast India half a century later.

"After that, we had the Communists come in, and they ruled for thirty-five years, which completely ruined the whole of the historical story," Vi said. "The second city of the British Empire, all the connections between Britain and India." The Communists had dismantled the statues of heroes of the Raj, which seemed to make her especially indignant.

"I think you were tempted a couple of times to go back to England, weren't you, Mum?" Jennifer said.

"Well, India has been very good to me. I'm very fond of Indian people. I'd be a nuisance without them. I can't cook or clean or iron or do anything. 'Madam, we're going to cook and clean for you.' I can't cook or anything, oh dear."

"You're a fugitive, aren't you, Mum? You're on the run."

But the guests always made it worthwhile, even if these days they were reduced in numbers and celebrity. The first family of Fairlawn had been the Kendals, an English theatrical family who traveled around India performing Shakespeare and stayed at the hotel on and off for thirty years. One of them, Jennifer, had married the outrageously handsome Bollywood star Shashi Kapoor. They spent their honeymoon here, and room 17 still had a plaque on the door that said, "Shashi Kapoor's Room." Ismael Merchant and James Ivory had stayed here once, working with the couple on *Bombay Talkie*, in which they costarred. Then there was Patrick Swayze and the cast of *City of Joy*, a movie about a Calcutta rickshaw puller, an idealistic American doctor, and a disastrous monsoon flood. One scene had been filmed in the reception area at the Fairlawn. Vi and Jennifer agreed that the Indian hero, played by Om Puri, had a credibility problem, since he was nine inches taller and weighed twice as much as any of the real-life rickshaw wallahs waiting outside on Sudder Street.

It was a more mixed crowd these days. "Japanese, Malayan, Thai," Vi said. "It's close by, you see, Bangkok."

"Lots of Australians," Jennifer said. "Lots of French and Germans, people from Spain."

"Which is nice."

"Which is lovely. We don't want it just to be for the English. That would be boring."

"Although we do get the odd British celebrity. Michael Palin, you know, from Monty Python. He was a nice man. The BBC were here. Tom Stoppard."

"Julie Christie."

"Sting."

"We did have one lord here, he was a Scotsman. Some politicians."

"Well, Prince Andrew was here, if you can call him a politician. And Princess Diana was here when she came to see Mother Teresa."

"And then there was that German, Günter Grass. He came here in 1971. I didn't like him. Very hard man, very anti-Bengali. The Germans are very hard people. He played havoc here, ran the Bengalis down. They're very sensitive, these Indians."

"Mum keeps well out of politics. She doesn't see the bad side of Calcutta. She lives in her own little world here. That's what's kept her so young."

Jennifer looked up irritably when a hotel employee came over with the register to ask her a question about some guests who had just checked in. She rolled her eyes when the man went back to the front desk. "My husband tells me I'm a real bossy boots," she said. "But someone's got to keep them under control. They're like children, really. They have to be told what to do and told off when they're naughty."

"I love people," Vi said, ignoring her daughter. "I want to enjoy the few years I have left; otherwise, you just sit here waiting to die. To be or not to be, that is the question."

I asked her what she did all day, other than sitting out here among the potted plants as the guests filed past to pay homage. "I just do bullshit all day," she chortled. "Look at all the bullshit on the walls. I just sit here and wait for my toy boys like you to come along."

As it turned out, the Duchess of Sudder Street didn't get to enjoy those extra few years. Six months after I left Calcutta, she died quietly in her private quarters at the Fairlawn Hotel.

PACKED AND PESTILENTIAL

V i Smith might have preferred to close herself off from the dark side of Calcutta, but for others, it was everything you needed to know about the city. Calcutta *was* the dark side.

One day, in the giant Barabazar market, I watched two blue-headed crows fighting over a dead rat. One would snatch it up in its beak, flap ten feet in the air, and drop it. The other would swoop down and repeat the performance. They would stop and circle the rat and peck at each other for a bit, then the first one would grab it again, and so it continued as the vendors went on selling their cheap T-shirts and underwear.

It might have been a symbolic scene from the documentary that Louis Malle made about the city in 1969, a tour de force of poverty porn that helped cement the idea of Calcutta as a hell on earth, afflicted by problems that were beyond imagination and beyond redemption. Here are some children splashing around in raw sewage. Here are some people banging drums and chanting about something in an alien language we don't understand. Here are some other people shouting slogans about Chairman Mao. Here are some crippled beggars lying in the street. Here are close-up shots of some lepers, who are even more repellent than the beggars. Here are some people at Nirmal Hriday, Mother Teresa's hospice, too weak to shovel rice into their mouths. Here are some people dying. Apart from the Maoist protesters, you can still see all those things in Calcutta today, but they're all that the filmmaker shows us, except for one brief passage that shows upper-class Indians in Western clothes absorbed in a horse race and blithely knocking balls around a well-watered golf course. Just in case we haven't gotten the point about the obscene cruelty of life. Claude Lévi-Strauss and Günter Grass painted, if anything, an even darker picture. For the French anthropologist, Calcutta was emblematic of the sickness of India: "filth, chaos, promiscuity, congestion; ruins, huts, mud, dirt; dung, urine, pus, humors, secretions, and running sores." *Tristes Tropiques*, indeed. For the German novelist, who showed up a couple of years after Malle to write *Der Butt* (*The Flounder*), the city was "a pile of shit that God dropped and called Calcutta." He had some helpful advice for tourists: "Let's not waste another word on Calcutta. Delete Calcutta from all guidebooks." His alter ego, Vasco (for Vasco da Gama, the Great Explorer), goes to Kalighat and says, "Chop off your cock in Calcutta (in the temple of Kali, where young goats are sacrificed and a tree is hung with wishing stones that cry out for children, more and more children)." While he's down at Kalighat, Grass also makes the obligatory stop at Mother Teresa's place to see some people dying, but Mother Teresa isn't home. He goes one step further than Malle by also turning his scorn on those genteel, sensitive, culturally confused Bengali writers who "read one another (in English) poems about flowers, monsoon clouds, and the elephant-headed god, Ganesha."

Not to deny that Calcutta was in a dire condition in the early 1970s. But what city wouldn't be after going through a quarter century of comparable horrors? Bengal had lost three million people to a famine part-engineered by its imperial overlords. It had suffered the aftershocks of Partition along religious lines, struggling to absorb millions of refugees from East Bengal who found nowhere to live but the pavements. And it was dealing with a historic crisis of identity that only deepened when fresh waves of migrants flooded in from the desperation of Bihar and Uttar Pradesh and native Bengalis found themselves reduced to only 40 percent of the population.

But all these European sophisticates also had more than two centuries of prejudice and cliché to build on. There was the foul climate and the terrible diseases it bred. The Black Hole, where a group of English prisoners, men, women, and children, died in 1756 (contemporary accounts put the number at 146, though later scholars estimated that it was probably closer to 43). The unspeakable Thugs, fanatics who strangled thousands of helpless travelers in the service of the goddess Kali. And darkest of all there was the goddess herself, black-skinned, fierce-faced, four-armed, with her blood-red protruding tongue, the piercing third eye in the middle of her forehead, and her necklace of human heads, an iconic image you still find painted on walls all through the back streets of the city.

Long before Malle and Grass and Lévi-Strauss arrived to pick at Calcutta's scabs, these dark notions of the place had been summed up for Westerners in the title of Rudyard Kipling's book *The City of the Dreadful Night*. Kipling writes of his nocturnal wanderings with the local police and his encounters with Dainty Iniquity and Fat Vice—thieves, prostitutes, and opium addicts. Yes, Kipling does call the city "packed and pestilential," but his contrary strand of respect for its deep complexities is usually forgotten. "Let us take our hats off to Calcutta," the book begins, in fact, "the many-sided, the smoky, the magnificent," with its "deep, full-throated boom of life and motion and humanity." "How long does it take to know it then?" he asks his police guide at the end of their tour. "About a lifetime," the man answers.

MULTIPLE PERSONALITIES

A*bout a lifetime*. Kipling's policeman was right. Everything in Calcutta seemed to be a metaphor that took time and effort to decipher. Or maybe a synecdoche, the word that Apu had learned in school. Everything had layers you didn't see on the surface, and sometimes they never became visible. In my wanderings in Calcutta I'd never felt more acutely the truth of what a friend had told me after my first three or four trips to India: that the more you go, the less you know.

Nothing perplexed me more than Kali and Durga, the goddesses who are most closely identified with the city. To the degree they served as metaphors, those metaphors were inevitably subjective. It all depended on which of the goddesses' attributes you chose to focus on. Calcuttans saw their multiple dimensions; the British, and later the European intellectuals, had an imaginative baseline that kept them focused on the darker ones.

Both Kali and Durga were known for acts of extreme violence. Durga, with her ten arms, each holding a different weapon, had killed the terrifying, shape-shifting buffalo-demon Mahisha, beheading him and impaling him on Shiva's trident. Kali, with her necklace of severed heads and her skirt of severed arms, led an army that vanquished the legion of demons. The Thugs invoked her as a patron; the Naxalites appropriated her as a symbol. But in killing demons, the goddesses were also protectors of virtue. Both of them represented the triumph of good over evil. They were creators as well as destroyers, and Durga's violent side is not what Calcuttans celebrate at her puja, the biggest of the year.

I asked Tapati Guha-Thakurta, an earnest and elegant academic expert on the Durga Puja, to tell me more about it. "You know, the myth is that she's the warrior goddess," she said. "But here she's considered to be the married daughter who comes down from the mountains with her children each year, leaving her husband's parental home, and then at the end of the puja she's given her farewell as she returns. So the mother-daughter-wife thing is parallel to her role as the killer of the demon. This has a long history in Bengal."

It seemed reasonable that a loving family would want to give their daughter an annual break from her husband, given that he was prone to wild and unpredictable moods. That was because Durga's husband was Shiva, a piece of information that left me deeply confused.

I often thought of Fanny Parkes sitting on the deck of her paddle steamer on the Ganges, trying to draw organizational charts that explained the hierarchy of the Hindu deities. In Calcutta, I kept genealogical notes of my own, trying to figure out where Kali and Durga fitted into this divine schema. My scribblings were evidence of a brain tied in knots.

Parvati ("daughter of the mountains") m. Shiva

Kali ("black goddess") and Gauri ("white goddess")—both
    manifestations of Parvati

Parvati = Gauri, but Gauri also = Durga (?)

But Kali also turns into Gauri (??)

Kali (aka Sati, aka Kalika, Chandika—too complicated, ignore)
    m. Shiva

Durga m. Shiva (so all marry Shiva? at different times?)

Durga's sons (Ganesha and Kartikeya) are also Parvati's sons.
    But not her daughters (Lakshmi, Saraswati)

Kali (Sati) later returns as Parvati

Kali born out of forehead of Ambika, who emerges from body of Parvati
    (so she's Parvati's granddaughter?)

But other stories say Kali springs from the forehead of Durga

So Durga = Gauri = Parvati = Kali (???)

Maybe there was just no point in trying to confine these riddles in neat boxes. In the end, all of them—Kali/Durga/Parvati/Sati/Gauri—were manifestations of the Great Goddess and mother, Devi, and expressions of shakti—divine energy. Ma Ganga, flowing past Calcutta to the ocean, was that power in liquid form.

But what brought Durga and Kali to Calcutta in the first place, given that it was nothing but a riverside swamp in the hazy millennia before the British made it their capital? The story involved a king named Daksha, the father of Sati (or Kali, or Gauri, or whatever), and as usual there were multiple variants, depending on which of the scriptures you consulted.

Sati/Kali was married to Shiva, but King Daksha despised his son-in-law as a wild-eyed, ash-smeared renegade and refused to invite him to a sacrificial ceremony at Kankhal, on the outskirts of Haridwar, where I'd seen my first body burning. Sati couldn't take any more of her father's insults and threw herself into the fire—as a result of which Kankhal is revered as one of the most sacred of all cremation grounds.

Maddened with rage and grief, Shiva tore out a lock of his hair and fashioned two fearsome, vengeful creatures from it. They laid waste to Daksha's celebration and left Kankhal strewn with corpses and body parts. Daksha was decapitated, though later, in an act of mercy, Shiva replaced his head with the head of a goat.

Shiva rampaged across the universe with his wife's incinerated body across his shoulders. Some versions say that his wild, whirling dance scattered pieces of Sati/Kali all over present-day South Asia. Others say that the gods were so alarmed by his rampage that they called in Vishnu to stop him, which he tried to do by hurling his discus at Shiva. But his aim was off, and the discus slashed the goddess's body to pieces instead. The places where they fell to earth became *shakti peethas*, places of pilgrimage. Four of the *peethas* were considered the most important, and one of these was on the banks of the Hooghly. Scholars debate the original location, but the modern temple, which was built in 1809, is in a congested neighborhood in South Calcutta.

One cliché I'd learned to avoid in India was "since time immemorial." As in, "Since time immemorial, Hindus have flocked to Kalighat to worship the goddess." It turned out that you couldn't get away from the British at Kalighat any more than you could in the rest of Calcutta. The reason there was a ghat here in the first place, and a temple beside it, was the entrepreneurial zeal of Major William Tolly of the East India Company, who expanded a small canal in 1775—thereafter known as Tolly's Nullah—to clear a silted-up tributary called the Adi Ganga and speed the way to the interior of Bengal. He charged boats a toll for the privilege, and a thriving market grew up around the ghat. The busy market was still there, selling religious items and all manner of Kali-themed trinkets like key chains and postcards and fridge magnets. But Tolly's Nullah was now a stinking ditch like countless others, though the government had been promising to clean it up.

I went down into the claustrophobic inner sanctum of the temple and joined the crowd that was circumambulating the goddess. There were empty, smoke-blackened niches along the walls, and the iron roof girders had a thick shroud of spiderwebs. An ancient TV set with a blank screen was suspended on a little cantilevered platform high on one wall, the kind you might see in a cheap motel room. Ceiling fans churned the sticky air. There were signs warning of "pickpocket and imposter" and instructions that said, "Broke Coconut Only in the Specific Place" and "Don't Touch Doubtful Article."

I bought my *prasad* and got my *darshan*. The effigy of Kali was fashioned out of black marble and enclosed in a metal-and-wire structure that looked like an old-fashioned elevator cage. There was definitely something unnerving about the Black One, with those three piercing eyes and the long tongue hanging out like a panting dog's. But to the Bengali worshippers, the tongue had a second meaning that was quite different. After Kali had wiped out the demon armies, her bloodlust was out of control, and the gods called on her husband, Shiva, to calm her down. He threw himself in her path, and in her frenzy, she stepped on him. Speechless with embarrassment, she bit her lip and thrust out her tongue and then, overcome by remorse, plunged into the Yamuna and emerged again as the gentle, nurturing Gauri. Even in her dark and violent persona, Kali was also an exemplar of the power of women. In the nineteenth century, a school of painters flourished at Kalighat that satirized the vanity and self-indulgence of the babus, the Bengali nouveaux riches who had profited from the presence of the East India Company. The paintings sometimes showed their women, both wives and mistresses, empowered by Kali's righteous energy, thrashing the babus or stomping them underfoot.

A thousand priests are affiliated with the temple at Kalighat, and one of them invited me to his brother's sweetshop, where an elderly lady in a windowless back room was scraping dough off a wooden tray and pressing spongy balls of *champakali* between her bare palms. They insisted I try some, and it was only polite to accept, though I thought the sweets were probably to blame when I spent most of the night that followed sprawled on my hands and knees on the bathroom floor, gasping over the toilet.

"Kali was dispersed in a hundred and eight pieces, and one of them came to earth here," my translator said, though others put the number at fifty-one.

I said I'd read about this. The pieces that had fallen on Kalighat were four toes from the right foot that were taken out once a year to be bathed during the summer full-moon festival of Snana Yatra.

The translator disagreed. "No, what fell here was her genital region."

I wasn't used to disputing points of Hindu theology, but I said, "Are you sure?"

She conferred with the priest for a while in Bengali.

"Yes, definitely the genitals," she said at last. "They are in the golden box in the temple, where you just went."

I double-checked later. Kali's genitals were in the northeastern state of Assam. Her toes were here in Calcutta. For the first time in all my blundering around in the mysteries of Hinduism, I found myself on the right side of an argument.

THE BOLLYWOOD GODDESS

The calendar of the great pujas is fixed by the movements of the moon. Saraswati is worshipped in January or February, Ganesha in April or May, Durga in September or October, and Kali three weeks after that. The Durga Puja, the biggest of them all, when thousands of clay-and-straw effigies of the goddess are immersed in the Hooghly, is another case of the perils of "since time immemorial," because British finger-prints were on this one, too.

The first great Durga Puja was organized by a local raja in 1757 to cel-ebrate the British victory at the Battle of Plassey, which gave Britain full military control over Bengal. The guest of honor was Robert Clive, the "con-queror of India," who had a rich menu of adjectives to convey his low opinion of Bengalis. Depending on their class, these included *servile*, *mean*, *submissive*, *venal*, *effeminate*, *luxurious*, *tyrannical*, *treacherous*, and *cruel*.

"Luxurious" presumably referred to the babus, who took over the Durga Puja in the 1850s, finding it a fine opportunity to show off their new money. At the end of the festival, British officials were invited to join them for an eve-ning of sherry and champagne.

The babus also dived into land speculation and real estate and created a number of caste-based neighborhoods in North Calcutta, which the British called Black Town, populating them with skilled artisans like cobblers, tai-lors, tanners, and potters. The potters came from towns and villages like Krishnanagar, along the east side of the Hooghly, using clay mud from the river as their working medium. They are still clustered in the neighborhood that the babus created for them, Kumartuli, which lies just north of the How-rah Bridge, and their specialty is to fashion the effigies that are immersed in the river during the Durga Puja and other great festivals.

All of them were from the same caste—*kumhars* are potters—and all of them seemed to be named Paul or Pal. The first man I stopped to talk to at one of the innumerable workshops that line the back alleys of Kumartuli was Akhil Paul, and he was from Krishnanagar. The most famous of them all was Gopeshwar Pal, who had traveled to the British Empire Exhibition in Lon-don in 1924 and could fashion a convincing horse's head out of clay in forty-five seconds flat. But what really impressed the royal visitors was the lightning speed with which he could turn out a lifelike statue of the Duke of Connaught. Later, he had gone on to Italy and learned how to sculpt in stone and bronze.

Stacked outside the workshops were purple-pink Ganeshas and blue Krishnas and no end of Shivas in various shapes and sizes and a delicate white Saraswati, symbolizing knowledge and wisdom, seated on her swan and playing a stringed vina. Akhil Paul was working on a small Kali. "Kali Puja is very big here," he said. "But we work all year round. The gods have to listen to our schedule, not just us to theirs." He grinned.

One of his crew was finishing off a ten-armed Durga who was still missing her head, and he described the various stages of the process: first, nail together a frame of wood and bamboo, then bind together bundles of straw to create the basic shape of the body, then add successive layers of clay. "There are fishermen who bring us the mud from Uluberia, downriver from the city," Akhil said. "They drop it here on the riverbank, and then a distributor sells it to us." The Hooghly was just a few blocks away.

Tradition says that it's auspicious to mix in a little mud from the doorway of a prostitute, which seemed easy enough to do, since Kumartuli is right next to the infamous brothels of Sonagachi. But I read about that detail only later, so I didn't ask him.

"Clay defines the art of Bengal in a way," Tapati Guha-Thakurta said. "We have so little stone here, and so much clay, because we can get it directly from the river. They use only unfired clay; that is a ritual injunction, they say. The purity of the clay is that which hasn't passed through fire of any kind. And there's a huge art in mixing different kinds of clay, which they give different names."

One of the workers was slapping a thick, sticky layer of clay onto the body of another Kali. On top of that, he would add a firmer, sandier clay, smoothing it out to give the body its final shape, sometimes mixing it with oil to make it glisten. A boy was using a fine-tipped brush to paint in the features on the head of a Durga, which had been made in a separate mold. The pointed nose, the yellow face shaped like a betel leaf, and finally the eyes, slanting and elongated and formed like leaves of bamboo, the moment at which the goddess came to life. With that she was ready for immersion. "The entire thing guiding it is that Durga comes from the river and then returns to it, so she has to be made from its soil," Tapati said.

On the last day of the festival, women would stroke the effigy with betel leaves, feed her sweets and paan, and beseech her to return the following year. Men would carry her on their shoulders to the river, and in she would go, sent back to Mount Kailash for another year of marital dramas—often tossed into the water quite unceremoniously, to judge from videos I'd seen of the event. "On the main ghats, in the past four or five years, they even have these giant cranes, so you literally just dip the goddess in that way," Tapati said.

The clay melts away from the effigy and sinks back to the riverbed, and people wade out to retrieve the frames and the straw and strip off the gold foil, the jewelry, and the ornaments—everything that can be saved and recycled. As Tapati described it, there was nothing very reverential about this process. "It's quite brutal, actually. The goddess is stripped apart. Her limbs fall off. She is literally dismembered."

It was partly a matter of city politics. The river was so shallow that garbage piled up in no time, and the authorities had come down on pollution like a hammer, insisting that the idol makers use only natural materials and lead-free paint. "But the sentiment of the community has to be maintained," Tapati said. "This is a practice you cannot stop. You can put an end to animal sacrifices, but you can never ban immersion. The goddess must go to the river."

Around the corner, at Sailen Paul's workshop, there was a notable absence of straw and clay.

"Those ones look like fiberglass," I said.

He nodded. These effigies might fly in the face of tradition, but they were unbreakable, made for shipping abroad. He said you could do customized "online idol booking," pay by credit card, and organize your own puja at home.

"I have sent already three shipments to London," Sailen said.

"NRB Durgas, we call them," Tapati said. "Nonresident Bengalis."

As we walked on through Kumartuli, there were many figures that had a distinctly secular look: statues of women with the features of Bollywood stars, men who looked as if they'd been copied from the works of Polyclitus or Praxiteles, others whose heroic chins jutted into the future like soldiers in a Soviet war memorial. And tucked away in a corner, either Batman or Superman; the clothing and features hadn't been painted on yet.

Tapati sighed. "It has all become very secularized." The groups that organized the Durga Puja had to bear in mind the competition for corporate sponsorship from the likes of Pepsi and Tata. Before immersion, the effigies would be displayed in extravagant booths, pandals, which more and more were designed with pop culture themes. Harry Potter's Hogwarts had been a favorite one year, until J. K. Rowling sued for breach of copyright.

Some of the effigies of Durga herself had dispensed with almost all the elements that made her recognizable: the yellow skin, the bamboo-leaf eyes. "She is being made more recognizably human," Tapati said. "It is what we may call the Bollywoodization of the goddess, with very *filmi* attire. She has to conform to public ideas of beauty."

And so did the public itself. The Durga Puja was a great street festival, strolling among the flashing lights and fireworks with family and friends, early snacks and blow-out dinners, Ferris wheel rides for the kids. You had to look your best. In the weeks before the Durga Puja, plastic surgeons worked overtime to meet the demand for nose jobs, chin lifts, and liposuction. I saw one doctor's pricelist: $1,500 for a boob job, $1,200 for a tummy tuck. At just $200, a shot of Botox seemed like a positive steal.

THE COIN COLLECTOR

So many millions of us had come here down through the millennia, pulled in by the magnet of the Ganges.

Xuanzang and Al-Biruni, Withington and Tavernier, to see the river's mysteries and tell their respective compatriots what they had seen.

A generation of Englishmen to explore it and map it and discover where it was born; other Englishmen to shoot at anything that flew over it or ran along its banks; others still to paint it and celebrate its beauty; the Raja of Harsil to log its cedars and grow his apples.

Men of the East India Company seeking their fortunes; young women looking for husbands; humanitarians shocked by famine; generals crushing rebellion; engineers to build bridges and railways and canals; residents and collectors to run the bureaucracy of empire.

Frenchmen to sell books; Englishmen to sell cakes and open hotels; writers and filmmakers to record and admire; writers and filmmakers to sneer; the Welshman William Jones, with his love of learning; the Welshwoman Fanny Parkes, wandering in search of the picturesque.

Poets searching for the meaning of life among the cremation fires and the naked sadhus; the Beatles seeking enlightenment, writing music, trying to kick drugs; retirees from Air India, drawn by the vibrations.

Mountaineers from New Zealand seeking new conquests of nature; Latvian bungee jumpers and yuppies from Gujarat in search of adventure; Israeli kids to numb their trauma after military service; hippies to learn yoga and the rudiments of the sitar; tourists to gawp at bodies burning.

Bishops and Jesuits who came bringing light to the heathen; soldiers who found a religion better than their own; politicians who used religion to seek votes; nomads who sold their milk to the pilgrims.

And the pilgrims themselves, in numbers beyond counting, flocking to Gangotri, to Haridwar, to Devprayag, to the Triveni Sangam at Allahabad, to the ghats of Varanasi, and finally to Gangasagar, south of Calcutta, where the creation story ended, the goddess met the king, and the river merged with the ocean.

I stopped halfway at Diamond Harbor, an hour and a half from the city, passing through a neighborhood called Lenin Nagar and parking outside the Stalin-Einstein Library ("AFERS XEXOR SERVICE"). A fisherman paddled himself out in an inner tube to check his nets. A middle-aged woman in a bright green sari jumped into my path and screamed in my face. The owner of a chai stall laughed and twirled a finger at his head.

At the village of Kakdwip, the river split in two around a long, narrow island. The channel to the east of it was called the Muriganga, the Puffed-Rice Ganges. The island might have been there for centuries, or it might have been formed from silt only a few years ago. In these last few miles before we reached Gangasagar, the Ganges had not always been a benign force. Navigation was treacherous; her sandbars were notorious. The captains of the East Indiamen marked their charts with the names and locations of familiar wrecks.

The vehicle that Ma Ganga rode on was a crocodile, and here in the delta it was a mortal threat. The English in Calcutta learned with horror of the local custom of fashioning a baby out of clay and placing it in the river to propitiate the beast. Ships had their prows carved in the shape of a crocodile for the same reason. Sharks, too, infested these waters and were equally fearsome. A writer in the 1920s described a ceremony at Gangasagar where pilgrims would walk into the ocean with the hope of being eaten by a shark, to placate these dark and powerful forces.

It was two miles from the jetty to Gangasagar. As we waited for the boat, I chatted with four young marine biologists with orange life preservers and aluminum suitcases, which contained the equipment they needed to set up testing stations to assess the health of the benthic life of the river. The pollution was not too bad this close to the ocean, they said.

The ferry finally arrived, and people piled on to it, pressing it lower and lower into the water. I guessed that the safety limit was no more than a hundred and fifty passengers. I stopped counting at four hundred. Boats capsized here with some frequency, as they did across the border in Bangladesh.

A jolly group of old ladies from Gujarat squeezed in beside me, next to the engine room. As the bungee jumpers in Rishikesh had said, no matter where you went in India, you always met Gujaratis. One of the old ladies had a decorative tattoo on her arm, lettered in Hindi. I asked her what it meant, and she said, "Hare Krishna, Hare Rama." They had come in a chartered bus with sixty people from their temple in the city of Surendranagar, doing a grand circuit of pilgrimage sites that would take them all the way south to the Ramanathaswamy temple in Tamil Nadu. They didn't care for the local food, so they had brought their own. They munched on five-rupee bags of roasted chickpeas that were dyed bright green and sucked on canary-yellow popsicles, colors that did not exist in nature. The old ladies tossed handfuls of fish food over the side of the boat, whispering a prayer.

There were tall electricity pylons planted in the shallow brown water of the Muriganga, and flocks of seagulls swooped and dived around us. The shoreline of the mainland was dotted with the slender chimneys of brickworks, and the island of Gangasagar was a flat strip of green. The forest station of Kotka, where I'd ended my travels in Bangladesh at another of the Hundred Mouths of the Ganges, was a hundred miles to the east.

At Kachuberia Ghat, the pierhead, we flagged a minibus for the forty-five-minute drive along a road that ran arrow-straight to the southern tip of the island. The driver was a chatty type. "If you walk along the river here, it is very beautiful," he said. "You will automatically remember all your memories." The major economic activity on the island was growing betel leaves and making paan. His vehicle ran on liquified natural gas. He made sure I noticed the solar panels outside a small Shiva temple. The local schools were good; the government had always supported education. As we approached the temple of Kapil Muni, the seer who had reduced the sixty thousand sons of King Sagara to ash, he pointed out a new helipad that provided weekly service for wealthy pilgrims from Calcutta. Near it was a guesthouse that had been built for the use of the chief minister of West Bengal. It was all built with tropical hardwoods, the driver said. It cost nine crores of rupees, about $1.5 million.

Two young priests were in attendance at the temple, which was low, narrow, modern, gaudy, and unprepossessing. Its predecessor had been washed away by the tides. In January each year, the three-day Gangasagar Mela, second only to the great mela at Allahabad, can bring crowds of a million or more to bathe in the chilly ocean waters, make their offerings of coconuts, and wash away the sins of a lifetime. Today there were only a handful of visitors. Near the temple, a few sheds had been built for the sadhus. A hammer-and-sickle flag was fluttering over one of them, printed with the initials CPI (M). Communist Party of India (Marxist), as opposed to the CPI (M-L), which added Lenin. "Those sheds are a haven of misconduct," Dodo snorted.

On the path to the beach, I bought a ten-rupee bag of rice and dal from one of the sadhus and then gave it back to him as a gift. He repaid me by smearing a fluorescent orange tilak on my forehead.

Some middle-class families were frolicking in the gentle surf, taking selfies on their iPhones. There was no sign of sharks. A pack of more than a dozen feral dogs were fighting over broken chunks of coconut, and a man in a T-shirt advertising Arizona Bagels was trawling a curious device back and forward through the water. It was like a gigantic rake studded with two rows of metal disks. He said his name was Ashok Paik, and he had grown up in Gangasagar. The disks were magnets, and he was collecting coins that had been thrown into the ocean as offerings—not the new rupees, which were made from base metal, but coins from the old days, denominated in annas. I'd seen vendors selling them from stalls along Chowringhee Road.

I asked him whether he was having any success, and he shrugged. "There are good days and there are bad days," he said. "It all depends. Everything is in the hands of our mother, Ma Ganga."

ABOUT THE AUTHOR

George Black is an award-winning author and journalist living in New York City. His work has appeared in *The New Yorker*, newyorker.com, *Harper's*, *Mother Jones*, *The Nation*, *The New York Times*, *The Los Angeles Times*, and many other publications. *On the Ganges* is his seventh book, and rivers run through most of them. His previous book for St. Martin's Press, *Empire of Shadows: The Epic Story of Yellowstone*, was a finalist for the 2013 *Los Angeles Times* Book Prize.